The Integration of Psychological Principles in Policy Development

The Integration of Psychological Principles in Policy Development

———◆———

Edited by
CHRIS E. STOUT

Westport, Connecticut
London

Library of Congress Cataloging-in-Publication Data

The integration of psychological principles in policy development /
    edited by Chris E. Stout.
        p.   cm.
    Includes bibliographical references and index.
    ISBN 0–275–95011–5 (alk. paper)
    1. Policy sciences—Psychological aspects.   2. Social policy—
Psychological aspects.   I. Stout, Chris E.
H97.I55   1996
320′.6—dc20   95–37645

British Library Cataloguing in Publication Data is available.

Library of Congress Catalog Card Number: 95–37645
ISBN: 0–275–95011–5

First published in 1996

Praeger Publishers, 88 Post Road West, Westport, CT 06881
An imprint of Greenwood Publishing Group, Inc.

Printed in the United States of America

The paper used in this book complies with the
Permanent Paper Standard issued by the National
Information Standards Organization (Z39.48–1984).

10 9 8 7 6 5 4 3 2 1

*With great hope and
expectation for a better
world for Grayson*

Contents

Healthcare Issues

Education Issues

Illustrations

Socioeconomic Issues

1

Introduction

Chris E. Stout

The goal of this book is to educate various policy makers, academics, political scientists, and others as to the beneficial use of various psychological principles (e.g., motivation and attribution theory, and social, clinical, educational, and industrial/organizational psychologies) within an integrative framework to aid in the development of policy that would likely yield less failure. Additionally, government, business, and community leaders will be able to learn more about various psychological applications as a means to conceptualize and address problems and develop creative problem-solving methodologies.

In adopting a twenty-first-century-based model, we need to shift our conceptual thinking and paradigms. It is my hope that focusing on technology, education, and quality outcomes holds much promise for beneficial, broad-based change to occur. The various chapters in this book offer an integrative, collaborative, synergistic approach to effecting such positive change. This is *not* just another volume of rhetoric without responsibility. It is quite easy to critique and argue. It is something quite different to identify problems and then provide possible solutions. The authors collected within this work do offer ideas, new concepts, and recommendations that are designed to help. It is also hoped that readers will be stimulated into reexamining how they approach issues.

PSYCHOLOGY'S ROLE

The formal involvement of psychology in policy, political, and global-cultural issues is not unique. There are various psychology-based international and inter-American societies. The American Psychological Association has Division 48, Peace Psychology, and an Office of International Affairs. These two branches offer some of the best research and policy opinion on various topics of global political interest. Foundations provide grants for various internationally collaborative projects. The MacArthur Foundation, for example, is funding a project examining environmental degradation effects resulting from *behavioral* factors. Sloan (1992) sees that "psychologists will participate in networks of interdisciplinary, international teams of researchers, activists, policy makers, and citizens focusing on particular regional problems. Within these teams and networks, the skills of psychologists are needed at various stages-in gathering information for advocacy purposes, in grant writing, in bringing a mental health perspective to bear on policy information, in designing media campaigns, in training service delivery teams, and in analyzing group resistance to change" (p. 7).

The economics of prevention are self-evident: "In the United States, $1 spent on immunization saves $10 in illness prevented. One dollar spent on preschool programs or prenatal care saves $3 later. But even such figures are not always persuasive. This is because the benefits usually do not immediately manifest on the ledger of the same administrator who authorizes the expenditure or during the term of office of its political champion. We must, nevertheless, remember that further savings will result from a larger pool of skilled, healthy, motivated citizens coming into the work force; savings in prison costs from a reduction in crime; and savings in fewer youngsters having children before they are prepared to raise them" (Schorr, 1993, 53–54). It is important to include outcome-based and results-based accountability for all programs, incorporate less bureaucratic and more responsive bureaucracies, better integrate services, strive for the foresight in leadership that keeps societal needs as the focus, and encourage bolder thinking (Schorr, 1993).

This volume begins with a varied theoretical foundation that ranges from innovations of public sector entrepreneurship and its consideration of responsibilities of society to new challenges within a constantly changing framework. Oliver offers a model that allows for analysis of individual entrepreneurs within the innovations of public policy. Next, Ptak examines the sociocultural foundations of education. She notes the reciprocity and interplay of cultural values and mores with educational programming and moral reasoning. Issues of diversity, cultural pluralism and diversity, concepts of community, and technological advances and disparities are discussed. Recommendations for the proper role of education in government and policy, with an eye to the future, complete her framework.

Lyons and Kisiel explore the difficult struggle of dealing with domestic violence and child abuse issues as they relate to public policy. A variety of theoretical approaches are presented along with meaningful and useful applications within judicial and legislative domains. The unique aspect of prevention, not just response, is provided also.

In this section, Morris provides a unique psychological focus on another topical and controversial area: welfare reform. His work is unique in that he delves into psychological aspects of causal factors of policy makers' beliefs and values and their subsequent impact on crafting policy. Additionally, he reciprocally examines the welfare recipients' behavioral responses. His resulting conceptual framework is powerful. Baumeister, Kupstas, and Zanthos specifically address poverty issues, but they do so in a political and economic context as well as with an eye to the future and a model of the New Morbidity. Finally, I have outlined some thoughts on the integration of the regulatory power of governments with the economic skills of private businesses, in tandem with a benevolent but responsibility-based person-citizen interaction.

Next, healthcare issues serve as one of the three foci of this book. Kemp provides a review of the history of community-based mental health systems along with a critique of associated successes and shortcomings, the current status of such systems, and some predictions. Theis reviews the issues of clinical application and policy development within the behavioral healthcare delivery system vis-à-vis issues of improvement and reformation. Paradigm shifts via policy principles, managed care, increased role of the consumer, and accountability of clinicians are explained.

Jones' perspective is to look at new relationships and behaviors in healthcare payment and delivery redesign. Her perspective is on societal changes and revolutions—both psychologically and economically within various care delivery systems. Lyons, Shasha, Christopher, and Vessey tackle the interface of managed care with decision science in what serves as a model and strategy of incorporating outcomes management, decision support, utilization review, and quality indicators within a context of continuous quality improvement. Measurement issues within managed behavioral healthcare serves as the common denominator of these aspects.

The final section of the book concerns educational issues. Harcum sets the stage with the assertion that successful public policy is hinged upon the tenet of human nature of the drive for free choice. The argument against behaviorism for a scientifically-based public policy is eloquently critiqued. In his contentions, Rybicki adopts a religiously based position vis-à-vis morality, values, and psychology's role in education. The Keiths support a position of utilizing schools as agents of change by proposing a new, research-supported model that creates linkages with urban schools, their students and communities, and "outside" agencies. It provides augmentation of resources, development (or reinforcing) of networked bonds among residents, educational institutions, businesses, and organizations, and an expansion of education beyond a focus on school students to include the broader. Wilhite considers the role of change agents in the actual transformation of service systems in serving the needs of children as well as their families, she further examines how schools could potentially serve in this capacity. The book concludes with an aptly titled chapter "New Directions." Monahan, Marino, and Miller take a look toward the year 2000 and beyond with review of various models with important academic and behavioral goals.

In conclusion, I would like to quote from Sullivan (1992, 527–528):

Government is the steward of the public welfare. ...Social justice [should be] a guiding principle of our stewardship. We are responsible for each other. We have rights, but we also have responsibilities. . . . Government has a positive role in society. It should be guided by the principle of subsidiary, which supports decision making at the lowest level of society—the individual and the family. . . . Government should enable and assist organizations [businesses] to function on their own and should only step in directly when it is beyond the capacity of the organizations to do so. Advocacy . . . must include both a political and a cultural dimension; political because it concerns the distribution of wealth and power, and cultural because it involves a conflict over values. . . . The promotion of democracy and the defense of human rights are important cultural focuses that create a sense of community and worldwide solidarity. Democracy can be understood as a political system that seeks to maximize personal participation, and it can be viewed as an institutional development enhancing people's ability to share in the decisions that affect their lives and the life of the whole community.

We need structural change, and this can [best] be brought about...if we opt for compassion and solidarity. The political task before us can be attained only through an ethical commitment to [collaboration and working together as global whole]. Senge (1990) reminds us that analysis does not equal vision. Analysts search for "why," and visionaries search for "why not." Vision is enhanced by involving others. Ten people working together are smarter than one working alone. Leadership is best served by teaching, not just stewarding. We need to conceptualize in the same visionary way as did the team responsible for the lunar landing, as did the group developing the microprocessor, as did signers of the Declaration of Independence. Our focus needs to be upon prevention and proactive intervention. In most situations it is easier (and less costly) to prevent the treatable than to treat the preventable. It is the responsibility of us all to do so.

To step out of the formal role of author and editor briefly, I wish to make note of the pride I feel in this work; it is with total thanks to my contributors. My goal was threefold: (1) not just to critique what is not working well with policy but to offer a varied collection of solutions and models of applications of psychological principles in doing so, (2) to collect a diverse group of experts, not individuals from just any one area or discipline, but academics, theorists, and practitioners whose expertise spans the top managed care firms, institutions of higher education, national consultants, schools, and healthcare facilities; and (3) to integrate this collection of pragmatic theorists into one volume with a general but common focus—making things better. I shall forever be thankful for the work of these individuals.

2

Conceptualizing the Challenges of Public Entrepreneurship

Thomas Richard Oliver

Innovation is a process of perception, cognition, and action. It begins when people notice—or are led to notice—an unusual occurrence in the world around them. Something has happened to create a previously unrecognized problem or an unexpected opportunity. If people are able to reach an understanding of the situation, a variety of actions become plausible. Action of any kind can occur only if a sufficient number of people are persuaded there is a need for change and a better way of doing things.

Thus, for a society and its constituent institutions to be responsive to new conditions and emerging challenges, there must be individuals who excel in "the art of anticipating the need for, and of leading, productive change" (Kanter 1983, 15). These are the *entrepreneurs*, who think deeply about problems, search for solutions, and struggle for their adoption. Their energy and ingenuity help provide the indispensable products for economic, political, and social transformation.

This chapter explores the nature of entrepreneurship as it occurs in the public sector. Over a decade ago, Nelson Polsby (1984) suggested that the tasks of entrepreneurs and other individuals who help transform our political system with innovative ideas were less appreciated and less well understood than they should be. In the years since, an extensive literature has emerged to spotlight the actions and contributions of entrepreneurs in the public sector. The intellectual process has been true to its subject—that is, rather independent, multifaceted, and somewhat chaotic. As will be described below, scholars and journalists have employed the concept of public entrepreneurship in many ways and for many purposes. At this time, there is no consensus on the boundaries of the phenomenon and no synthesis of its origins, motivations, or impact on government and citizens.

By considering how the thoughts and actions of public sector entrepreneurs resemble those of their counterparts in business and industry, I have attempted to bring the concept back to intellectual roots established two centuries ago. Notwithstanding the obvious differences in public and private institutions and the factors of production, this analogy can take us quite far in understanding the inherent challenges facing individuals who seek to change public policy and their potential responses to those challenges. Through this conceptual lens, the success of the aspiring entrepreneur and enterprise as a whole depends on the performance of five tasks:

- Identifying a market opportunity
- Designing an innovation
- Attracting investment
- Creating market demand
- Monitoring the market

In the sections below, I present this model for analyzing the work of individual entrepreneurs in public policy innovation. The basic tasks can be approached in a variety of ways depending on the circumstances facing the entrepreneur. What is an appropriate strategy or tactic in one situation may be unnecessary or fruitless in another. I will illustrate some of the variations in entrepreneurial tasks by recounting the actions that led to several prominent innovations in American health policy.[1]

THE ENTREPRENEURIAL FUNCTION

Entrepreneurship is the process of introducing innovation to society. An innovation can be a new idea, process, product, or service (Kanter, 1983). It establishes a new production function-the doing of new things or the doing of things that are already being done in a new way (Schumpeter, 1939, 1947).

Entrepreneurs develop and market innovations in pursuit of profits that greatly exceed normal returns to investment (Schumpeter, 1939). In their pursuit of profits, however, they perform a social function as well. "Entrepreneurs, by definition, shift resources from areas of low productivity and yield to areas of higher productivity and yield" (Drucker, 1985, 28). Defined in terms of demand rather than supply, entrepreneurship changes the value and satisfaction consumers obtain from resources (Drucker, 1985).

In even broader perspective, entrepreneurs are the architects of social change. They serve as transformational leaders whose creative responses to problems and opportunities expand and rearrange the existing set of preferences, rather than adapt to them (Hargrove, 1989; Jones, 1989; Schumpeter, 1939; Tenenbaum, 1991). The new preferences they create and the means for meeting those preferences are essential to economic evolution and social learning (Deutsch, 1985; Gilder, 1984; Schon, 1971; Schumpeter, 1939; J.L. Walker,

1981).[2]

It would be a mistake to think that change is either smooth or harmonious: "On the contrary, we must recognize that evolution is lopsided, discontinuous, disharmonious by nature-that the disharmony is inherent in the very *modus operandi* of the factors of progress" (Schumpeter, 1939, 102). In the eyes of Joseph Schumpeter (1942), entrepreneurship is "creative destruction": No matter what value an innovation delivers to society at large, it will almost invariably produce relative gains for some members and relative losses for others.[3] This uneven pattern of costs and benefits poses special challenges for entrepreneurship in the world of politics and public policy, as we will see below.

Public Sector Entrepreneurship

The entrepreneurial function is traditionally associated with private business and industry (e.g., Gilder, 1984; Kanter, 1983). Others see it as a distinctive and pervasive impulse in American society (Tropman & Morningstar, 1989). According to Peter Drucker (1985, 27), "Entrepreneurship is by no means limited to the economic sphere although the term originated there. It pertains to all activities of human beings other than those one might term 'existential' rather than 'social.' And we now know that there is little difference between entrepreneurship whatever the sphere."

Indeed, the phenomenon has universal appeal, and for over a quarter-century social scientists have applied their concepts of entrepreneurship to activities in government and other institutions that deliver public services. A number of scholars refer to public sector entrepreneurship as an important phenomenon but give it only limited attention in their studies of the broader policy-making process.[4] Other studies examine the behavior of individuals who carry out entrepreneurial activities but do not explicitly label their subjects entrepreneurs.[5] There is now a rapid growth of interest in public entrepreneurship as a subject of inquiry in its own right, and a rich literature now exists or is developing throughout the social sciences. Recently, efforts have begun to construct general models of the concept for scholars and participants in policy innovation (e.g., Roberts & King, 1991; Schneider & Teske, 1992).

At the present time, however, there are problems to overcome in developing a synthesis of the concepts and theoretical propositions about public entrepreneurship. Researchers do not agree on the essential qualities of entrepreneurs or entrepreneurship in the public sector. In various studies, the term entrepreneur and the concept of entrepreneurship have been applied to diverse actors who in fact engage in very different activities and perform very different functions in the political system. These studies refer to elected officials who seek to build political capital and boost career ambitions (Dahl, 1961; Loomis, 1988; Mollenkopf, 1983) or who enact innovative policies (Bardach, 1972; J.L. Walker, 1977); individuals who attempt to supply collective goods for citizens or interest groups in exchange for personal or political profits (Fiorina & Shepsle, 1989; Frohlich, Oppenheimer & Young, 1971; Salisbury, 1969; Schneider & Teske, 1992); political leaders who are able to take actions free from the influence of both economic elites and political constituencies (B.D. Jones, 1989; Jones & Bachelor, 1986); governmental aides and analysts who formulate agenda items to aid politicians and advance policy objectives (Meltsner, 1976; Norris & Bembry, 1995; Polsby, 1984; Price, 1971); administrators of public corporations whose initiatives blend corporate efficiency together with moral leadership in the public interest (Tenenbaum, 1991); officials in administrative agencies who seek to expand institutional or personal power (Doig & Hargrove, 1990; Downs, 1967; Lewis, 1980; Milward, 1980; Nakamura & Smallwood, 1980; Ramamurti, 1986) or who wish to reorganize governmental services (Osborne & Gaebler, 1992); and individuals outside of government who create policy alternatives and seek opportunities to promote them before public officials (C.A. Arnold, 1989; Eyestone, 1978; Feldman, Putnam, & Gerteis, 1992; Gray, 1992; Kingdon, 1984; Oliver, 1991a; Roberts & King, 1989a; J.Q. Wilson, 1973).

There are gaps in knowledge as well. Very little is known about the supply of public entrepreneurs-when and why they bring an innovation into the political marketplace, and where they are most likely to emerge (Baumgartner & Jones, 1991; Schneider & Teske, 1992). An obvious incongruity is that the great majority of studies suggest that public entrepreneurship is usually carried out by governmental officials, whereas many of the most significant innovations rely on the ideas and energy of individuals and groups outside of government.

There appears to be considerable disagreement among theorists as to what motivates entrepreneurial behavior in the public sector. Frohlich, Oppenheimer, and Young (1971) and Schneider and Teske (1992) postulate that entrepreneurs are activated by "political profits," whereas Roberts and King (1991) and C.A. Arnold (1989) show that entrepreneurs are driven by the innovative idea itself and by the anticipated social benefits. Clearly, entrepreneurial "profits" may extend well beyond material benefits to a fulfillment of social or ideological purposes, satisfaction in political participation, higher status, or even altruism (Eyestone, 1978; Kingdon, 1984; Ramamurti, 1986; J.Q. Wilson, 1973, 1980).

The existing literature also presents disparate views of the scope of entrepreneurial activities and functions in the process of innovation. Some scholarly studies-perhaps conforming to popular opinion of what is "entrepreneurial"-suggest that entrepreneurship consists of simply proposing a policy change or addressing a salient issue (Schneider & Teske, 1992; Weissert, 1991). A more conventional notion is that the entrepreneurial function involves generating a policy proposal as well as political advocacy and negotiation on its behalf (Eyestone, 1978; Kingdon, 1984; Loomis, 1988; Meltsner, 1976). Still others argue that the concept requires not only the creation and advocacy of an innovation but also successful adoption and implementation (Roberts & King,

1991). This comprehensive view is well suited for studies concerned with how leaders affect policy performance, not simply the direction and flow of social resources. It also suits cases where the innovation is not a single statement of policy but a long-term course of action to reform a system of public and private services (Oliver, 1991a). Nonetheless, defining entrepreneurship by the scope of involvement and success of the innovation process is to miss the essential impact of these activities-a change in societal preferences and the creation of a problem-solving opportunity-and to rule out many interesting and important cases of leadership in policy innovation.

Given the lack of consensus as to who entrepreneurs are and what they do, entrepreneurship in the public sector has become an umbrella concept that covers up important distinctions and at the same time ignores common elements for those who seek to build more exacting theory and promote understanding of this phenomenon. We therefore need a more fundamental understanding of public entrepreneurs-of their motivations, their cognitive skills and political resources, their collaboration with other participants, their strategies to alter existing patterns of politics and public services, and their ultimate functions in policy-making and implementation.

Searching for the Essential Public Entrepreneur

Given the abundance of literature and diverse purposes of inquiry, it would be inappropriate to assert the superiority of any single model of public entrepreneurship. Nonetheless, the few studies that combine a general intellectual framework with sufficient detail on the individual cognition and behavior of entrepreneurs point in a common direction (Arnold, 1990; Bardach, 1972; Doig & Hargrove, 1990; Frohlich et al., 1971; Roberts & King, 1991). They adhere to the notion that the essence of public entrepreneurship is policy innovation-establishing new goals, procedures, organizations, or programs in the public sector.

Thus, public entrepreneurs are individual leaders in the process of policy innovation. They recombine intellectual, political, and organizational resources into new products and courses of action for government (Oliver, 1991a). Their activities and functions differ from those of other leaders in the public sector: Whereas other leaders may place priority on responding to constituencies, maintaining order, or accumulating power, public entrepreneurs specialize in identifying social problems and finding solutions (Polsby, 1984). They are "irritants in fixed systems" (Duhl, 1990). By drawing attention to new possibilities and then pushing for action, public entrepreneurs can break up routine interactions in governmental agencies and the policy process and provoke significant change on an issue.

Public entrepreneurs also differ from other participants in the process of policy innovation. Their interest and involvement extend beyond the traditional "enlightenment function" of researchers and policy analysts (Weiss, 1989) to political advocacy and strategy. Public entrepreneurs trade in the world of ideas as well as the world of action; indeed, their crucial function is translating ideas into action by coupling innovative policy proposals with problem situations and political opportunities (Kingdon, 1984; J.L. Walker, 1981).   In ideal circumstances, these individuals might prove instrumental in all phases of innovation from creating a proposal to fixing problems in the course of implementation (Bardach, 1977; Roberts & King, 1991). In so doing, they share roles with other actors in the political system: They may probe and adapt the ideas and inventions of intellectuals, recruit powerful champions, mobilize other advocates, and supervise and aid administrators throughout the process of policy innovation (Oliver, 1991a).

In sum, we find prototypical entrepreneurs "defining a policy problem, recommending a policy proposal, mobilizing supporters, and shepherding the proposal through a complex policy process characterized by uncertainty and ambiguity" (B.D. Jones, 1989, 11). They undertake entrepreneurial tasks from a variety of positions inside or outside of government. Although their actions would not be sufficient to bring off the whole enterprise by themselves, entrepreneurs are often critical actors in the process (Eyestone, 1978). They help orchestrate, but cannot entirely replace, the contributions of inventors, capitalists, and managers to the public enterprise.

ENTREPRENEURS AND HEALTH POLICY INNOVATION

The sections below will illustrate the tasks of public entrepreneurship with examples from the area of health policy. The entrepreneurs and their initiatives span many years and various purposes. Through their ideas and actions, they have touched the lives of millions of people and provoked serious discussion about the adequacy of our systems of medicine and public health.

Abe Bergman, a Seattle pediatrician described as "a political activist as well as a doctor" (Redman, 1973, 27), triggered action leading to diverse innovations such as the Consumer Product Safety Commission, the National Health Service Corps, child-proof packaging of medicines and toxic household products research and legislation leading to a definition of sudden infant death syndrome (SIDS) and public recognition of its social costs, expansion of the Indian Health Service, and other public health programs at all levels of government.

Paul Ellwood, a Minnesota physician trained in pediatrics, neurology, and rehabilitation medicine, was drawn into policy analysis and achieved prominence by coining the term health maintenance organization (HMO) and persuading the Nixon administration to endorse and promote the development of these prepaid health plans (Falkson, 1980; Brown, 1983). He was even more influential in stimulating HMO development and healthcare competition in Minnesota and throughout private industry in the United States (Oliver, 1990, 1991a). More recently, he founded the Jackson Hole Group and, with Alan Enthoven as a key partner, put forward the intellectual framework and many of the structural changes that found their way into major proposals for healthcare reform in the early 1990s.

Philip Lee, a California internist, left the Palo Alto Medical Clinic in 1963 to direct the health division of the Agency for International Development and then in 1965 became the first assistant secretary for health in the Department of Health, Education, and Welfare (DHEW), a position he returned to in 1993 with the Clinton administration. He helped lay the foundation for the field of health services research by initiating plans for the National Center for Health Services Research (with assistance from Paul Ellwood) and founding the Institute for Health Policy Studies at the University of California, San Francisco (UCSF), after serving as chancellor of UCSF from 1969 to 1972. Throughout his career, Lee has been a persistent critic of the practices of pharmaceutical companies in Third World countries. He also contributed to an important policy innovation as chairman of the Physician Payment Review Commission (PPRC), where he and his colleagues combined the roles of technical analyst and political advisor to help Congress reform the Medicare physician payment system in the late 1980s (Oliver, 1993).

John Kitzhaber practiced emergency medicine for thirteen years in southern Oregon before taking up politics as a full-time career. As president of the state senate, he crafted and oversaw the passage of a legislative package known collectively as the Oregon Health Plan in 1989. The most notable provisions created the Oregon Health Services Commission, which was charged with soliciting community input and establishing a ranked list of health services for state Medicaid coverage (Fox & Leichter, 1991; Kitzhaber & Gibson, 1991). Kitzhaber helped ensure the adoption of implementing legislation and fought for a federal waiver to allow the state to extend coverage of basic health services to all Oregonians in poverty and deny coverage for low-priority services. Kitzhaber's ability to articulate the case for explicit rationing of health services made him a national celebrity and helped him win election as governor of Oregon in 1994.

Bergman and Ellwood operated entirely from outside the political system, whereas Lee and Kitzhaber occupied positions within government. Only Kitzhaber possessed any formal authority to initiate and adopt new policies. What they have in common is that they all chose (at least periodically, if not permanently) to leave the professional realm of patient care behind and take up the practice of "political medicine."[6] They recognized that government could do more to improve or harm lives than physicians acting alone or in concert ever could.

These health policy entrepreneurs are counter examples to John Gardner's assertion (1986, 16) that "most professionals become specialists, and they have a powerful impulse to deal with only those aspects of a problem that fit their specialty. Leaders are generalists. An additional handicap of professionals is that they have generally had no occasion to develop the political sensitivity that leadership requires-may indeed have been schooled to be contemptuous of things political."[7] Observing how these leaders identified opportunities for innovation and took actions to bring them about may provide useful lessons about the tasks of public entrepreneurship.

A CONCEPTUAL MODEL OF PUBLIC ENTREPRENEURSHIP

An entrepreneur seeks a policy change that is significant in terms of (1) large scale and visibility, (2) break with preceding habit, and (3) lasting consequences (Polsby, 1984).[8] Whether an aspiring entrepreneur is promoting a legislative proposal or attempting to establish an innovation through other institutional channels, the challenges are essentially the same.

The proposed change, if accorded any legitimate chance of adoption, "stirs the pot" and activates both proponents and opponents (Duhl, 1990). An entrepreneur, working individually or from a core group, must recruit supporters and generate resources to place the issue onto the appropriate institutional agenda and then build and maintain a winning coalition. The fate of the proposed innovation is in many hands; usually, the entrepreneur must receive support from many officials who have the prerogative to give or withhold it (Bardach, 1972).

This study adopts the view that entrepreneurship in the commonwealth is analogous to entrepreneurship in the private marketplace. The basic function is to develop and market an innovation. Although the institutional pathways and specific tools of public entrepreneurship differ from private initiatives, I suggest the essential qualities of thought and action are very similar. This section describes how the entrepreneurial function is achieved through five tasks: identifying a market opportunity; designing an innovation; attracting investment; creating market demand; and monitoring the market. It explains the key strategies and tactics involved with each task and shows how these strategies and tactics may vary depending on factors such as the resources initially available to the entrepreneur, the nature of the proposed innovation, and the nature of the political environment.[9]

Identifying a Market Opportunity

Entrepreneurship consists of "action in uncertainty" (Gilder, 1984, 247). Donald Schon (1971) argued that by the late twentieth century, the predictability of the ideas and institutions governing our lives was forever lost as new technology and forms of social organization moved modern society beyond the "stable state." Change is unsettling; for most people, it is uncomfortable or even threatening. In contrast, Peter Drucker (1985, 28) noted that "entrepreneurs see change as the norm and as healthy. Usually, they do not bring about the change themselves.   But—and this defines entrepreneur and entrepreneurship—*the entrepreneur always searches for change, responds to it, and exploits it as an opportunity.*"

So innovation is itself a response to changes somewhere else in the environment—in basic knowledge, available technology, social conditions, or performance of the existing repertoire of private and public institutions. What sets entrepreneurs apart from other leaders in the political system is the nature of their response to change. Instead of searching for tried-and-true methods of the past, entrepreneurs exhibit a wider "horizon" of choice in planning a course of action. They have an ability to choose not only among tried possibilities but also untried ones (Schumpeter, 1939).   At the outset of the innovation process, entrepreneurs are free to choose where and how to initiate action. In the course of their normal duties and careers, they may often confront issues that demand immediate attention and resolution. These issues may even be the source of the idea for innovation.[10] Acting *as entrepreneurs*, however, leaders do not merely react to situations, nor do they simply approve or reject others' proposals for action. "They do not choose among paired alternatives; they define those alternatives. They select problems to attack from the full list of major and minor ailments in society" (R.D. Arnold, 1990, 7).

Most entrepreneurs are not pure opportunists in the sense that they rarely, if ever, stumble into the innovation process by complete accident. Most spend a lot of time, often many years, studying issues and developing policy ideas (Kingdon, 1984; Polsby, 1984; Weissert, 1991).   Scholars suggest that entrepreneurs possess uncommon powers of rational observation and pattern recognition, which enable them to dissect gaps in current operations and detect new needs based on emerging developments (Doig & Hargrove, 1990; Gilder, 1984; Schumpeter, 1934; Tropman & Morningstar, 1989). Through experience or careful examination, they map the allocation of resources and the political contours in their chosen area. They must understand the existing set of programs and practices, analyze their purposes and performance, and determine possibilities for change (Bardach, 1972). The experience of entrepreneurs most commonly fits the prescription attributed to Benjamin Disraeli: "The secret of success in life is for a man to be ready for his opportunity when it comes."

While chance favors the prepared mind, the opportunity to bring a proposal to the attention of policy-makers is still a matter of chance. What factors determine if the issue of concern to the entrepreneur will make it onto the governmental agenda and allow the proposed innovation (and competing alternatives) a hearing? Certainly, it is easier to pursue an issue that is receiving active attention from governmental officials and other participants in the policy community than to place a new item on the agenda. Opportunities for innovation arise most frequently from unexpected problems or from the routine needs of political leadership (Kingdon, 1984; Polsby, 1984). These two sources of demand offer public entrepreneurs potential "windows of opportunity" to push new products in the political marketplace.

Problem-Driven Opportunity. The least predictable, but probably the most powerful, source of policy innovation is the stream of problems that press themselves onto the already crowded governmental agenda. Problems are conditions that people find unacceptable and want to change. They emerge in several ways: Citizens or participants in a policy community may detect a "performance gap" in a given area based on crises, indicators, feedback from current policies, or comparison to similar policies or jurisdictions (Kingdon, 1984; J.L. Walker, 1974, 1981).

From the standpoint of the entrepreneur, an opportunity for "problemistic innovation" (Cyert & March, 1963) can occur for one of two reasons. In the first situation, there is sufficient ambiguity in the nature of the problem or what can be done about it so that the entrepreneur can offer his or her proposal as a plausible solution. The greater the uncertainty, the more likely a leader will be able to define a situation and offer a corresponding solution (B.D. Jones, 1989). In the second situation, the nature of the problem becomes defined in a way that dictates a solution similar to what the entrepreneur is promoting, or it provides an opportunity if the entrepreneur can design an innovation that conforms to the agreed-upon definition of the problem.

An example of innovation resulting from the first type of problem-oriented demand is the Oregon Health Plan, which guarantees a basic set of health services to Medicaid recipients but denies coverage for low-priority services. It grew out of a crisis in public opinion when state Medicaid officials informed the unemployed and uninsured mother of a seven-year-old boy suffering from leukemia that the program would not pay for a bone marrow transplant because the state legislature eliminated the transplant program earlier that year. The boy's death shortly thereafter reignited the transplant issue (though earlier denials of coverage to other transplant candidates had not) and brought the glare of national media attention to state policy makers. It was from that situation that John Kitzhaber, the president of the state senate, crafted a proposal to expand enrollment in the Medicaid program and set up a process to determine priorities for explicit rationing of services (Fox & Leichter, 1991; Kitzhaber & Gibson, 1991). Kitzhaber changed the issue from uncaring government-which would require policy makers to come up with money to pay for identifiable "needed services" without respect to other unmet needs-to an issue of fair allocation of scarce resources and how to establish an ethically defensible process for determining what medical needs were most deserving of governmental assistance.

The comprehensive reform of the Medicare physician payment system in 1989 also resulted from problem-oriented demand, but of a vastly different kind. These problems were detected from indicators showing that Medicare spending per beneficiary for physician services increased at unprecedented rates in the early 1980s. The rate increases failed to slow even after a fee freeze in 1984. In addition, physician expenses began to rise more quickly than hospital expenses after the 1983 reform of the Medicare hospital payment system. A great deal of research demonstrated distortions in relative payments for different services, unexplained variations in physician practice patterns, and a substantial volume of inappropriate services. The increased costs of the program were forcing increases in premiums for Medicare beneficiaries, who were already spending one of every six dollars of after-tax income on health services (Oliver, 1993). These problems were hardly noticed by the general public but gained the attention of experts in the health policy community and of politicians who served on the congressional committees responsible for oversight of the Medicare program.

Politics-Driven Opportunity. Opportunities for innovation can also occur in response to demand from within the political system. This kind of demand arises from shifts in the national mood, anticipation of and reaction to elections, interest group pressure, and the ideological preferences and priorities of officials (Kingdon, 1984; J.Q. Wilson, 1973).

Political sources of demand can be explicit or latent in character. Perhaps the clearest window of opportunity occurs when officials in the executive or legislative branch authorize a formal commission or task force to study a policy problem and recommend solutions. This presents aspiring entrepreneurs both inside and outside the commission a chance to promote innovations of their own design. The creation of the PPRC in 1985 signaled congressional intent to act on physician payment issues in the wake of the 1983 reform of the Medicare hospital payment system. Phil Lee, appointed as chairman of the commission, and his staff sensed the need for a fairly comprehensive approach to the problem and committed themselves to work in that direction. On the outside, the PPRC gave William Hsiao at the Harvard School of Medicine an opening to further develop a resource-based fee schedule to replace payments based on the fees submitted by physicians themselves.

The formation of a commission does not guarantee a receptive market for would-be innovators, however. Commission members must decide between incremental and nonincremental courses of action, and they must obtain the support of political leadership for their recommendations to have a chance of adoption. The fate of recent healthcare proposals from President Bush's Advisory Council on Social Security and from President Clinton's massive healthcare reform task force is a vivid reminder that initiation is no guarantee of success. The purpose of a commission may be purely reactive and call for transactional-not transformational-leaders (Burns, 1978). It may provide a forum for a particular set of interests to voice their concerns, it may mediate the demands of competing interests and negotiate a short-term resolution, or it may be no more than a symbolic gesture (Alford, 1975; Edelman, 1964). At best, the politicians who create a commission will take a wait-and-see attitude; only after they observe the level of agreement, assertiveness, and credibility of the commission will they commit real resources for innovation.

Many sources of demand for innovative proposals are less explicit but highly predictable, since governmental officials need to follow up on election promises and take actions they can claim credit for in the next election (R.D. Arnold, 1990; Fenno, 1973; Kingdon, 1981; Mayhew, 1974; Polsby, 1984). A new administration presents perhaps the most obvious set of opportunities for aspiring entrepreneurs in virtually all areas of public policy. Paul Ellwood was able to take advantage of this avenue to innovation when he made connections with high-level health officials in the Nixon administration. They were actively searching for a strategy to fend off pressure from liberal Democrats and organized labor for tax-financed national health insurance, and Ellwood's idea of creating HMOs to provide more comprehensive insurance coverage and greater efficiency through market competition met their ideological and intellectual tests. In 1970, the newly appointed secretary of health, education and welfare, Elliot Richardson, authorized grants for the development of HMOs. Two months later, President Nixon endorsed HMOs as a centerpiece of his "National Health Strategy" and the wheels of innovation were under way (Brown, 1983; Falkson, 1980). According to Ellwood, the simple endorsement by the president did more to stimulate HMO development in the private sector than the national legislation that followed over two years later.

Aside from the obvious demand created by elections and a change in partisan composition, another less visible source of demand is turnover in key positions (Kingdon, 1984; March & Olsen, 1989). Abe Bergman saw an opportunity created by legislative turnover in his effort to establish a National Health Service Corps to bring doctors to underserved rural areas and inner-city neighborhoods. In 1969, Senator Warren Magnuson, a legislative powerhouse, took over the chairmanship of the HEW Appropriations Subcommittee and Bergman seized the moment to provide him with an informal group of health advisors and a host of new policy options (Redman, 1973). At the same time, Representative Paul Rogers was seeking to take up the mantle of health policy leader in the wake of Representative John Fogarty's death and Lister Hill's retirement from the U.S. Senate in 1968. Rogers was not even chairman of a health subcommittee but was given free rein by the chairman, who had little interest in health affairs. As a result of Rogers' ambition, "he needed ideas for new legislation, and welcomed any visitor with an imaginative proposal" (Redman, 1973, 89). Bergman was easily able to persuade Rogers to introduce legislation jointly with Magnuson to create the new medical corps.

Issues recycle in government and officials spend much of their time considering proposals to expand, maintain, or cut back existing policies and programs (Cobb & Elder, 1972; Kingdon, 1984). Reauthorization of a major piece of legislation is another predictable opportunity for entrepreneurs. Ironically, it may be harder to substantially modify an existing policy than to initiate an altogether new policy (J.Q. Wilson, 1973), a point to which we will return below.

Finally, many demands from the political system are not really explicit at all. Instead, legislators and their staffs (the same can be said of the heads of administrative agencies) routinely search the environment for discretionary items they can place on the policy agenda (Loomis, 1988; Polsby, 1984; Price, 1971; Salisbury & Shepsle, 1981; J.L. Walker, 1977). Although "slack innovation" (Cyert & March, 1963) might serve electoral needs, much of it appears directed at the other goals of political leaders such as making good public policy or enhancing their reputation within the policy community (Kingdon, 1981; J.L. Walker, 1977).

Entrepreneurial Opportunity. Few of the market opportunities that public entrepreneurs might act on will be the result of their own endeavors. Yet innovations do occur when there is no pressing problem or special receptivity from the policy makers who generally set the governmental agenda. Paul Ellwood was able to trigger the fastest HMO development in the nation in his home state of Minnesota by persuading medical and civic leaders of the worth of the idea and providing technical assistance to the new organizations. The success of his voluntary efforts pressured state lawmakers to approve enabling legislation and created the foundation for profound competition and restructuring in the Minnesota healthcare market (Oliver, 1990; 1991). Abe Bergman helped pull together a grassroots coalition to define SIDS attract governmental funding for research, and educate local officials so that grieving parents who lost their babies would receive compassion and social support rather than legal harassment (Bergman, 1986).

The advantage one gains by creating an opportunity through entrepreneurial supply is that there are likely to be few if any competing proposals. The innovation can be judged on its own merits in relation to the status quo—a comparison more easily controlled by the entrepreneur—instead of facing the complications of multiple proposals and rapidly shifting stakes.

Even when entrepreneurs cannot directly create their own market opportunities, they can do preliminary work so that when windows of opportunity do arise in the problem or political streams, they will have an easier time linking their proposals to the perceived needs for action. They seek ways to "soften up" public opinion, experts in the policy community, or key policy makers with media coverage or research that better documents a problem or highlights a solution (Eyestone, 1978; Kingdon, 1984). These activities may help push the problems they are concerned with higher on the agenda or plant a seed that leads to future opportunities. This sort of behavior indicates that there is more strategy than meets the eye in loosely coupled systems of decision making (Cohen, March, & Olsen, 1972; Kingdon, 1984). The promoters of solutions do more than chase problems and decision opportunities when they arise—they often help create them.

Designing an Innovation

Social problems, political interests, or sometimes the sheer power of a good idea can create an opportunity for policy change. Whether a proposed innovation turns out to be an idea whose time has come depends largely on whether there is an available, worked-out design to match the problem definition and the political climate (Eyestone, 1978; Kingdon, 1984; J.L. Walker, 1977; 1981).

An entrepreneur may or may not be the *inventor* of the idea for innovation (Schumpeter, 1939). Indeed, the ultimate origin of the idea is for practical purposes unimportant (Kingdon, 1984). The critical thing is how well entrepreneurs and supporters take their ideas forward. They will be in the best possible position to take advantage of a market opportunity if they can design a blueprint for action that meets the tests of both technical and political feasibility.

Technical Feasibility. Entrepreneurs may develop an innovation that is very specific in design, or they may propose something that lacks precision engineering. They tread a fine line in this area: They must be prepared to demonstrate that rearranging critical resources such as money, personnel, clients, or decision-making authority can "invigorate the existing ecology of programs and practices" and produce better overall results (Bardach, 1972, 184). On the other hand, entrepreneurs who are able to maintain a certain ambiguity in their design can attract broader investment and market support during the critical early stages of innovation (Cobb & Elder, 1972; Eyestone, 1978). The issue of technical feasibility is debated primarily by experts in the policy community. The interests and forces pushing an issue forward can go for naught if a proposal is incompatible with the intellectual convictions of experts and policy makers and their knowledge of past efforts to deal with the problem at hand (Polsby, 1984). The consensus or division of opinion among policy specialists acts as a filtering device for proposals; it can be a serious impediment if experts disagree on the causes of a problem or the credibility of a solution (Brown, 1991; J.L. Walker, 1981).

Clearly, expert research and analysis are not value free. It is used more to support existing positions than to enlighten and persuade policy makers to change positions (Weiss, 1989). Indeed, there is seldom unanimity on the workability and effectiveness of an innovation of any importance. Perhaps the most influential kind of information in policy making is incontestable documentation of the nature and magnitude of a problem (Brown, 1991). This can help keep a proposal moving forward even when disagreements arise about the likely consequences of the innovation.

A major challenge for the entrepreneur in the area of technical feasibility, therefore, is to inject the highest- quality information possible into the debate. Entrepreneurs recognize that the risks outweigh any possible advantages of using intentionally selective or biased information. They almost universally appear to rely on rational, not manipulative, persuasion, to influence others to support an innovation.[11] Andrew McGuire, the initiator of a national campaign for fire-safe cigarettes, said, "One can never underestimate the need for the highest ethical standards in all advocacy work." A related principle is "Getting and using accurate data is absolutely necessary. Spurious data or exaggeration of data is to be religiously avoided" (McGuire, 1989, 74).

The quality of information was cited by Phil Lee as a critical factor in the influence of the PPRC and the ultimate adoption of Medicare physician payment reform. The most useful information generated by the commission was the data and analysis that pinpointed and verified key problem areas and simulated the effects of policy options. These helped consolidate support for the commission's recommendations and refute the claims of interest groups opposed to various provisions (Oliver, 1993).

Political Feasibility. Credible evidence on the technical merits of an innovation is an increasingly important, but still not unnecessary, condition for moving a proposal toward adoption in the political system. Gilder (1984, 247) asserted that technical knowledge and "settled expertise" are overrated because in the realm of innovation, belief precedes knowledge. Private sector entrepreneurs must be able to "act boldly in the shadow of doubt" about the precise requirements and consequences of their enterprise. In all likelihood, this is even more true when it comes to governmental action.

John Kingdon (1984) listed several criteria for political feasibility: financial affordability, congruence with community values, acceptability to specialized publics and the mass public, and receptivity of critical politicians. "Hard data" on the anticipated costs of an innovation have always been important to an entrepreneur's cause (Bardach, 1972), but affordability is probably of greater importance today than at any time in the past. Advocates may have to demonstrate that new policies and programs will be "budget neutral" or even reduce net governmental outlays so that policy makers will not be forced to identify new revenue sources or cut other programs. Budget neutrality was a key selling point for reform of the Medicare physician payment system, as it was for overhauling the federal tax code three years earlier (Mucciaroni, 1991; Oliver, 1993). Similarly, the principal thrust of the Oregon Health Plan was to contain the rising costs of the Medicaid program; Neil Goldschmidt, governor of Oregon at the time, referred to Medicaid as "the monster that ate the states" (Fox & Leichter, 1991, 13).

A perhaps even more formidable task for the entrepreneur is to design a proposal with a favorable combination of benefits and costs. This task cuts to the core of political feasibility and may be the singular challenge in public entrepreneurship. An entrepreneur can advance the prospects of innovation and prevent some foreseeable dangers by first mapping the interests and alliances in the policy area (Bardach, 1972). It is important to evaluate the organizational history of the issue and either take advantage of, or attempt to avoid, alliances with proven track records. One can then assess the magnitude and intensity of the current stakes to understand how they may promote or threaten the prospects for innovation.

The entrepreneur must be aware that political decisions are based on the perceived, not the true, consequences of a policy. What matters most for political feasibility is not whether the *overall* benefits of an innovation exceed its costs. Rather, the pattern of support and opposition will depend on the *perceived distribution* of its benefits and costs-their magnitude, timing, and certainty (Arnold, 1990; J.Q. Wilson, 1973, 1980). There are three kinds of benefits and costs-geographic, group, and general-and most policies will include some combination of all six effects. Geographic and group effects are more noticeable than general effects.

Logically, the entrepreneur is best off with a design that provides concentrated benefits (large, immediate, and direct) and diffuse costs (small, delayed, and indirect). In contrast, it will be extraordinarily difficult to attract the support of policy makers for a proposal that imposes concentrated costs in order to provide diffuse benefits (R.D. Arnold, 1990; Olson, 1989). Concentrated interests systematically outweigh diffuse interests in the politics of policy making and, in addition, politicians expect punishment for decisions that impose costs or take away existing benefits far more than reward for providing new benefits.

This kind of analysis helps explain why the ideas of Paul Ellwood and Alain Enthoven for reforming the U.S. healthcare system through "managed competition" have been stymied for nearly two decades, even when politicians who rhetorically support "market solutions" have held the keys to governmental power (Oliver, 1991b). R. Douglas Arnold (1990) argued that proposals to use marketlike incentives rather than command-and-control regulation fit into a class of "politically repellent policies" where citizens do not see a tangible connection between the proposed policy instruments and the intended effects. The Jackson Hole version of managed competition would impose some immediate costs by cutting small insurance companies and brokers out of the system, encouraging the growth of health plans that limit patient choice of physicians and hospitals, and placing a cap on the tax deductibility of private health insurance, while most of the promised benefits (financial savings) are indirect and longterm. Systematic thinking here runs head-on into political perceptions. Even if policy makers believe in the efficacy of market incentives, they do not trust citizens to rally on behalf of these policies and counteract the certain opposition of a smaller but more intense set of organizations and individuals.

This logic of collective action leads to the conclusion that it may be easier to mobilize support for an entirely new policy with fairly uncertain consequences than to substantially reform an existing policy where citizens or groups will intensely defend their more certain, established interests (J.Q. Wilson, 1973). An entrepreneur who hopes to overcome entrenched interests and establish an innovation to serve the general good must, at the very least, employ tactics to make potential beneficiaries aware of their stakes and to make the costs less visible. The example of Phil Lee and the PPRC in physician payment reform shows that a more feasible route to innovation is to design a package that provides something positive to an important constituency that faces overall losses. The American Medical Association (AMA) supported the development of the new Medicare fee schedule; in exchange, the AMA had to accept limits on how much physicians could charge patients over the amount paid by Medicare and on Medicare spending for physician services (Oliver, 1993). This strategy of blending benefits and costs defuses some opposition and lessens the chance that a powerful group will lobby against a whole package that contains some provisions the group definitely wants.

Attracting Investment

A good idea is nothing without the resources to bring it to fruition. John Gardner noted that "it is a familiar failing of visionaries and of people who live in the realm of ideas and issues that they are not inclined to soil their hands with the nuts and bolts of organizational or social functioning....Good leaders don't ignore the machinery. Every leader needs some grasp of how to 'work the system'" (1986, 12-13).

Abe Bergman sounded a similar warning to aspiring entrepreneurs, suggesting that even if they have the desire to move from the world of ideas into the world of political action, they need additional equipment for the challenges ahead: "A frequent shortcoming of well-meaning social change agents is their failure to study the battlefield before marching into action. Anyone who works for social change must first know where the power to effect change lies. Speeches, petitions, mass meetings, newspaper headlines, are all totally useless unless they result in some tangible action" (Bergman, 1986, 68).

In the private sector, entrepreneurs are unlikely to develop and market an innovation of any importance without considerable help from others in adapting existing technology, financial support, management, and marketing. They need essential resources to move from a promising design to a viable product. The reality is that successful entrepreneurs act less like "mountain men" than leaders of a "wagon train" in their pioneering activities (Tropman & Morningstar, 1989). This is even more true for entrepreneurs in the public sector. Whether armed with a vague idea or an exquisite prototype, a public entrepreneur needs two valuable resources: institutional access and political capital.

Recruiting Investors. In any given arena for policy deliberation, only a limited number of issues and ideas are in "good currency" and are likely to be attended to (Schon, 1971). An entrepreneur needs to recruit influential insiders because they are the institutional gatekeepers who ultimately control which issues move from the governmental agenda at large to the agenda for policy decisions. One quickly learns that political leaders are active participants in agenda building, not simply arbiters of the policy disputes among outside forces (Cobb & Elder, 1972).

The U.S. political system, which divides power among different institutions and levels of government, offers numerous points of access to aspiring entrepreneurs. This access is offset, however, by the potential number of veto points opponents may exercise throughout the process of innovation. There really is no single marketplace of ideas in the Madisonian system, and the resulting need for cross-cutting agreement or at least deference among governmental leaders and institutions may be regarded as either the genius or curse of U.S. politics (Ferman, 1990; Hayes, 1992; Shafer, 1989). To navigate the system and identify the most favorable arenas for action, entrepreneurs must either be "inside-dopesters" or collaborate with someone who is (Eyestone, 1978).

In addition, access to an arena must be accompanied by the power and inclination to force action. "To effect change, one must either possess power oneself or find someone with power willing to 'push the button'" (Bergman, 1986, 46). Entrepreneurs often have no formal authority of their own (Oliver, 1991a; Tropman & Morningstar, 1989). So they need to recruit partners who do possess formal authority and other forms of political capital and convince them to invest their resources and skills to underwrite the development and marketing of the innovation. Entrepreneurs must find investors who not only favor the innovation but will make it a priority based on the anticipated electoral, ideological, or other special benefits. The prestige and passive assent of a prominent investor is not especially weighty compared to the cues sent through active enthusiasm for the enterprise. One looks for investors and subordinates who will help build a coalition through their powers of persuasion and position. Many studies of policy innovation acknowledge the critical importance of these policy champions or opinion leaders (Angle & Van de Ven, 1989; Roberts & King, 1991; Rogers & Kim, 1985; Szanton, 1981).

John Kitzhaber, as Senate majority leader for three terms, was in a position to champion his own proposal for the Oregon Health Plan. He was also a close friend and political ally of the speaker of the Oregon House and they cooperated on crucial decisions (Fox & Leichter, 1991). The other entrepreneurs usually found equally influential investors to underwrite their innovations. Abe Bergman makes no secret of the "power of Warren Magnuson" as his key to success in various innovations (Bergman, 1986). He had previously helped Senator Magnuson move into the area of consumer affairs with his work to improve lawnmower safety and flame-retardant sleepwear. Bergman gained enough credibility that when he brought up his idea for the National Health Service Corps, Magnuson agreed to lend him staff support and eventually his legislative expertise and clout. The senator was the ideal investor: He could endow an entrepreneur at once with the resources of access, seniority, and staff. Observers of physician payment reform stress the critical contributions of Senator Jay

Rockefeller, who after a private meeting with Phil Lee became determined to enact the legislative package in the 1989 budget reconciliation bill. Rockefeller resurrected the physician payment proposals several times during the conference committee deliberations and was a key influence in the exhaustive negotiations that concluded only hours before congressional adjournment. Potential investors with nominally similar positions may differ significantly in the amount of political capital they can deliver to the entrepreneur. In the private sector, though money from one person is as good as money from another, some investors can provide additional resources such as a marketing or distribution infrastructure. Political resources are even more differentiated, and the entrepreneur must use good judgment in seeking someone to champion his or her innovation. Individuals who can lend resources to the entrepreneur and enterprise draw their power primarily from their formal institutional position-perhaps as a chairperson or senior member of a committee-but also from their style, reputation, and partisanship. They may have the ability to call hearings, or wield jurisdictional control, or they may simply have a reputation for being serious and skilled policy makers. An alert entrepreneur will also avoid investors who might provide earnest support but weaken the prospects for attracting other investment or selling the product. Eric Redman (1973) noted that the proposal for a National Health Service Corps would have been dead in 1970 had a summer intern for a far more junior and liberal Democratic senator succeeded in drafting a bill before aides to Senator Magnuson found out about it. The government-run program would have attracted much greater scrutiny from conservatives if someone other than Magnuson-a member of the Senate's "Inner Club"-had introduced the idea first. Paul Ellwood claimed his success in getting President Nixon to endorse HMOs was largely attributable to the extraordinary skills of two lower-level investors, Assistant Secretary Lewis Butler and Undersecretary John Veneman in the Department of Health, Education, and Welfare.

Establishing an Enterprise. As entrepreneurs acquire access and political capital from investors, they need to convert those resources into an ongoing capacity to refine and market the innovation in the broader political marketplace. Commonly, they recruit other analysts and advocates into an "enterprise," a group or network of supporters who can attract further investment, promote the innovation, respond to criticism and in turn critique competing alternatives, solicit feedback, and help coordinate information and action as a larger coalition is built. The aim of the entrepreneur should be to develop a network with complementary resources and skills in analysis, marketing, and management (Bardach, 1972). The combination of people and resources represented in the enterprise will be an important determinant of the ultimate size and strength of the coalition backing the innovation.

The enterprise can be very small or relatively large, and it can be developed through an existing organizational base, a new organizational base, or ad hoc collaboration. Abe Bergman was able to come to Washington, D.C., and set to work with an accomplished network of committee and personal staff loyal to Senator Magnuson. In addition, he regularly "consulted the pros" like Mary Lasker and Mike Gorman, the unofficial but unparalleled lobbyists for biomedical research and other health issues. To address the issue of SIDS, Bergman recognized the need for new organizations to change the policy environment; to supplement his regular contacts, he helped establish and lead an emerging grassroots movement through the SIDS Foundation (Bergman, 1986).

Phil Lee headed a highly unorthodox, yet highly organized enterprise created within the Congress to deal explicitly with physician payment issues. The PPRC simultaneously advised the three main committees responsible for Medicare and served as a central point of access for participants across the health policy community.

Paul Ellwood built up a core enterprise at the American Rehabilitation Foundation—later called InterStudy—that became the touchstone for HMO development in the Twin Cities and throughout the country. His style was to bring in bright, interested professionals and analysts and let their ambition and creative tension run as freely as possible. InterStudy produced policy proposals and technical assistance and in addition served as the "farm system" to develop managers for the fledgling HMO industry (Oliver, 1991a). The Jackson Hole Group is an effort to link a similar small think tank to a more coherent network of change agents, most of whom are again in the private sector.

John Kitzhaber worked primarily from his legislative base, but after the initial plan was enacted in 1989 he created a new enterprise for implementation. He turned the formulation of the basic health services package over to the newly created Oregon Health Services Commission. He had also for several years been a member of a citizens group called Oregon Health Decisions that attempted to critique the current allocation of health care resources. This group worked with the state commission to solicit public input through phone surveys and dozens of community meetings across the state. Kitzhaber intentionally withdrew to the background; his objective in setting up this process was to get ordinary people to buy into the idea of rationing healthcare (Fox & Leichter, 1991).

The methods of Ellwood and Bergman in particular indicate that entrepreneurs who are outside of government must rely to an extraordinary extent on persuasion to accomplish anything. Private sector entrepreneurs can use financial inducements or simply replace uncooperative employees, suppliers, and distributors; in contrast, public entrepreneurs must focus on "coaching" the other players (Duhl, 1990; Tropman & Morningstar, 1989), and sometimes they will be reduced to mere "cheerleading" as events leave their control.

Creating Market Demand

Because any investor is likely to calculate potential as well as currently known preferences in the marketplace (R.D. Arnold, 1990), entrepreneurs must be prepared to demonstrate the superiority of their product to the status quo and other legitimate alternatives. In almost all situations, entrepreneurs must sell their design for innovation not only to interested investors but to a broader coalition of policy makers, organized interests, and various segments of the public.

Where there is a favorable balance of preferences in the marketplace, the entrepreneur must maintain it as policy makers approach a decision to adopt the innovation or not. Where the balance of preferences is uncertain or unfavorable, the entrepreneur must seek ways to create, activate, or change the policy preferences of selected individuals and groups. Because of the inherent uncertainty of innovation, entrepreneurs inhabit a realm where supply creates demand (Gilder, 1984). Consumer tastes and preferences in the political market are not fixed; they depend to some degree on the available options (B.D. Jones, 1989; J.Q. Wilson, 1980, 1990). New products in the political market-proposals for policy innovation-create new preferences and alter existing ones among governmental officials, their staffs, interest groups, and the general public. Hence, at times the entrepreneurs are actively involved in creating the widespread demand to which they appear to be responding (Doig & Hargrove, 1990).

Entrepreneurs can improve the market perceptions of an innovation by enhancing the visibility of the benefits or obscuring the costs. They can shape policy preferences to fit the proposal through one of three basic strategies: (1) persuasion, (2) choice of arena and procedures, or (3) bargaining and modification (R.D. Arnold, 1990).

Persuasion. Mere attention to an issue, rather than a favorable resolution of an issue, amounts to a hollow victory for an aspiring entrepreneur (Eyestone, 1978). The basic challenge is to persuade a sufficient number of individuals and groups to register their support for the innovation.

Entrepreneurs full of conviction and brimming with enthusiasm may become frustrated trying to generate demand for their ideas even among friendly audiences. It may prove unexpectedly difficult to get individuals and groups to do more than register support if they recognize that any resources and effort they commit to adoption will produce broad benefits that flow to many other parties as well (Bardach, 1972; Frohlich et al., 1971; Olson, 1965).

It is helpful to keep in mind, however, that a group will support or oppose a proposal for its own reasons; thus, adoption does not depend on a harmony of interests or "meeting of the minds" (Bardach, 1972). The skillful entrepreneur will be able to identify a variety of material and ideological preferences and tailor arguments to those preferences.

One tactic of persuasion is to link the proposed innovation to popular existing policies. Paul Ellwood and his collaborators, for example, initially tried to get Congress to add a "Part C" HMO option to the Medicare program. By the same token, the entrepreneurs must be prepared for opponents to link a proposal to unpopular policies and motives.   Abe Bergman sought Senator Henry Jackson's co-sponsorship of the National Health Service Corps bill to defend against the possibility that the Pentagon might come out in opposition and jeopardize passage due to a non health issue. The unquestioned support from Jackson, a hawk on the Vietnam War, immunized the bill from allegations that the National Health Service Corps was merely a way for doctors to dodge military service, which was still mandatory at the time.

Another tactic of persuasion is to construct favorable arguments about governmental responsibilities and capacities. Medicare physician payment reform and a host of other major health policy innovations have come about only when the attentive public and policy makers judge that the private sector has proven incapable or unwilling to control healthcare costs (Oliver, 1993). Similarly, the National Health Service Corps was acceptable even to most conservatives because it addressed a clear market failure-rural areas and inner cities were unable to attract physicians despite demonstrable medical needs. The geographic benefits for underserved rural districts represented by conservative legislators of course muted their ideological concerns about governmental intervention in private medical practice (Redman, 1973).

Entrepreneurs may also attempt to publicize selective benefits or costs to mobilize support for their proposal. Abe Bergman decided that the treatment of SIDS parents by law enforcement officials (and neighbors) would only improve only by showing how ignorant coroners were interpreting SIDS cases as intentional homicides. Local officials might not have changed their ways based on high-minded appeals; but creating "villains" prompted a rapid response (Bergman, 1986).

A final tactic of persuasion is to attempt to expand the scope of conflict by framing the issue in a way calculated to bring new parties into the debate (R.D. Arnold, 1990; Schattschneider, 1960).   John Kitzhaber took the risky step of voting against a proposal to restore money for Medicaid transplants after the initial crisis in order to trigger a statewide debate that included not just advocates for the poor and medical care providers but business, labor, and ordinary citizens. Depending on the balance of preferences, entrepreneurs may conversely try to contain the scope of conflict and "let sleeping dogs lie" (Polsby, 1984).

Choice of Arena and Procedures. Entrepreneurs must know when to do battle and how to make the battleground one of their own choosing. The arena can have a decisive effect on how a proposal is defined by outsiders and on the chances for favorable action by insiders (Baumgartner & Jones, 1991). Entrepreneurs must scout out ways to give their proposal a hearing before the most sympathetic committee, agency, or level of government. They need to seek the arena where the interests supporting their innovation carry the greatest weight (Bardach, 1972). Abe Bergman and his collaborators at first sought to establish the National Health Service Corps by simply earmarking additional appropriations to the Public Health Service, a move Senator Magnuson could easily carry off from his subcommittee position. It was only after the legislative counsel persuasively argued that the Public Health Service had no authority to place physicians in normal communities that they pursued new legislation (Redman, 1973).[12] John Kitzhaber gained a strategic advantage for the legislative consideration of the Oregon Health Plan when he created the new Senate Committee on Health Insurance and Bioethics and appointed a freshman senator and ally as chairman in order to avoid the less sympathetic chairman of the existing Human Resources Committee (Fox & Leichter, 1991).

There are procedures in the policy process that can affect how traceable benefits or costs are to policy makers. To weaken the chain of causation from a policy choice to political perceptions, entrepreneurs can maneuver to delegate difficult choices to other governmental bodies such as commissions or executive agencies. They can also attempt to bundle a decision that would impose concentrated costs with other more politically attractive policy decisions. Finally, entrepreneurs can argue for rules that restrict changes in proposals and thereby protect the integrity of the innovation while actually increasing its chances for adoption (R.D. Arnold, 1990).

John Kitzhaber and other legislators in Oregon delegated the ranking of health services to a new commission and at the same time restricted the legislature to either accepting or rejecting the rankings as a whole without any modifications when the commission submitted its list (Fox & Leichter, 1991). Similarly, congressional leaders routinely incorporated politically difficult choices in physician payment reform into the annual omnibus budget reconciliation process. The PPRC did its own bundling by designing a package with balance billing restrictions to satisfy Medicare beneficiaries, the resource-based fee schedule to please most physicians, and budget limits to protect the interests of taxpayers. Controversial decisions such as setting a conversion factor for the fee schedule and determining annual budget limits were delegated to the Health Care Financing Administration or to the PPRC (Oliver, 1993).

Bargaining and Modification. Abe Bergman is fond of quoting Albert Camus, who chided religious authorities by saying, "You seek a world in which no children starve; I seek a world in which fewer children starve" (1986, 136). Entrepreneurs are unlikely to make much headway on an issue if they are unprepared to compromise. In most cases, they cannot afford either the intransigence of agitators, who often sacrifice immediate gains for abstract ideals, or the unprincipled conduct of negotiators, who are more concerned with resolving momentary conflict than the quality and long-term viability of the solution (Dahl, 1984). Their underlying approach to politics is what I would call "pragmatic idealism." Though they may have an ultimate goal that is quite fixed, they must be flexible as to the path and number of steps chosen to get there; they must be ends-fixed, means-flexible.

Entrepreneurs may agree to modify their prototype at different times and for different reasons. They may introduce or offer modifications in the design of their initial proposal or in the heat of final formulation, amendment, and decision. They may employ this strategy in order to attract additional investors who can then persuade others to join the cause. Or they may propose modifications to co-opt potential adversaries and create enough disunity to prevent a serious opposition campaign (R.D. Arnold 1990). Advocates of budget limits for Medicare physician services agreed to drop automatic "expenditure targets" and substitute discretionary "volume performance standards" for calculating fee updates; this was viewed as a largely semantic difference by many, and indeed Congress has followed a default formula in setting the annual volume performance standards (Oliver, 1993).

One tactic available to entrepreneurs is to scale back the scope of the proposal or phase in its provisions to reduce costs and uncertainty about the consequences. Another modification is to reduce the apparent costs of the innovation by providing outright compensation to groups or areas who would incur sizable costs; or more commonly, one might attempt to spread costs out over a larger constituency, delay them, or design them as later-order effects in a chain of causation stemming from the policy decision (R.D. Arnold, 1990). Abe Bergman and his allies consistently presented the National Health Service Corps as a relatively small, elite program that would serve as a demonstration rather than immediately fill all the unmet needs for physician services. In a predictable move, Congress determined that reductions in fees for physician specialties under the new Medicare fee schedule would be phased in over five years while increases for undervalued specialties were accelerated (Oliver, 1993).

The entrepreneur can modify benefits in the proposal as well, aiming to make them more visible to important group or geographic constituencies. The expected advantages of each bargain, of course, must be weighed against the possible loss of supporters and resources within the entrepreneur's coalition (Bardach, 1972).

Monitoring the Market

The characteristic and charismatic work of entrepreneurship is finished when prudent investment and skilled marketing lead policy makers to adopt an innovation. Entrepreneurs typically have had to struggle to develop a design that is technically sound and create a favorable pattern of political preferences.

Early success does not guarantee long-term success in the marketplace, however. The market is inherently unstable, and innovations commonly exhibit dynamic growth or decline (Gilder, 1984). If entrepreneurs are able to help move the innovation through implementation and institutionalization, the odds of long-term performance appear to increase (Roberts & King, 1991; Oliver, 1991a).

At the national level, it is extremely difficult for entrepreneurs to have a substantial role in implementing the innovations they have pushed onto the agenda and into reality. Abe Bergman, for example, was never asked to play an advisory role in the National Health Service Corps, although he did help communities in Washington State recruit physicians from the program. Similarly, Paul Ellwood had little participation in the government's HMO program and instead concentrated on technical assistance to individual plans in the Twin Cities and throughout the country. Phil Lee was able to help monitor and fine-tune the progress of physician payment reform, but the principal implementation functions rested with the Health Care Financing Administration and private insurance carriers. Congress' decision to not only maintain the PPRC but expand its mandate from Medicare to Medicaid and private sector healthcare issues signified respect for the commitment and capacity of Lee and his fellow commissioners and staff and their influence in the health policy community. John Kitzhaber elected to take a far less active role in implementing the Oregon Health Plan; it is not clear whether he viewed this as necessity given his other obligations or as a desirable way to increase others' investment in the program.

We can conclude that despite common limitations on their scope of involvement, entrepreneurs are potentially valuable in several implementation roles. First, they can be *educators* and share their knowledge of the initial philosophy and design with executives charged with administration and with street-level bureaucrats and clients. Second, they can be problem *fixers*; if they have generated sufficient resources in the course of the enterprise, they can use them to "fix" implementation games that might dissipate the effectiveness of the new policy (Bardach, 1977). Their influence may rest on valuable information they can provide, or it may rest on their ability to call in key investors who were involved in adopting the innovation and who are willing to spend further political capital to ensure better accountability or coordination to prevent reinvention of the policy (Rogers & Kim, 1985). Third, they can serve as *conduits* to provide credible evaluation and feedback from implementors to the leaders and institutions who authorized the innovation. The implementors want recognition of the technical complexities and political constraints of turning a vision into reality, and the designers and investors want to maintain a favorable climate of political opinion and market preferences. Thus, a consummate entrepreneur can improve the interaction of participants across the policy community and help ensure an evolution of the innovation that is more, not less, effective (Majone & Wildavsky, 1984).

NOTES

1. The development of this conceptual model is part of a larger project on *entrepreneurship and Health policy innovation,* funded by an Investigator Award in Health Policy Research from the Robert Wood Johnson Foundation of Princeton, New Jersey.

2. Gilder (1984) pointed out that the potential for financial and epistemological profit go hand in hand-great risks by entrepreneurs can yield great gains in knowledge.

In this view, entrepreneurs contribute to social progress by exposing new ideas to the possibility of failure, and if they indeed fail, they have still helped test hypotheses about economic life.

3. The economic perspective on entrepreneurship and innovation implicitly offers normative support for the phenomenon. Observers of entrepreneurship in political markets have also generally imbued the concept with favorable meaning.

Because innovations, by definition, gain short-term approval in the economic or political market and thereby meet a presumptive test of efficiency does not warrant an uncritical view of innovation and entrepreneurship. Some observers acknowledge that since innovation benefits some and injures others, we should divest ourselves of any preconceived value judgment and assess each case of innovation on its own merits (Doig & Hargrove, 1990; Rogers & Kim, 1985; Schumpeter, 1949).

Furthermore, from a historical perspective, the adoption of one innovation may foreclose market opportunities for what are in the longterm, more efficient alternatives. One innovation may trigger additional changes whereas another may forestall changes that come to be regarded as appropriate or necessary, hence one cannot assume the efficiency of innovation (Deutch, 1985; March & Olsen, 1984; March & Olsen, 1989).

4. This group of studies includes Eyestone, 1978; Kingdon, 1984; Nakamura and Smallwood, 1980; Oliver, 1990; Polsby, 1984; J.L. Walker, 1977 and 1981. These studies refer to creative leaders in policy innovation with labels similar to "public entrepreneur," such as "issue entrepreneur," "policy entrepreneur," "political entrepreneur," or "bureaucratic entrepreneur."

5. These include, for example, R.D. Arnold, 1990; Bardach, 1977; Burns, 1978; Mucciaroni, 1991; Riker, 1986; Rogers, 1983; and Schon, 1971. The entrepreneurial leaders are labeled as "insurgents," "vanguard roles," "fixers," "transformational leaders," "change agents," "herestheticians," "instigators," "coalition leaders," or simply "political leaders."

6. This is the term Abe Bergman (1986) used to describe his activities to promote public action on heath problems.

7. All four entrepreneurs appear to be atypical professionals. Bergman and Ellwood both earned professorships at major medical schools through clinical research. Lee published numerous articles on his clinical research before he entered governmental service. Kitzhaber is among a very few physicians who have sought high elective office.

8. My definition of innovation follows those of Polsby and James Q. Wilson. Wilson (1989, 222) contended that "innovation is not any new program or technology, but only those that involve the performance of new tasks or a significant alteration in the way in which existing tasks are performed." See also the definition by March and Simon (1958, 174). Others are less restrictive, arguing that changes of a technological or administrative nature are innovations if those who develop and implement the changes consider them to be new, although they may have been developed earlier in another location. This conception is summarized by Roberts and King (1991, 150).

9. In this simplified model of a complex process, the entrepreneurial tasks presented below do not necessarily proceed in routine order. One task is not necessarily a functional prerequisite for the next task. The substantive activities associated with each task, and the timing of each task, may overlap considerably with other tasks. This is consistent with other characterizations of loosely coupled systems (Cohen, March, & Olsen, 1972; Kingdon, 1984; March & Olsen, 1984; Polsby, 1984; J.L. Walker, 1977,

1981).

10. Abe Bergman, for instance, was spurred to action in the late 1960s when young children were continually brought to the outpatient clinic he directed (at Children's Hospital in Seattle) for treatment of terrible burns suffered when their pajamas caught on fire. He and a colleague experimented with flame retardant materials and then took the results to U.S. Senator Warren Magnuson. In short order, new regulations on children's sleepware were added through the Flammable Fabrics Act Amendments of 1967. Earlier, an opportunity to present evidence of lawnmower injuries to Senator Magnuson set in motion legislation that established what is now the Consumer Product Safety Commission (Redman, 1973).

11. On the ethical difference between rational and manipulative persuasion, see Dahl, 1984.

12. The Public Health Service did staff medical clinics for merchant sailors, the Indian Health Service, and other "traditional beneficiaries" of the federal government.

3

Sociocultural Foundations of Education

Laura Ptak Cook

Education is not just a set curriculum,
it is formation of good people.

A Student Teacher

Education of character does not mean schools should develop a unit on values or moral reasoning and glue it onto existing curriculum. Nor does it mean children should be taught to behave. What it does mean is that the very profession of teaching calls on instructors to try to produce not merely good learners but good people.

Educational programs reflect the life and condition of society; for education cannot be removed from the social, historical, or philosophical forces that ultimately shape its direction. Educators must be aware of the relationship between education and society; thus the study of the sociocultural foundations of education is essential in the training of teachers, counselors, administrators, congressmen and women, and governmental policy developers.

The Western world has historically integrated its cultural values with the need for education as a way of perpetuating the democratic way of life. Yet, many of the actualities of our society conflict with the very ideals we have proclaimed. Issues of assimilation, acculturation, and equality of opportunity constantly and vividly manifest themselves in the classroom, displaying the gap between our democratic ideal and the reality. To understand these issues and others faced by society today, for example, the drive for social status, the role of pressure groups in redirecting educational programs, and the speed of integration, one needs to study the sociocultural foundations of education from an interdisciplinary perspective, considering sociology, economics, and history as well as psychology.

CULTURAL VALUES AND EDUCATING

One salient characteristic of American society is its heterogeneity. Peopled by representatives of many and diverse cultures, the United States is often described as a loose collection of cultural elements held together by an ideology that is vaguely described as "the American way of life." Many have attempted to define "the American way of life," but as population increases and subsequent shifts take place in social, political, and religious institutions, the old sentiments that once held the heterogeneous mass together are being challenged and in some cases altered.

In the United States, education itself is a value; it is to education that citizens often turn as they seek satisfaction and meaning in life. The degree to which the school meets this cultural expectation is likewise being challenged. Since values tend to codify a society's committed way of life, they provide meaning, identification, and focus. An understanding of the values of a social group is therefore essential before any meaningful curriculum can be initiated. It is important to realize that American "core" values reflect the middle-class Puritan ethic and that because of the heterogeneity of our society, there are many Americans whose first contact with this value orientation occurs in public school. For those to whom these values are new, the task of education is acculturative, and the discontinuity between the school and other socializing agents in the community may have far-reaching effects on the behavior and participation level of individuals as adults.

American education is forced to deal with cultural pluralism. The curriculum tend to be programmed around the values of the society supporting the educational institutions. It is important, then, for the teacher to be aware of the values available and to develop with the student a set of criteria for value selection. There is nothing more crucial for an educator, nor more vital to the successful transmission of culture, than an understanding of the value structure of the culture and society.

An overview of American values merely provides a point of reference from which a teacher can develop insight into the complex nature of that which motivates, identifies, and gives continuity to a culture and its social relationships. Each subcultural group has fairly distinct values that tend to separate it from other groups.

A Californian school trustee (Associated Press, 1994) illustrated this when he remarked: "We have students who can tap into the Internet and CD-ROMs in their own bedroom and have a vast array of information at their fingertips, but the unfortunate   people who live in hovels with the entire family sharing one or two rooms—how is that kid supposed to do his homework? Still they're graded the same. Some students are simply in a better environment to succeed than others, and it is unfair to grade students on their homelife" (p. 14).

In a very real sense each school and its community has a "character" that reflects a value structure possibly distinctive and unique. The educator newly assigned to a school has an obligation to become familiar with the culture of his school and its community to determine any discontinuity between the values of the community's dominant culture and those of the subculture represented in the school. Should a marked discrepancy exist, the functioning of the school as an institution within the community will be seriously jeopardized.

This is not to suggest that particular values should be taught in schools—if, indeed, they can be taught-but, rather, to promote an awareness of the importance of values in determining the goals of the school in order to ensure a "cultural fit" with the goals of the community. It is important for educators to remain cognizant of these different value systems and to provide a cultural slant to instruction while guarding against cultural bias. Generic, multicultural, all-cultural values must be the focus. Interpret the needs of the students and teach accordingly. Use the information you obtain from observing the existing community value systems and then find the best method to gain the interest of the students and the best technique to communicate the information to them. Keep the culture in; use it not as a means to separate groups, but to relate them, to educate them. To carry out this philosophy, educators must understand the nature of culture, how it is learned, how it shapes students, how education varies in different cultures, and what the variances are. Such cultural information must be considered in decisions made at all levels of instruction to enable educators to provide learning experiences for pupils from varied cultural backgrounds. "Education is to be thought of as that part of the enculturative experience that, through the learning process, equips an individual to take his place as an adult member of his society" (Hershovits, 1948, 73).

Specific cultures should be seen as *part* of the dominant culture, albeit an independent part, with a great variety of other cultures helping make up an intricate system that is the *true* "American way of life." Education must create productive members of a society of many cultures. This belief needs to move from a verbalized ideal to an obtainable reality.

CULTURE AS A SOCIAL CONTROL

The urge to learn is basic in most children. Knowledge must be acquired by learning; this learning must be organized and directed. The process of educating the young in any society is patterned. Culture provides patterns for the behavior of an individual and "groups" within the society, and groups and individuals put these patterns into action.

An individual cannot exist without society and society cannot function without controls; thus, the individual's very existence depends upon societal control. It is important to differentiate the conceptual significance of *enculturation* from that which we shall assign here to the word *education*; it is equally important to set off both these terms from the designation *schooling*.

Enculturation continues throughout the life of an individual. It includes that which he or she receives through others as well as what is acquired without direction. Education is necessary to bring on individual's behavior into line with the specific requirements of a culture. It is true everyone must train the young of the society (this is obtained through enculturation and education); however, in very few cultures this training held outside the household. Generally it is obtained through schooling.

Unfortunately, many agree with Skrtic (1991) that schools as institutional "machine bureaucracies" acculturate new teachers into an institutional mold that values conformity, conservatism, and rigidity in instructional methods and devalues individual differences. When individual students do not conform to the rigid classroom structure, conflict results. One response to this conflict could be to make classroom instruction more student–centered and more responsive to student needs. However, schools as institutions have generally been reluctant to transform themselves; their actual response has often been to "classify" nonconforming students, relegating them to an ineffectual system of assessment and educational services. By isolating nonconforming individuals from the regular classroom and placing the blame for this isolation on the students themselves, schools preserve the structure and the rationale for the traditional system of classroom instruction.

Educational institutions are concerned with training the young in such a way that societal stability is preserved. Through education, individuals achieve status. As they do so, the problems of formal education become compounded. As individuals become oriented and educated into the existing order, they begin to believe that maintenance of the status quo and its corresponding group power structure is essential. Education, in a formal sense, therefore creates the paradox whereby human beings on the one hand are trained to perpetuate the existing order in a way that creates cultural continuity and, on the other, are expected to develop minds capable of reconstructing society in order that it may adapt to present and future needs. There must be a continuous focus on the role education plays in the social organization of our society. Maintaining a prosocial, as opposed to a pro-cultural viewpoint, is key.

The crucial importance of public education has never been so well understood as it is today. Organized labor, since its earliest beginnings, has ardently believed in the rightness of universal free public education. Labor has supported public schools because it has believed that educated citizens are necessary to the success of political democracy. Labor has also supported public schools because it is convinced that the education of poor children and rich children in the same school is the only system of education consistent with democratic beliefs (*AFL-CIO Proceedings*, 1963). More than a century before the Supreme Court held that segregated schools were essentially unequal schools, organized labor sensed the same principle and held that no equality of educational opportunity was possible so long as children from different economic backgrounds were educated in separate school systems. They therefore demanded universal free public education in which the children of the rich and the children of the poor would attend classes "under the same roof."

Organized labor also sensed very early that there was a relationship between education and economic opportunity, in that there was reciprocality between society and education. This is true and good, and community involvement should be encouraged, but at what level? Where should societal government edict lie in the educational domain?

EDUCATION AND THE GOVERNMENT

Political scientists and professional educators have for some years had differences in their thinking about the proper place of education in the structure and process of government. Some political scientists and governmental administrators have advocated that education be established as a branch of state and local government exactly in the same manner as are public works, public safety, and public welfare. They point to the fact that on the state level the budget for education and the laws governing education must be voted by the same legislature that prescribes for other public agencies, and they argue that the financing of education should be a part of overall state fiscal planning and operations. They call attention to the fact that the taxes paid to support public safety, public works, and public education come from the pockets of the same local citizens. They conclude therefore that schools should be organized and operated as a department of municipalities and of states, run in similar fashion to the several departments and responsible to the mayor or the governor in the same way.

On the other hand, educators generally contend that education is unique in many respects, some have gone so far as to suggest that it should be a fourth branch of government, in addition to the legislative, judicial, and executive branches (Chandler, Styles, & Kitsuse, 1982). This group recognizes that as for the executive and judicial branches, the policies and laws governing the operation of schools and the funds available for them to do their work are dependent on legislative action. Within those policies and within that budget the executive and the judicial branches have a large degree of independence from the legislative branch and from each other. Many professional educators would have education equally autonomous.

It seems timely to examine relationships of education and government in view of increased recognition of the importance of education to the individual and to the nation, concern in many states as to the support and control of rapidly expanding higher education, and multiple proposals for federal support for schools and colleges. Some believe, however, that education should be free from local government regulation, particularly partisan politics.

The history of education in this country presents several classic examples of what has happened when, local or state, partisan political leaders have attempted to use schools or educational institutions to strengthen their political power, either by making educational appointments on political rather than professional qualifications or through spending school funds to influence partisan political ends rather than to achieve educational benefits. Sooner or later it has become apparent to citizens that such operations do not result in maximum educational returns for each taxpayer dollar. In such cases students are denied full benefit of the money appropriated for schools because top priority in decisions as to staff and finances is predicated on spurious criteria. The remedy is for citizens to rebel and vote out those who are in power. This usually happens, as some governors, mayors, and political party leaders have learned to their sorrow. This type of reaction comes more slowly in a large city than in a smaller community, but it happens just as surely.

Citizens of this country time and again have demonstrated their conviction that partisan political considerations should not control the operation of educational institutions. They place educational well-being above political party loyalty in cases of conflict. They recognize that those attending school are in most instances minors for whom the state has established lay member boards of trustees who are charged with the duty to see that pupils receive their heritage of good schooling. Most communities are allowed to pick their local trustees, and state board of education members are in a number of states selected by citizens. In turn, lay boards are given authority over the program and operation of the schools in their charge. The state, through legislation, sets up the limitations of power and indicates the obligations of these trustees, much as it does for the trustees who have responsibilities for minors in other ways. The educational trustees as the people's representatives are expected to safeguard the interests of minors who attend schools-not to protect or to advance vested or selfish interests of individuals or groups. Trustees of public education, generally, are readily and directly responsible to the people, so that they may receive the penalty of early removal from office if they fail to carry out the educational trusts vested in them by local citizens.

One result of strong feelings about established traditions concerning education has been that many persons have said that education and politics must be kept completely separate. Such a notion reflects the misconception that politics means the use of governmental office to advance partisan political interests above the general welfare of the people. For what have been considered the best interests of education some have pressed this point of separation of education and politics, and with great success. But candid observation reveals that in certain situations education and politics have been kept so completely separate that a different kind of problem has arisen.

At the state level, in some states, governors and legislators have not concerned themselves sufficiently with the problems of education to appreciate their importance. In such cases it has apparently been assumed that educators and boards of education can solve all educational problems. Consequently, when education needs have been presented for consideration by educators and by the boards of education, the proposals have been looked upon as presentation of self-interest groups, especially when tax increases are requested. In such situations, governors and legislators have sometimes resisted more or less automatically instead of carefully examining forward-looking educational programs. Thus, educational leadership has been denied to school executives and to state boards because they are so far separated from the executive and legislative branches of government. This situation is by no means universal, but it is problematic.

After giving consideration to all levels of political involvement, from complete government guidance to semigovernmental influences to radical, comprehensive government uninvolvement and everything in between, two main groups of reformers emerge.

The first can be classified as traditionally-administratively oriented. Goals include changing administrative personnel, introducing new systems, and recruiting from outside the school structure. This group is generally made up of school professionals. The second group can be labeled as nontraditionally-community oriented. This group rejects pure administrative reform and demands redistribution of power in the school system through decentralization (delegation of decision-making power to local districts within the city) and increased community control. Community role is manifest in local election of school boards with discretion over personnel and budget. This group is mainly comprised of nonschool professionals and lay local community groups.

The latter group tends to connect its powerlessness to the growth of a centralized professional bureaucracy that controls the policy process to the exclusion of the group. Accordingly, they seek more fundamental reform, expanding the role of the community by concentrating greater decision making in an independent local school district. They see the large citywide school system as unable to respond to the diversified needs in areas throughout the city. The emphasis is in balancing power between professionals and parents and/or local residents. Those who seek the reform of the total structure are concerned primarily with the need to redistribute power within the system, to include the very people who are most directly affected by school policy. They support the method of representation where members are elected by constituent groups: Parents vote for parent representatives, teachers for teacher representatives, and so on. So local schools can be run by local people as a safeguard against corruption or a takeover by self-interest groups.

The groups most resistant to change are, understandably, the professionals who have a vested interest in maintaining their status and power under the present structure. The community group sees the professionals as monopolizing a good share of the policy process and reluctant to relinquish control. Teacher unions and organizations vary in their relative strength in different cities as do boards of education, and accordingly, the leadership of resistance may vary. The coalition of established education groups, however, can be anticipated in every large city. Special interest groups in education would be generally supportive of the system as would be parent associations. This does not mean, however, that community control is not without controversy as well.

Local control does challenge some of the basic concepts associated with the traditional city reform movement, a movement originally conceived to root out corruption and control of the system. It nonetheless remains a movement that has not yet adjusted to the many changes faced by the urban community in the present era. Additionally, there is no procedure to guarantee that the community will be qualified and educated enough to effectively handle the management and regulation of relevant issues. Fears about community control of the schools can be expressed in two other general areas also. First is the concern that integration will be abandoned or made impossible to achieve under community control. Second is the concern that parochialism will be encouraged (Mayor's Advisory Panel, 1967). The administration suggests the latter will stimulate local ethnic conflicts. Perhaps if an ad hoc structure replaced the bureaucratic structure and if perspectives based on distributive justice rather than utilitarianism prevailed, schools might indeed be more accommodating to learner diversity and teachers might be trained in the skills necessary to address such diversity. But until then...

Proper Involvement of Education in Government

How can education have its rightful consideration in government and its appropriate support by governmental officials without being dominated or controlled for partisan political ends? How can and should education be involved in politics? Politics may be beneficial or harmful in serving the interests of the people. Good politics result in good government for the people; bad politics bring about government detrimental to the best interests of the people. One major purpose of politics in a democracy is to make desirable opportunities and services available, not to a privileged few, but to all citizens. Good politics operates so that persons appointed to render public services and to purchase materials and services for governmental activities make appointments and award contracts on the basis of the ability to perform the service or to deliver the best goods at the last cost rather than on the basis of "pull and power." Bad politics operates so that government is used as the means of securing privilege for the few at the expense of the many.

It is necessary to bear in mind that there is not one relationship of education to government but several. Different principles and, perhaps, different practices should be used to deal with these relationships.

Instruction by qualified teachers—what is taught and how it is taught—must be independent of control by government officials . This principle is important because there is danger that the power to control instruction might be used as a means of perpetuating individuals or their party in power. The danger is illustrated by what has happened in the use of control of instruction to establish and retain power in totalitarian governments. Educational institutions must be free to develop curriculum and instructional methods as a safeguard to individual freedom. Thus, generally, policies governing instruction in schools and colleges are entrusted to the people who are elected to boards of education in special, nonpartisan elections.

Instructional policies and procedures must be relatively stable and not interrupted as the result of political changes. Education is for the benefit of all students, whatever their political ideas. It is a long process that needs to be continuous year by year. For this reason, governing boards should not change majority membership precipitously.

Instruction must be closely integrated with and responsive to the ideas and ideals of the home and the community. As discussed earlier, formal schooling has been established to supplement and complement the education provided by the home and the community. Local lay boards for elementary and secondary schools and representative lay boards for higher education have been given broad authority over curriculum so that home and community ideas and ideals might be reflected in educational programs. There is some danger that in carrying out this principle laymen may not accept the advice and leadership of trained people in specialized fields even when it would be wise to do so. Generally, however, the principle has been accepted in the belief that it is a safeguard against control by professional educators.

Education must be readily and directly responsive to public action because of its importance to the individual and to the nation. This belief has led rather generally to having local and state school boards elected or selected separately from other government officials—evidence that a distinction between education and other governmental functions is made in the minds of many citizens. More than that, it reflects the realization that schools are important to individuals whose education cannot be stopped or handicapped and then at a later time remedied. If school conditions need changing, people want to make the changes directly, without having to vote out of office a political party that may be reasonably effective in other respects. Here is perhaps the strongest argument for electing school boards responsible for operating instructional programs separately from other officials.

Now for a look at the relationship of education to government as it relates to securing the necessary policies and financial support for the school. It is important for schools that attention be given to educational needs equal to that given other enterprises supported by and controlled through governmental action and that executives and legislators be informed and concerned about educational problems. It is important that these officials accept as an important part of their responsibility the function of planning and providing for schools. Congress is in charge of education bills. The Elementary and Secondary Education Act, for example, was instituted with the aim of improving the nation's schools with the authorization of eight programs (Department of Education, 1965). These programs will help the United States reach the "by-the-year-2000" goals established by Congress. Congress is also charged with deciding how much money to allocate to which geographical areas to assist in reaching these goals. A handful of states have passed laws allowing the state board of education to take control in cases of serious academic deficiencies or financial mismanagement (Zuckman, 1993), but few have done so. Regional divisions, antagonisms, and jealousies often block concerted efforts to fund all public schools adequately and fairly. Unfortunately, and not uncommonly, the bottom line remains fiscal, at all levels.

Education also has a responsibility to government. Public schools do not exist only because the government provides them. The schools, in turn, must educate so that good government is provided. Students are prepared to participate in all aspects of the government. This includes active participation by individuals in the selection and support of those who operate government for the betterment of all.

Current Relations

Certainly education today is not all it could be. The conflict between democratic ends and bureaucratic means, as Skrtic (1991) suggests, creates problems in society in general and schools in particular. This contradiction is inevitable in contemporary Western societies. The frequent result is the bureaucratic exclusion or isolation of those individuals or groups of individuals who do not fulfill institutional expectations.

The best solution would be a careful integration of the private sector and the public sector. Education at the local level would be state influenced. The Tenth Amendment to the United States Constitution delegates plenary power for education to the various states. Consequently, state legislatures have far-reaching state constitutional and statutory authority to shape a wide range of state educational policies.

Chase and Sweitzer (1978) observe: "The chief responsibility of the state board of education is to develop major policies for all publicly supported programs of the state as indicated in state constitutions and/or statutes and to see that such policies are followed. In carrying out this responsibility, it is important that the state board of education cooperate with other educational and governmental agencies" (p. 4). Given this constitutional and statutory authority, the authors assert that the state policy makers (state boards of education), state education policy practitioners (state education agency staffs), and specifically chief state school officers (state superintendents of public instruction) have considerable potential for key leadership roles in educational policy formation and implementation. The integration is both feasible and reasonable.

It appears that many schools are agreeable and on several occasions have tried to accomplish this goal but have found it impossible to do so completely due to lack of adequate finances-the bottom line, again. On the other hand, were the federal government be willing to give grant money, not all schools would react to this positively. Worry concerning loss of control over teaching related to religious or cultural issues at the local level may result if funding were to come from the federal government. Federal government meddling could result in an overall protocol that would not suit local needs.

This system of consolidation of state, local, and community statutes should encourage cooperation, not conflict. Educational reform must not fall victim to division or political gridlock. A delicate balance between state and local entities as well as administrative and community-oriented policies will exit, must exist.

FUTURE EDUCATIONAL EXPECTATIONS

Perhaps in the future a true synthesis of these views can be achieved through an awakening of interest in what schools could be, without losing touch with what schools are and what they have been.

It is to be hoped that such beliefs will provide the foundation for the continuing development of critical thought about education and the problems of schooling. Collaborative problem solving of individual cases would be the rule, not the exception.

True, there is often an inequitable distribution of educational resources. True, it is likely the stubborn will of a range of self-interested bureaucracies works against a common purpose. True, sometimes a rigid, unresponsive classroom culture exists. But before content and organization completely fail to evolve with the changing world, and before knowledge of and respect for students have failed the test of reality, schools need to respond to the dazzling array of needs and potentials youngsters bring to school today. Too many schools are organized with a mythical child in mind. When the child who arrives at the schoolhouse door does not look or act anything like this imagined child, does not have its experiences or skills, then the child is too often deemed unteachable by inflexible and narrow schools.

No one denies the need for reform. The fact that schools are in crises is broadly experienced and widely understood. It is in this context of stagnation and unresponsiveness that teacher unions hold walkouts and strikes.

Strikes become the catalyst that forge a workable coalition of parents, community groups, business leaders, and government representatives. They become a vehicle for people to express their anger and frustration with the full range of school problems. The presence of reform coalitions guarantee that regardless of any agreement between the board and the union, there will not be return to business as usual. Coalitions are able to hammer out a reform package and a successful legislative strategy.

The reform legislation is, of course, only a step toward real school improvement. The real work of school improvement is long term and complex, and no single step can turn around years of failure. Problems continue. Everyone uses the language of reform, but there remains a long road to travel if power and resources are really to shift from the center to the base. Local initiatives are still routinely frustrated, and the central office still regularly issues commands. Furthermore, the people who have the power to propose and implement dramatic change will not necessarily do it. They seem to lack imagination, always requesting the same things such as higher test scores, or less truancy the same way. If groups do not think of something dramatic or of dramatic ways to change, "there is little chance they can create dramatically different schools. And if the schools do not break with their tradition of failure, then failure will remain their constant companion" (Ayers, 1991, 43). A teacher's imagination and energy must be captured. Partnership between parents and teachers must be built. That there is concern over these issues is a positive thing. It is now necessary for that energy to bring about change in specific schools. The solution to the problems in a democracy is more democracy, and the people with the problems are the people with the solutions. Experience in changing things will bring wisdom to the next steps. Options are open. Long-term change can proceed.

4

Domestic Violence and Social Policy: Integrating Theory and Practice in the Prevention of Spousal and Child Abuse

John S. Lyons
Cassandra Kisiel

Although violent crimes have been slowly declining with the aging U.S. population, violence still pervades our society. Nowhere is the cost of this violence more dramatic and tragic than in the home. The reported rates of domestic violence and (incestuous) child abuse have been increasing despite the overall reduction of violence. Approximately 15-20 percent of the general population reveals some form of childhood incestuous abuse (Bagley et al., 1984). Twenty-five percent of women report experiencing physical violence and/or sexual assault at the hands of their partner (Gelles, Straus, & Harrop, 1988). Although spousal and child abuse are often considered separately, the evidence suggests that these forms of domestic violence often co-occur, with as many as 45-60 percent of child abuse cases also involving wife abuse (McKibben, DeVos, & Newberger, 1989). Domestic violence or violence occurring in the home in which the perpetrator is a family relation of the victim, is becoming one of our most pressing social problems. Thus domestic violence, in all its forms remains a significant threat to the health and well-being of women and children in this country. As such it has become a focal point for local, state, and federal policy initiatives.

Attempts to understand the problem of domestic violence and child abuse have resulted in a variety of theoretical perspectives to explain the phenomenon.

Each theory of domestic violence has somewhat different policy implications. The present chapter will outline the different theoretical approaches to this problem and evaluate the policy responses at various levels-legislative, judicial, political, and organizational-in an effort to assess how well these theories can be translated into meaningful action, namely, in the creation and implementation of public policy toward spousal and child abuse. This goal, however, requires the integration of theoretical perspectives, the specification of their policy implications, and a review of the extant policy options for addressing domestic violence.

DEFINING DOMESTIC VIOLENCE

The problem of domestic abuse has been approached from several vantage points. Confusion arises from a lack of clarity in the definition of domestic violence. Much of this vagueness surrounds definitions of child abuse that can vary substantially in terms of impact: from failure to provide an adequate home environment (i.e., neglect) to severe physical abuse resulting in mortality. Spousal violence can include physical violence as well as nonviolent sexual activity between marital partners where one partner has stated a desire not to participate. These broad definitions and the concomitant lack of consistency across research studies makes drawing conclusions for the scientific literature difficult. The consistent application of laws also requires some definitional clarity. For purposes of the present chapter we will define domestic violence as physically harmful behavior in which the perpetrator and the victim are related through blood or marriage or through an intimate relationship. This definition, therefore, includes both spousal and child abuse.

The important implications of this definition are twofold. First, the behavior considered within our framework must be physically harmful. Thus, psychological harm is not included. Second, both the victim and the perpetrator must be related or in an intimate relationship. in this definition, other violence that occurs in the home is not considered domestic violence.

THEORETICAL PERSPECTIVES

Ethological/Sociobiological Theories

Drawing from earlier theories, a strong relationship has been posited between aggression and biology. Some of these theories (e.g., instinct theory) have now been abandoned, but ethological and more sociobiological approaches still have validity. Applying the findings from primate studies, child maltreatment may be linked to parents' failure to receive expected reproductive returns, possibly due to a child's limited capacity to provide these returns (Burgess & Garbarino, 1983). This may be particularly applicable to violence initiated against very young children who can be demanding to care for yet are unable to provide much to the caretaker in return.

From a sociobiological viewpoint, violence is often used as a means of survival and a way of maintaining order (Bigelow, 1972). Accordingly, there is a genetic predisposition toward some form of aggression across species (E.O. Wilson, 1978). Power and control are achieved through success in competition. The same logic applies to spousal abuse. Violence becomes a survival-based means of maintaining order and control in the family. In most mammals, including humans, the male of the species is responsible for establishing and maintaining the organizational hierarchy. In nonhuman species, however, violence of this nature is frequently between males within the hierarchy, rather than across gender.

Within human organizations, threats of aggression or force underlay some social systems. Applying this to domestic life, when order is breached in the marital dyad or in the family unit, force may be used to restore balance. Gunn (1991) proposes a social dominance theory that accounts for violence in a social system or between individuals by power imbalance. Therefore, domestic abusers may be seeking control or power they have failed to achieve through lesser forms of aggression. This theory bears some resemblance to Dollard and Miller's (1939) earlier frustration hypothesis, positing aggression as a product of frustrated drives. Although "drive" terminology may not sufficiently explain the concept of aggression, one can see how this theory is applicable in the case of the domestic abuser who may fail to achieve the control or power he desires within the context of his familial relationships or carried over from other facets of his life.

Social Control Theory

The perspective of social control theory represents a shift in focus from the individual to the environment. According to this theory, aggression, as a function of the human condition, is managed through social controls. These controls are posited to be based on various social bonds (relationships) to which one is committed. These bonds include attachment to significant others, investment in societal goals or aspirations, involvement in conventional behaviors, and commitment to moral beliefs (Hirschi, 1969). Individuals are differentially "bonded" to society based on these relationships. The stronger these bonds, the more committed one remains to social values and the less likely one will violate these mores. The assumption here is that human motivation for deviance is consistent across all individuals. Therefore, domestic violence is fully determined by the absence of secure environmental (culture-based) controls. Families who are embedded in a supportive family and community network would be less likely to experience family violence. Further, the more attachments *outside* of the home, the more visibility of behaviors increases and, therefore, decreases the likelihood of violence *within* the home. Degree of emotional connectedness within and outside the family should also serve to curb violent acts. This theoretical perspective is consistent with the observed isolation of many families in which sustained patterns of abuse are occurring.

Propensity for violence within the home is also influenced by one's level of commitment to one's family and to the community. The length of marriage and presence of children would likely influence one's degree of commitment to one's family and therefore reduce the risk of committing acts of violence. This theory predicts increased likelihood for violence against children perpetuated by stepparents and nonparental relatives whose level of commitment to family is less than a parent's.   Research also suggests that the greater one's commitment to one's job, the less likely one would be to violate the law (Hirschi, 1969). This theory argues that any involvement in conventional activities such as work or family and social activities would increase one's chances of conforming to the law.   Empirical evidence has revealed that the degree of importance one places on activities with significant others mitigates one's tendency to engage in spouse assault (Williams & Hawkins, 1989).

Lastly, moral beliefs, the extent to which people believe they should obey the rules of society, vary in the degree to which they can control violent behavior in individuals. This may be influenced by ambiguity within moral codes for violence within the family.   There are some instances in which hitting is tolerated as a form of punishment. Use of ranges of physical punishment can vary widely in severity of the punishment and in the age at which children continue to receive corporal punishment for misbehavior.   Therefore, this normative variation (i.e., lack of consistency as to how much violence is tolerable) can become a basis for justifying violence (Gelles, 1983). It also has been posited that moral beliefs may be neutralized prior to an act of violence within the family, allowing the individual to act out aggressively in certain instances. The risk of arrest for domestic assault would likely serve as a moral deterrent to this form of violence. However the deterrent power of arrest would likely be influenced by how much one has to lose as the result of the social consequences of arrest and by the degree of risk one perceives for arrest (Sherman, Schmidt, & Rogan, 1992). Perceived risk of arrest and the perceived severity of consequences have been found to be positively correlated with a tendency to refrain from spouse assault (Williams & Hawkins, 1989).

It is clear that this theory has certain appeal by it power for accounting for observed patterns of domestic violence, yet it is insufficient to explain the phenomenon fully. For example, different individuals subjected to identical social controls can vary in their likelihood of engaging in domestic violence. Although varying perceptions of risk can account for some of these observed differences, these perceptions are by no means complete explanations.   In modifying this theory, it appears that domestic abuse may also be subject to certain individual differences that make it differentially influenced by social controls. Social controls may be minimized because these acts often have less visibility within the community and outsiders may be less willing to intervene in "private" affairs. However, attachment influence of family may, on the other hand, be a different mechanism of social control than attachments outside of the family. This theory has yet to be researched (Williams & Hawkins, 1989).

Emotional Labeling and Social Learning Theory

The process of emotional labeling has been proposed to account for the interaction between physiological arousal and the cognitive labelling of emotions (Schacter & Singer, 1962). Emotional labeling may be related to domestic violence in cases where males possess a combination of physiological arousal and coercive control over the arousing person (spouse or child). Males may be more likely in this situation to label their emotion as anger and act on this response (Navoco, 1975). Thus, frustration, hurt, and perhaps even lust may be falsely labeled as anger and precipitate violence as a behavioral response to the mislabeled emotion.

Social learning theory originated with Bandura (1983), who saw individuals as acquiring aggressive behaviors through observational learning, external reinforcement for such behaviors, and internal (emotional) responses. L.E. Walker's "cycle theory of violence" (1979, 1984, 1987) is based upon the social learning and tension reduction paradigms. She conceptualizes a three-phase cycle, including: (1) the tension-building phase, consisting of minor battering incidents and a buildup of tension in the relationship; (2) the acute battering incident, where there is an uncontrollable discharge of tension sometimes provoked by the fear of the battered woman; and (3) the calm, loving respite that consists of a shift in feelings on the part of the abuser and the abused. The batterer exhibits caring behaviors and the battered woman shifts from angry and frightened feelings to viewing her abuser as dependable and loving.

The fact that often child abusers were abused children supports the major component of the social learning theory. Of course, not all perpetrators of domestic violence were victims, and not all victims become perpetrators, so this model remains somewhat simplistic and cannot be a complete explanation.

Existential Theory

Existential theory requires some brief discussion as it provides a bridge between the individual's perspectives (emphasized in the sociobiological and, later, in the psychopathology models) and the social conditions (emphasized in the theory of social control). In existential terminology we all strive for power and control, in essence to transcend the limits of the human condition. As an extreme form of this quest, one may seek complete control over another human being through violence. This condition may arise from insufficient external factors such as societal power imbalances or lack of adequate stimulation (Fromm, 1973).

Thus existential theory would be consistent with data that suggest domestic violence is more commonly reported in low-income population (see the next section below). In existentialism the use of violence represents the vehicle for establishing one's meaning vis-à-vis one's community and family.

Sociological Theories

Bundled together, sociological theorists move almost entirely outside the focus of the individual and extol the importance of external circumstances infringing upon the individual. This perspective has several vantage points from which to view domestic abuse. Trends in domestic abuse are related to economic, demographic, and social factors in various communities. It has been clearly established that poverty and low income are significantly associated with an elevated risk of child abuse (National Center on Child Abuse and Neglect, 1989). The concept of social impoverishment has been discussed as a major contributing factor in families at high risk for abuse This includes low socioeconomic status often characteristic of abusing families and is associated with their having inadequate social supports, including less positive day-to-day interactions with others. Other significant variables associated with domestic abuse trends include unemployment status, minority status, single-parent (female) households, early parenthood, large families, and overcrowded and transient housing (Creighton, 1988; Garbarino & Kostelny, 1992). Further, marital instability as well as inadequate parental attention have also been associated with increased domestic abuse (Hallett, 1988).

However, a potential bias in domestic violence data is that impoverished families may be more often targeted and brought to the attention of authorities, whereas those in more affluent positions are better able to keep their family problems secret (Hallett, 1988). It therefore appears safer to say that these sociological trends are associated with levels of reported abuse (O'Toole, Turbett, & Nalepka, 1983). This does not necessarily extrapolate to all domestic violence (both officially reported and unreported).

Understanding societal structure is also important in exploring these trends. Theories of patriarchy have explained wife assault and child sexual abuse as specific manifestations of male power or dominance (Walby, 1986). Straus (1973) has blamed family violence on the "sexist organization of society," which legitimizes males' use of force against women. He further notes that wife assault is influenced by antagonism between the sexes created by the polarized socialization of males and females. Increased distance between husbands and wives, influenced by the greater career independence of women as well as the high level of attention required by children, particularly the young, may also fuel tension between the sexes and create a climate for abuse (Dutton, 1991).

Another important contribution in this regard is the exploration of the societal value of violence as a means of influencing domestic abuse. Cultural norms tend to legitimize violence between family members (e.g., condoning corporal punishment) (Dutton, 1991). Further, legal procedures have been reported to contribute to women's sense of helplessness and lack of power in abusive relationships by not coming to their rescue or punishing them for their report of violence.

Feminist Theory

Feminist theory has, in one sense, elaborated upon some aspects of sociological theory of domestic abuse by reifying the negative impact of the patriarchal organization of society. Gender-based trauma, in particular, is an important emphasis for feminist scholars. Within feminism, however, there are several ways of conceptualizing this issue. Liberal feminists think of female oppression as a product of rigid sex role conditioning and focus on political action as a means of changing these roles. Cultural feminists strive for a "feminization" of culture (striving for peace and harmony) as a means to overcome violence. Radical feminism emphasizes male dominance as all-pervasive and stress separatism for women. Radical feminists are responsible for much of the collective action and advocacy against gender-based violence (Enns, 1992).

One concern of many feminists regarding domestic abuse is that women are unfairly stigmatized and may be revictimized by the very medical system that is intended to serve them (Warshaw, 1992). Part of the stigmatization comes from many of the pejorative psychiatric labels such as "battered woman's syndrome" or "self-defeating personality disorder," which tend to place blame on the victim rather than focusing on the overwhelming trauma she may have encountered (Warshaw, 1993). The feminist approach is often one of increasing awareness regarding the specific needs of women.

Feminist theory has little to say with regard to understanding the phenomenon of cross-gender child abuse. Given the co-occurrence rates of spouse and child abuse and the increased role of women in the abuse of their children, this silence may reflect a limitation of the feminist theories.

Psychopathology Theories

Theories based on psychopathology stem from a medical model focusing on the psychiatric status of the perpetrator or victim of violence. It is increasingly evident that parental substance abuse is a major contributor to family dysfunction. Parental alcohol abuse is highly associated with child maltreatment

(Famularo et al., 1986), marital conflict (Reich, Earls & Powell, 1988), and domestic violence (Fitch & Papantonio, 1983). Other forms of substance abuse among parents have also been associated with child maltreatment, particularly when combined with other adverse social circumstances such as teenage pregnancy and economic hardship (Regan, Erlich, & Finnegan, 1987). Parents or spouses who maltreat also suffer from co-morbid mood and substance use disorders to a large degree (Famularo et al., 1992). More than half of all murders of relatives involve a perpetrator who is intoxicated at the time of the crime (American Psychiatric Association, 1994).

Domestic abusers are more likely to suffer from narcissistic or borderline personality disorders (Rosen, 1991). In particular, traits of narcissism such as "interpersonal exploitativeness" or "an attitude of entitlement" are often found in these individuals (DSM-IV criteria). Child abusers consistently appear to suffer from low self-esteem likely as a result of their own childhood mistreatment. From a self-psychology perspective, abusers may be expressing their narcissistic rage toward their victims (Kohut, 1973).

Understanding the psychological makeup of victims is a murky and controversial topic. It is almost impossible to study individual characteristics of victims without being subjected to the accusation of victim blaming. However, theorists from a psychoanalytic approach have written extensively on the masochistic character structure of women who are abused by their partners. This is posited as numerous studies reveal that many battered women have experienced abuse prior to their marriages or return to their partner despite repeated abuse (Young & Gerson, 1991). However, this perspective is hotly debated by feminist scholars. It appears common, though, that victims of domestic victims show a dramatic reduction in self-esteem. Devaluations of self by the victim is often found to be a repetition of earlier childhood experiences (Rosen, 1991). Such devaluation not only is re-experienced by the victim as a result of the current abuse but may actually cause the victim to seek out ongoing abuse in order to master her earlier experiences (Freud, 1920).

Victims of domestic abuse may suffer from an intense narcissistic wound that may cause them to seek out or remain in abusive relationships (Kohut, 1973). What becomes cloudy, however, is determining how much of a victim's disturbance is influenced by prior experience, which may cause her to seek out current abusive experience, or is simply related to her current experience of abuse. That is, one must question to what extent any observed differences in personality or psychopathology are a risk for abuse or indicate a result of the victimization.

Family Systems Theory

Conceptually located between those theories that emphasize the characteristics of individuals and those that place the causation in the society or environment, a systems perspective focuses on the family and as an interconnected unit without putting any one individual at blame. The family systems theory views violence in the family as an output of a dysfunctional family and social system (Straus, 1973). According to this view, violent ways of reacting may have originated within an earlier generation of the family and carried down through the generations or may be adapted from aggressive ways of relating in a particular social system, such as that often seen within inner-city families.

Within a systems approach, each family member has an integral role in the transmission of violence. Certain individuals can serve to provoke conflict, whereas others can serve to diffuse it. However, each part plays an equivalent role in the generation of conflict. Therefore, although a child is unlikely to seek out abuse (as suggested with battered women) or to provoke abuse due to past experience, he or she does contribute to the environment that can precipitate the abuse perhaps by helping to trigger some mechanism in the abuser. Violence is seen as a cycle or pattern that can be broken only if the family system is restructured (Gelles & Maynard, 1987).

INTEGRATING DISPARATE THEORIES

Although each theory alone may not be sufficient to explain domestic spousal and child abuse, together they offer potentially important contributions. To integrate these theoretical perspectives it is useful to recognize that domestic violence is likely multiply determined; that is multiple causes act concomitantly and interactively. Further, consideration of the various types of causal relationships can provide a structure for integrating these theories. Three basic types of causes contribute to the problem of domestic violence. **Predisposing causes** are underlying factors in the individual or environment that set the stage for violence. **Precipitating causes** are factors that are operative at the moment of violence. **Maintaining causes** are factors that support the ongoing cycle of violence in a family.

Each type of cause suggests different interventions to prevent domestic violence. If predisposing causes can be addressed, then primary prevention can be achieved. That is, if the underlying causes of domestic violence are altered, less violence will occur. If precipitating causes can be addressed, then violence can also be prevented. Precipitating causes can also be addressed for purposes of secondary prevention. Given that most of the precipitating causes are individual difference variables, then secondary prevention intended to ameliorate precipitating causes must focus on treatment interventions with perpetrators of domestic violence and their families. Addressing maintaining causes will likely lead to secondary prevention of domestic violence. That is, once violence occurs, initiatives directed at altering maintaining causes have the potential for reducing future violence. Table 4.1 places the contributions of the theoretical perspectives discussed above into the framework of predisposing, precipitating, and maintaining causes.

Of the predisposing factors, only one is an individual difference variable personality disorders, while the remaining four are societal—social learning, social bonds, acceptance of violence, and gender politics. Four of the five identified precipitating causes are individual. And, the one social variable—social control—relies on the individual's perceptions of the existing controls to mediate their impact on the individual. Thus one could reasonably argue that all precipitating causes of domestic violence exist within the individual. The opposite is true for maintaining causes—all can be seen as existing within the environment.

Table 4.1
Integration of Theoretical Perspectives on Domestic Violence by Type of Causal Relationship

Predisposing Causes	Precipitating Causes	Maintaining Causes
Personality Disorders	Loss of Control	Social Learning
Social Learning	Alcohol/Drug Intoxication	Consequences
Social Bonds	Social Controls	Family Systems
Social Acceptance of Violence	Transient Emotional States	
Gender Politics	Mislabeled Emotions	

PUBLIC POLICY FOR DOMESTIC VIOLENCE

Several factors determine the successes or failures of current policies surrounding spousal and child abuse. Issues range from deciding what constitutes abuse to determining who is a valid witness to how an abuser or victim is handled in the system. The most salient issues surrounding child abuse policy concern mandatory reporting laws. These laws are intended to optimize identification of cases of child abuse so that efforts at secondary prevention can be achieved.

Child Abuse

Identification of Child Abuse. While policies appear to be adequate in their coverage of abuse, what has become a murky issue is that of identification of substantiated cases. Cases of child abuse are initially identified by healthcare or social service agents. Although there are specific sets of symptoms that are often indicative of trauma-related experiences, it appears that other variables tend to bias a professional's tendency to identify abuse as having occurred. Social class and race, in addition to degree of injury, have been shown to be important factors in these decisions by professionals of all levels of experience (Martin, 1983; O'Toole et al., 1983). There is even evidence to suggest that the specific symptoms exhibited by the child will influence reporting (Dingwall et al., 1989). In general, there appears to be an expectation that impoverished families will be more likely to abuse their children. Repeatedly, lower-class families are more often subject to surveillance by public authorities (Becker & McPherson, 1986; Goldberg & Warburton, 1979; Irvine, 1988), whereas more affluent families are more able to keep their family lives private. Although the great degree of surveillance is a benefit, that it is likely biased in favor of those with more wealth or power in society is a drawback. This lends itself to the notion that there is likely underreporting or underdetection of abuse cases within middle- to upper-class families. More consistent application of these laws is necessary to achieve equal treatment of all families.

Reporting of Abuse. Within the United States there are mandatory reporting laws for child abuse that vary from state to state, ranging from criteria that are very strict (e.g., having to come into contact with observable behavior in children) to unrestrictive (e.g., having reasonable cause to know or suspect abuse). These laws are beneficial because they bring the issue of child abuse to public attention. They also enable official action to be made with greater ease by any number of professionals. This translates into the increased recognition of child abuse as a salient issue.

However, there are many shortcomings of the current mandated reporting statutes. In general, the wording of these statutes is often vague, imprecise, and difficult to interpret (Kalichman & Brosig, 1992). Further, the lack of consistency across states as to what is mandated as abuse leads to much definitional confusion. Additionally, many professionals believe these laws compromise confidentiality with patients (Finkelhor, 1984). All the above factors often lead to inconsistent reporting among professionals.

A majority of professionals indicated that at some point they failed to make official reports of abuse when indicated. Mental health professionals and criminal justice agencies are among the worst compliers in this regard (Finkelhor, 1984). The tendency to report abuse appears to increase when there is physical evidence of abuse, when a child acknowledges the abuse in a confirmatory report, and when a child is of younger age (Kalichman & Brosig, 1992). There may therefore be under-reporting of suspected abuse of children of older ages.

There also appears to be inconsistency in children's tendency to report abuse. Younger children may be less apt to report such experiences because of less emotional and cognitive maturity. These variables influence children's ability to judge right from wrong, to comprehend when an act is considered sexual abuse as compared to affection, and to take action to protect themselves (Reppucci & Haugaard, 1989).

A major problem with reporting statutes is that they merely identify abuse cases. If effective interventions designed to prevent further abuse are not undertaken within a reasonable time, then the reporting has less effect. Murphy and others (1992) reported a substantial re-reporting rate for unsubstantiated cases of child abuse, suggesting that the court decisions missed actual abuse and did not prevent future problems. Particularly when healthcare providers have multiple experiences with cases that did not receive appropriate follow-up after reporting, their morale and decision-making can be negatively affected. Services for both victims and perpetrators of domestic violence have badly lagged behind other service sectors.

Testimony of Abuse. In addition to the issue of whether a child is willing to report incidents of abuse, is the issue of whether a child's testimony is considered credible. A main argument against having children appear as witnesses is their lack of competency and increased suggestibility (Weissman, 1991). However, these arguments have been debated as overly simplistic (Wescott, 1991). Evidence does not indicate that children are more suggestible than adults given the circumstances. Other arguments against having children appear as witnesses include memory retention, the effect of trauma upon children's thinking, and developmental (e.g., language) abilities of children. In addition, concern has been expressed about the emotional impact of the testimony itself on children (Terr, 1986). However, the current movement is to bring as much evidence as possible into the courtroom, which means putting young children on the witness stand. In favor of this, it appears that children may be more apt to remember seemingly irrelevant details that would assist in court (Neisser, 1979) and may be *less* likely to respond to prejudices and verbal suggestions they do not yet comprehend, typically those that might influence adults (Allport & Postman, 1947).

Outcome of Legal Proceedings. Consequences are thought to be both a powerful deterrent and an effective means of secondary prevention. Ideally, consequences should be consistent with the action, quick, and fair. Three primary dispositions can be determined in the aftermath of legal proceedings for child abuse cases: The abuse can be found to be unsubstantiated; the child can be returned to the home under supervised care; or where abuse is proven, the child can be removed from the home and placed into temporary custody. Murphy and others (1992) reported that 31 percent of cases were dismissed, 63 percent were removed from their homes, and only 6 percent were ordered treated within their homes.

One problem with court proceedings is the time they take. One estimate of the length of time a child is in the legal system from the time the official report is filed to the time the case is resolved is an average of five years; complex cases take longer. Delays occur prior to arraignment and prior to disposition (Bishop et al., 1992). Further, after a disposition is made, it may take an average of an additional year and a half for a child to reach permanent placement. What appears to happen is that the legal system loses its sense of urgency because the child is out of immediate danger (Bishop et al., 1992).

The biggest drawback of this system is that the child's welfare—allegedly the goal—is somehow lost in this process. Thus, although the purpose of the delays is to sort out the best interests of the children, their needs are somehow lost in the shuffle. Children are often shifted from temporary placement to placement without regard to their need for a stable, nurturing environment (Cooper, Peterson, & Meier, 1987). Empirical evidence has revealed that time delays are associated with increased social and emotional dysfunction often manifested in symptoms such as anxiety, hyperactivity, enuresis, or nightmares (Golden, 1977). These delays still occur despite over two decades of advocacy by concerned professionals as well as the passage of federal and state laws mandating more frequent reviews of foster care (Bishop et al., 1992). Not only do these delays need to decrease but there needs to be a more concerted effort to assess the reason for these delays and their impact on children's development.

Although the aim of the legal proceedings is to ensure the safety of the child, repeated mistreatment occurs after the final disposition. Rates of reabuse as substantiated in official reports of further mistreatment have ranged from approximately 15 percent to 70 percent (Ferleger et al., 1988; Herrenkohl et al., 1979; D.P.H., Jones, 1987); further, they may occur in the family of origin or in the family to which the child is displaced. Not only does the actual reabuse have detrimental effects on the child but so does the child's return to court. This issue speaks to some problems assessing the safety of the family environment. There is an apparent need for more careful assessment and surveillance of foster-care families or families to which children are displaced. A judge's decision to dismiss a case and return a child to the family of origin is often based on parental compliance with court orders (Bishop et al., 1992). However, a new criteria for decision-making is necessary because this route is not always successful.

Factors shown to be associated with reabuse in family of origin include prior history in court and the family's degree of psychopathology (Bishop et al., 1992). It is likely in the best interests of the court to determine which families have a high probability of returning to court because of reabuse. This determination might prove to be a useful time- and cost-saving procedure for the legal system.

In some families pathological dynamics are so entrenched that the patterns of abuse continually reoccur. Such families are labeled untreatable because they are found to be unresponsive to treatment (Jones, D.P.H., 1987). Identifying these families early on is crucial to the welfare of the child. The untreatability of families tends to correlate with severity of abuse and extreme parental psychopathology, including major personality disorders, psychoses involving the child, addiction problems, or mental retardation (Jones, D.P.H., 1987). Reduced motivation for treatment among families (e.g., greater degree of missed appointments) may also be an indication of reabuse risk. Further, parents with no income source or with their own history of abuse have a greater likelihood for reabuse (Ferleger et al., 1988). With these families it may be important to attend to these identifying characteristics and then make an informed decision for the best interests of the child.

It also appears that types of treatment programs offered to families influence rates of reabuse. Cases where some form of psychotherapy is offered in addition to supportive services reveal less reabuse (Ferleger et al., 1988). Those who were offered only case management indicated higher rates of reabuse (Herrenkohl et al., 1979; Morse, Sahler & Friedman, 1970; Rivara, 1985). This indicates a need to reformulate treatment approaches for targeting abusers.

Spousal Violence

Arrest as a Deterrent. An issue of utmost controversy surrounding domestic violence policy is the use of arrest as a deterrent. Whereas arrest was previously used as a last resort because of its long-term consequences for the victim, it is now being increasingly implemented. Evidence has revealed that arrest has worked better than separating or advising couples; therefore it has been argued that police should be allowed to make warrantless arrests in misdemeanor domestic violence cases (Schmidt & Sherman, 1993). Historically, abusers have not been arrested if the abused person is afraid to press charges for fear of retribution; in such cases no legal action is taken. The current pro-arrest policy under debate would require police to arrest domestic offenders even if the victim does not want to sign a criminal complaint. This shift in arrest criteria from subjective wish of the victim to objective analysis of probable cause of arrest has drastically increased the number of domestic violence cases that have come to legal attention (Menard & Salius, 1990).

However, there is murkiness, here too, in implementing these policies. What is defined as probable cause to arrest varies from state to state, and thus implementation becomes difficult. Often an identification bias brings cases from lower-class and minority households that are under greater surveillance (Schmidt & Sherman, 1993), perhaps leading to an underarrest of middle- or upper-class cases.

Another complicating factor is that arrest appears to operate as a deterrent in some instances, but not in others. It appears to reduce domestic violence in some cities but increase it in others; it reduces violence among employed people but increases it among unemployed individuals; it reduces violence in the short run but can increase it in the long run for the same victim or someone else. These findings are consistent with social control theory, which emphasizes the degree of social bonding a person has with his or her community. An interesting spousal violence policy development regarding the criminal justice system has occurred in the past several years with the implementation of "stalking" laws. These laws provide for stricter sanctions for repeated following when combined with any threatening behavior. Although these laws have not been on the books long enough for researchers to study their effects, they do offer the potential for both deterrence and secondary prevention through incarceration of the perpetrator.

Mediation. State action is increasingly downplaying the use of mediation between abused and abuser, emphasizing the nonnegotiable, serious nature of crimes of abuse (Menard & Salius, 1990). This action also serves to protect the safety of the victim. Mediation is increasingly performed by court personnel, particularly in criminal cases. More supervised mediation is being offered in civil court disputes, and this also serves to protect the victim. The concern of policy makers is now to offer effective, affordable alternatives to mediation. This is often facilitated by counselors or advocates serving the interests of the client by obtaining complete and accurate information and by being increasingly sensitive to the safety of the victim. Problems have arisen when courts have misrepresent the battered woman by failing to gain enough accurate information (Menard & Salius, 1993), but states are increasingly responding to this issue.

Another improvement is that courts are often providing victims with advocates to facilitate their participation in the system and to provide them with more direct access to community resources. The result is that the courts can more effectively assess and respond to cases (Menard & Salius, 1993). This effectiveness is, in essence, facilitated by increased communication among law enforcement, court officials, and community activists to better serve the needs of the victims.

CONCLUSION

The many policy efforts in the area of domestic violence have emphasized case finding and consequences. From the review of theoretical perspectives this focus reveals a relative absence of initiatives directed toward predisposing and precipitating causes of violence toward spouses and children. Thus comprehensive policy initiatives toward the prevention of domestic violence must also address these other classes of causes. First, changes in the social environment should be fostered. Lowering the tolerance or acceptance of violence, decreasing alienation particularly among impoverished Americans, and working through problems with gender hierarchies and politics should all facilitate a general reduction in domestic violence. Also, although the improving program choices for victims of domestic violence is an important undertaking, the development and demonstration of effective treatments for perpetrators of domestic violence should also be addressed. Teaching anger management and marital and parenting skills may facilitate positive adjustment to family roles. Court-mandated chemical dependence treatment as a response to domestic violence should also be evaluated. In sum, by integrating the various causal pathways to domestic violence and designing interventions that address these causes, it should be possible to reduce the horrible costs of violence that afflicts too many families.

5

Psychological Perspectives on Welfare Reform

Michael Morris

Writing a chapter on the relevance of psychological issues to welfare reform is an intriguing task. A review of the scholarly and research literature on welfare policy reveals a domain that is dominated by sociologists, economists, political scientists, and professors of social work, with psychologists generally conspicuous by their absence. This is ironic, given that it is impossible to discuss welfare reform without raising, at least implicitly, three questions that are undeniably psychological in whole or in part. First, how do the values, attitudes, and beliefs of policy makers and the public concerning poverty and dependency shape the reforms that are proposed and adopted? Second, to what extent do the behavioral responses of welfare recipients (and potential recipients) to various policies confirm or contradict the expectations that underlie those initiatives? Finally, what are the implications of the answer to the second question? These questions will provide the conceptual framework for examining welfare reform in this chapter.

The welfare program that will be focused upon in this review is Aid to Families with Dependent Children (AFDC). Indeed, for many if not most Americans, the AFDC and welfare are virtually synonymous. Rightly or wrongly, AFDC functions as a lightning rod for Americans' fears and concerns regarding such value-laden issues as the work ethic, self-sufficiency versus dependency, race relations, illegitimacy, violent crime, substance abuse, and the deteriorating social fabric of the inner city. When compared with other public assistance programs such as Food Stamps, Medicaid, Supplemental Security Income, and housing assistance, AFDC clearly emerges as the most controversial program by a wide margin. Thus, it should not be surprising that AFDC and the population it serves have been the primary targets of welfare reform proposals and legislation in recent years (e.g., Chilman, 1992; Corbett, 1993; Cottingham & Ellwood, 1989; Ellwood, 1988; Garfinkel, 1992; Gibbs, 1994; Wiseman, 1993).

The bulk of this population consists of single parents (usually mothers) and their children. Indeed, single -parent households accounted for 93 percent of all AFDC families in 1992, and 90% of all AFDC recipients. (The remaining AFDC households are two-parent families in which the principal wage earner is unemployed.) Overall, children under eighteen represented two-thirds (67 percent) of the AFDC caseload in that year (Committee on Ways and Means, 1993). In essence, then, AFDC is a program for poor single mothers and their offspring.

Although the number of AFDC recipients increased 27 percent from 1972 to 1992 (from 10.7 million to 13.6 million), a slightly *smaller* percentage of the U.S. population was actually on AFDC in the latter year (4.95 percent) than in the former (5.13 percent). On the other hand, the percentage of U.S. children on AFDC grew from 11.2 percent to 13.1 percent during that period (Committee on Ways and Means, 1993).

It is not the size of the AFDC population, however, that is at the heart of the controversy surrounding the program. Public concern is rooted elsewhere, with the following facts playing a prominent role:

- In a society where the most single mothers are employed either full or part time, very few AFDC mothers work. In 1990, for example, 70 percent of all single mothers worked full time or part time, whereas only 6.7 percent of AFDC mothers did (Committee on Ways and Means, 1993).
- Recent decades have seen a significant increase in the proportion of AFDC mothers who have never been married (Besharov, 1989); from 1976 to 1992, for example, the percentage grew from 21 percent to 52 percent (U.S. General Accounting Office, 1994b).
- Long-term welfare dependency characterizes a substantial percentage of those who are on AFDC at any given point in time. Indeed, it has been estimated that at any given point 65 percent of those receiving AFDC will eventually total eight years or more in the program (Committee on Ways and Means, 1993; see also Gottschalk, McLanahan, & Sandefur, 1994).
- Current and former teenage mothers account for nearly half of all single mothers on welfare (42 percent in 1992). In turn, teenage motherhood is associated with a variety of characteristics (e.g., being unmarried, not having a high school degree, having little work experience) that are positively correlated with long periods of AFDC dependency (Committee on Ways and Means, 1993; U.S. General Accounting Office, 1994a, 1994c). These facts reflect the more general finding that teenage childbearing generates significant long-term economic hardship for the mother and her children, and that this hardship is greater now than it was several decades ago (Butler, 1992).
- Although research shows that many, and perhaps most, daughters of AFDC mothers do not grow up to be AFDC mothers themselves, it also indicates that they are *more likely* to become AFDC mothers than those who did not experience AFDC as children (Committee on Ways and Means, 1993; Gottschalk et al., 1994). This evidence is consistent with, but does not prove, the claim that welfare receipt can foster social and behavioral dynamics that generate intergenerational welfare depen-

dency.

- The rate of AFDC receipt among blacks is disproportionately high when compared with the percentage of the U.S. population they represent. Although blacks comprised just 12 percent of the population in 1990, they accounted for 40 percent of all AFDC family heads in that year. Blacks on AFDC are also more likely than whites on AFDC to exhibit long-term dependency on the program, and they appear more prone to intergenerational AFDC receipt as well (Committee on Ways and Means, 1993). These latter findings are to be expected, given that blacks are more likely than whites to display characteristics that are associated with AFDC dependency, such as unmarried teenage motherhood and low levels of education and work experience.

Placed within the context of American political and social culture, the circumstances just described combine to form a virtually seamless "story" that is seen by many as justifying, indeed demanding, major changes in the welfare system. As is the case with all such stories, the rough edges of missing, ambiguous, or inconsistent data tend to be smoothed over or ignored in the process of producing a narrative that reinforces and confirms the ideological bent of the host culture at a certain point in time. In this case, a story that reflects the current zeitgeist regarding welfare reform would unfold roughly as follows:

In a nation in which the majority of single mothers are employed outside of the home, often at very low wages and at great personal sacrifice, it is inappropriate for the government to support able-bodied women and their children without expecting the mothers to take steps to become more economically self-sufficient. The failure of U.S. welfare policy to address this issue has in effect contributed to an environment in which many low-income, teenage females see out-of-wedlock pregnancy and long-term AFDC motherhood as acceptable, and perhaps even desirable, options for themselves. In the inner city especially, these dynamics have played a major role in producing an intergenerational, welfare-related underclass among blacks, characterized by relatively low levels of marriage and "legitimate" employment and by high rates of family dysfunction, violence, crime, and substance abuse.

Anyone with even a passing knowledge of the history of public assistance in the United States recognizes that concern over the work ethic of the poor is not new; its heritage dates back centuries (e.g., Katz, 1983; Piven & Cloward, 1971; Trattner, 1984). The work effort of poor *women* is a relatively recent source of public distress, however. Indeed, when Aid to Dependent Children (ADC-the forerunner of AFDC) was established in 1935 as part of the Social Security Act, the intention was to keep the program's adult beneficiaries *out* the labor force so that they would not compete with men for employment and could devote their energies full time to child rearing. It was anticipated that the bulk of the ADC client population would be widows and their children, and that ADC would eventually become unnecessary as widowed families were increasingly covered by Social Security in future decades. It was only during ADC's early years, however, that such families dominated the caseload. As the percentage of divorced, separated, and especially unmarried mothers on the rolls grew significantly over time, it became clear that ADC was not going to wither away of its own accord, despite the fact that the employment levels of single mothers not in the program were increasing.

It is against this background that discussions of welfare reform are taking place in the 1990s. Although liberals and conservatives have not reached a consensus on how to modify the system, the overall goal of reducing welfare dependency (i.e., increasing self-sufficiency) has emerged as the organizing theme linking the analyses of both groups (e.g., Ellwood, 1988; Jencks, 1992b; Mead, 1992). Consequently, in the sections that follow this theme will provide a framework for reviewing the various strategies for reform that have been proposed.

PROMOTING SELF-SUFFICIENCY: INTERVENTIONS AND EVIDENCE

Welfare reform discourse typically pays silent homage to an equation frequently encountered in psychology: Performance = Ability x Motivation (Campbell & Pritchard, 1976). Replace "performance" with "economic self-sufficiency," and the formula captures the way Americans like to think about solving the "welfare problem." That is, interventions are designed to affect the ability and/or motivation of recipients or potential recipients. Whether conceptualized in terms of performance or self-sufficiency, however, the formula is incomplete if it does not include the structural variable of "opportunity" alongside the two individualistic factors of ability and motivation. Accordingly, all three dimensions will be addressed here.

Ability-Oriented Strategies

The overriding goal of most ability-oriented strategies is to increase the "human capital" (Becker, 1964) of the target population. As used by economists, human capital refers to the "capacity of individuals to perform functions that are of value to themselves or others" (Watts, 1993, 247). The rationale underlying this approach is straightforward: To the extent that welfare recipients possess low levels of education, work experience, and job-relevant skills, they will have difficulty finding mainstream employment that will enable them to become economically self-sufficient. Taken as a whole, ability-oriented strategies attempt to remedy this problem by providing various combinations of education, work experience, skill training, on-the-job training, job counseling, and job-search assistance. Less intensive programs frequently include little more than loosely supervised individual or group job-search activities, whereas more intensive ones stress a network of coordinated training, support, and case management services.

Virtually all the major proposals for welfare reform in the 1990s place a heavy emphasis on ability-oriented approaches. Over the years countless studies have been conducted to evaluate the impact and cost-effectiveness of programs having this focus. Although it is beyond the scope of this chapter to examine fully the results of this complex body of research (for recent reviews see Blank, 1994; Burtless, 1989; Greenberg & Wiseman, 1992; Gueron & Pauly, 1991; Morris & Williamson, 1986; U.S. General Accounting Office, 1993), some general patterns can be discerned in the data that have major implications for current discussions of welfare reform.

First, ability-oriented interventions tend to have a modest positive impact on the income and earnings of AFDC recipients, as well as a modest negative impact on their welfare dependency. Second, these programs appear to be much more successful at increasing the *number* of hours that participants work in relatively low-skilled jobs than at enhancing their ability to obtain higher-skilled (and thus better paying) employment. These dynamics severely limit the positive impact the ability-oriented approach can have on participants' earnings. Working one's way out of poverty is very hard to do when the vehicle being used is a low-skilled job (Haveman & Buron, 1993).

Third, the overall income of program participants does not usually increase as much as their earnings do because welfare payments are reduced as one's earnings rise. Fourth, among participants who benefit economically from ability-oriented interventions, reduced welfare dependency does not usually mean a total escape from welfare. In most cases the earnings gains experienced by participants are simply not large enough to lift their families above the poverty line or to make them ineligible for AFDC for sustained periods.

Finally, some ability-oriented programs appear to have a much greater or lesser impact than others. For example, there is little evidence that mandatory unpaid work experience for AFDC recipients is very effective at increasing earnings or employment levels or in reducing welfare dependency (Brock, Butler, & Long, 1993). In contrast, major gains on all these dimensions were achieved in the National Supported Work Demonstration, an expensive, twelve-to-eighteen month voluntary work experience program for long-term AFDC mothers (Hollister, Kemper, & Maynard, 1984). This intensive program was characterized by close supervision of participants, assignment of participants to work teams, and standards for job attendance and performance that were gradually but steadily increased during the period in which participants were enrolled. More recently, the evaluation of a major welfare-to-work initiative in California (GAIN) suggests that the most successful implementation of the program occurred at a site that emphasized, among other things, both basic education and job-search activities in working with participants (Riccio, Friedlander, & Freedman, 1994).

Optimists as well as pessimists regarding the ability-oriented strategy can find a measure of support for their predispositions in the results just reviewed. On the positive side, it is clear that this approach has a beneficial impact on many recipients' economic well-being and welfare dependency. And in a minority of cases, ability-oriented programs can actually help individuals escape from AFDC on a fairly permanent basis. Even recipients with a history of long-term dependency can benefit significantly. Furthermore, many of these interventions are good investments from a government-budget perspective because the cost of implementing these programs is offset by subsequent decreases in welfare expenses and increases in tax payments from participants who have increased their earnings.

On the other hand, pessimists can point to the research evidence indicating that in general, the ability-oriented approach is simply not potent enough to achieve the ambitious goals the public has for it, which is to enable most participants to get off welfare and enter the ranks of the nonpoor on a sustained basis. Put more bluntly, the strategy does not represent a panacea for the dual problems of dependency and poverty in the United States, regardless of how congruent it may be with core American values concerning the relationship between self-development and self-sufficiency.

It is also disappointing that most of the positive impact of ability-oriented interventions does not seem to be attributable to substantial increases in the skill levels of participants. Program graduates typically remain in relatively low-skilled jobs, but gain economically because they work more hours than they did previously. Thus, in practice these programs function more as motivation-enhancing interventions than as ability-enhancing ones. Increasing the skills of welfare recipients has proven to be an extremely difficult task, and doing so on a large scale would probably require an investment of government dollars far in excess of what is politically feasible even in periods of enthusiasm for progressive welfare reform.

In view of the preceding analysis, what is the future likely to hold for ability-oriented approaches in welfare policy? The components of this strategy (basic and vocational education, job search, skill training, etc.) will continue to be implemented in various combinations across the country as the federal government, philanthropic foundations, and individual states seek a mix of program elements that can produce a breakthrough in effectiveness (Wiseman, 1993). The probability of such a breakthrough occurring is slim, however, given the results of previous research. Thus, improvements in the performance of the ability-oriented strategy are likely to be incremental at best, rather than dramatic. This would be a worthwhile achievement, to be sure. In the long run, however, it might be even more worthwhile if the public began to acknowledge more readily the limited role this approach can play in the lives of most AFDC recipients.

Motivational Strategies

In many respects motivational strategy is where the "action" has been in discussions of welfare reform for more than a decade (e.g., Gibbs, 1994; Mead, 1986, 1992; Murray, 1984). As a psychological concept, motivation encompasses a complex set of issues focusing on the choices individuals make as revealed through their behavior (Campbell & Pritchard, 1976). In the concrete terms of policy debate concerning AFDC, motivation is generally regarded as the willingness of recipients to exert effort toward economic self-sufficiency. Thus, motivational strategies attempt to reward behaviors consistent with self-sufficiency and/or punish (or, at least, not reward) behaviors inconsistent with it.

Historically, liberals have tended to favor reward-oriented "carrots" whereas conservatives have preferred punishment-oriented "sticks" in dealing with AFDC recipients. Although this distinction still holds today, at a more general level many liberals have shifted in a conservative direction on motivational issues in recent years (e.g., Ellwood, 1988; Jencks, 1992a). The result has been the growing consensus, described earlier, that it is appropriate and desirable for society to *require* welfare recipients to take steps to achieve self-sufficiency in exchange for the economic assistance they are given. Although this consensus, at least as it pertains to AFDC mothers with young children, has not, by any means, been endorsed by all of those on the political left, even dissenters acknowledge that the political and cultural zeitgeist has become increasingly supportive of policies that deal with welfare recipients in a coercive fashion (e.g., Lynn, 1993; Piven & Cloward, in press).

It is important to recognize that motivational strategies and ability-oriented approaches are closely related. To the extent that the former are successful, the percentage of the AFDC population participating in the latter will increase. Indeed, this increase in participation represents the primary goal of many motivational interventions. What this means, however, is that the ultimate impact of motivational programs on self-sufficiency is very often dependent on the potency of the ability-oriented interventions into which they channel participants. This reality is sometimes overlooked by policy analysts and is frequently neglected by the general public; its relevance should be kept in mind when considering the interventions discussed in the following sections.

REWARD-ORIENTED APPROACHES

At first glance, using positive incentives to encourage self-sufficiency would seem to be preferable to employing other motivational approaches, since the latter (e.g., punishment) can frequently produce unwanted side effects in the target population such as resentment and hostility. Within the structure of AFDC program itself, the positive approach that has received the most attention over the years involves manipulation of the benefit reduction rate. This rate is the percentage by which AFDC payments are reduced as a family's nonwelfare income increases. Thus, when the rate is high, the net economic gain to welfare recipients from working is relatively low, and when the rate is low, the economic gain is relatively high. Thus, low benefit reduction rates provide recipients with a financial incentive to exhibit high levels of work effort.

Over the past three decades Congress has modified the reduction rates several times, and in many states additional changes have been made in AFDC regulations that, at a practical level, amount to rate manipulations. It does not appear that these changes have produced major shifts in the work behavior of AFDC mothers (e.g., Hutchens, 1986; Moffitt, 1992). In part this is probably due to the fact that the costs to recipients of increased work effort often involve more than just the size of their AFDC check. For example, Food Stamp benefits are likely to decrease, while child- care costs and rental expenses for subsidized housing are likely to increase. As Pavetti (1993) observed in her study of current and former AFDC mothers in the Boston area, "The majority of women interviewed feel that it simply doesn't pay for them to go to work...their description of the benefits of going to work focus more on enhanced self-esteem, providing a role model for their children, and not having to deal with the welfare department" (pp. 8-9). To the degree that Pavetti's findings are generalizable to AFDC recipients nationwide, the limitation of the benefit reduction rate as a policy device to financially reward self-sufficiency becomes clear. Its impact is diluted, both objectively and subjectively, by the various economic incentives for nonwork that remain.

The research findings just reviewed, in conjunction with the current popularity of more coercive methods for dealing with AFDC recipients, have lessened the attention the benefit reduction rate has received from federal policy makers in recent years.[1] At a more general level, however, the use of positive financial incentives to motivate self-sufficiency continues through the mechanism of the income tax system. Perhaps the most prominent example of this approach is the Earned Income Tax Credit (EITC), which is a refundable credit available to low-income families with children who file federal income tax returns. Established in 1975, the EITC functions as an earnings subsidy and is designed so that the subsidy increases as a family's earnings increase, up to a point. Thus, high levels of work effort are rewarded with high subsidy levels. On the other hand, no subsidy is provided if the family has no earnings.

Because the EITC is not counted as income when determining benefit levels for AFDC, Medicaid, Food Stamps, and low-income housing programs, it bypasses the motivational problems associated with the benefit reduction rate. Moreover, because the EITC is available to all low-income families with earnings, not just those on AFDC, the stigma associated with participating in a welfare program is absent.

In recent years the EITC has been strengthened considerably; for example, the subsidy rate has been raised and the range of earnings over which the subsidy is applied has been expanded upward. Employed AFDC recipients benefit from the first change (assuming they file tax returns), but not from the latter.

Relatively little research has been done on the impact of the EITC, a situation that is likely to change as the program's expansion attracts increased attention from policy analysts. Concerns have been raised, for example, over the ways in which the program might influence marriage and separation rates, the reporting (more specifically, the misreporting) of family income, and the work effort of those EITC-eligibles whose earnings are relatively high (Scholz, 1994). These concerns notwithstanding, there seems to be general agreement that the EITC provides an unambiguous positive incentive for AFDC recipients to increase their work effort. Virtually no AFDC households have the "relatively high earnings" that could raise doubts about EITC's implications for work effort.

Indeed, perhaps the most serious limitation of the EITC as it pertains to AFDC recipients is that its function may not be fully understood by them, even when they participate in and benefit from it (Blank, 1994; Riccio et al., 1994; Scholz, 1994). There are several aspects of the program that contribute to its complexity and abstruseness, and to the extent that these features interfere with an individual's ability to appreciate how increased earnings are rewarded by the EITC, the positive impact of the program on work effort is diminished. Insofar as future research confirms this to be a problem, educational efforts that target the AFDC population would clearly be an appropriate policy response.

OBLIGATION-ORIENTED APPROACHES

As a group, the initiatives discussed in this section most fully reflect the climate of frustration that characterizes policy makers and the public when confronted with long-term welfare dependency. The overriding emphasis is on *requiring* individuals to engage in certain activities while *discouraging* them from engaging in others. Translating these behavioral wish lists into specific, concrete policies has proven to be a tortuous process, however. In fact, many of the most ambitious obligation-oriented strategies are still at the proposal stage or are in the form of demonstration projects in various states across the country (Wiseman, 1993). It will probably be close to a decade before the empirical dust from much of this research begins to settle in a coherent fashion. Nevertheless, even in embryonic form these strategies raise policy issues that are sufficiently crystallized to warrant their review.

Mandatory Work, Education, and/or Training

Mandatory Work, Education, and/or Training is, without question, the obligation-oriented approach with the longest lineage. At a rudimentary level, policies aimed at requiring able-bodied recipients of public assistance to engage in labor-related activities can be traced back over 300 years to the workhouse in colonial America (Trattner, 1984). It was not until the 1960s, however, that women on welfare became a major target population for such requirements. Since that time the pressure to involve AFDC mothers in work-focused endeavors has grown. As a result of the passage of the Family Support Act (FSA) in 1988, states are obliged to offer a variety of educational, work, training, and job-search activities to AFDC recipients, who in turn are required to participate in them except in cases where the state lacks the resources needed to accommodate all those who are eligible. States are expected to focus their resources on AFDC households that are at the greatest risk for long-term dependency. The overall spirit of the FSA is perhaps best captured by Moffitt (1993), who notes that it: "aimed to change the culture and character of the AFDC experience. AFDC was to be transformed into a program in which work, training, and education were to be an integral and inseparable part of welfare recipiency. Being on welfare was to be intrinsically linked to preparation for self-sufficiency off the rolls" (p. 9).

Requirements of this sort are justified in a variety of ways. Perhaps the most basic argument involves deterrence: To the extent that individuals find the obligations burdensome, they will avoid going on welfare unless they absolutely have to. Consequently, the ranks of the "truly needy" on the welfare rolls will be maximized, while the number of malingerers will be at a minimum. A second line of reasoning focuses on the previously discussed norm of reciprocity and emphasizes mandatory work. Specifically, welfare clients are seen as owing something to society in return for the assistance they receive, and engaging in labor represents one way of paying society back. Third, *requiring* recipients to participate in work, training, and education may be the only way of ensuring their involvement in activities that will ultimately benefit them. Finally, strictly enforced obligations send a message to recipients and nonrecipients alike, which is that work is to be strongly preferred over dependency and that welfare should not be perceived as a way of escaping from the obligation to work. In this fashion the importance of the work ethic for the society as a whole is reaffirmed.

Given the various rationales that underlie mandatory programs, evaluating the success of this strategy is not a straightforward endeavor. On the one hand, Gueron and Pauly (1991) have observed that "there are no rigorous studies that allow a direct comparison of the impact [on participants' earnings and dependency] and cost-effectiveness of mandatory and voluntary broad-coverage programs or of programs that are more or less stringent in imposing program requirements" (p. 45). It does appear, however, that mandatory programs generate higher participation rates than voluntary ones (Mead, 1990). For those who subscribe to the reciprocity justification for work requirements, as well as for those who believe that such requirements are necessary to achieve high participation levels, this is welcome news.

There is also evidence, based on empirical estimates generated by Moffitt (1993), that a strictly enforced work and training requirement covering a large percentage of the AFDC population would significantly decrease the entry rate of eligible families into the AFDC program. The extent to which this decrease could be attributed to the reluctance of malingerers (rather than the truly needy) to subject themselves to work obligations is a heavily value-laden question that is not readily resolvable by appeals to research data.

Finally, and perhaps most important, in the GAIN project cited earlier, the greatest positive impact on participant earnings occurred at the site where program staff most consistently sought to "communicate a strong 'message' to all registrants... at all stages of the program, that employment was central, that it should be sought expeditiously, and that opportunities to obtain low-paying jobs should not be turned down" (Riccio et al., 1994, 6). This site was also characterized by very strict enforcement of GAIN's participation requirements, in which individuals' welfare grants could be reduced if they failed to participate in the program with "good cause."

Interestingly, the available evidence indicates that most participants in mandatory work programs find the work meaningful, like working for their welfare benefits, and believe that a work requirement is fair (Brock et al., 1993). This finding, when viewed in conjunction with previous research on the values of welfare recipients (Morris & Williamson, 1992), suggests that traditional characterizations of the AFDC population as uniformly low in their commitment to the work ethic are probably greatly overstated. Nevertheless, for a variety of political, logistical, and economic reasons, the participation of a large percentage of AFDC adults in mandatory work, training, and education activities has never occurred on a nationwide basis in the United States. Although some aspects of the political landscape have certainly become much more supportive of this policy objective in recent years, many obstacles remain, especially in terms of the federal government and states having the resources available to provide services to all recipients who are subject to mandated participation. Consequently, it is an open question whether recent and future welfare reforms can actually be implemented in a fashion that, in Moffitt's words, changes "the culture and character of the AFDC experience" in this regard (Brock et al., 1993; Chilman, 1992; Gueron & Pauly, 1991).

Child Support

Although AFDC mothers are the major target of contemporary welfare reform debate (e.g., Gibbs, 1994), the absent fathers of AFDC children have also become a focus of obligation-oriented policy measures. It is in the area of child support payments where this is most evident. Prior to 1975, child support was almost exclusively a state and local issue, with local court judges deciding whether child support should be paid, how much should be paid, and what sanctions should be applied to nonpayers. Over the past two decades, however, the federal government has become increasingly involved in this domain. States must now develop and use specific guidelines for determining child support awards, and these amounts are supposed to be routinely withheld from the father's paycheck.

In the case of AFDC, the custodial family receives the first $50 each month of the child support payment, with the remainder being used to reimburse the state and federal government for the welfare benefits provided to the family. In some instances the support payments may actually be large enough to make a family ineligible for AFDC, in which case all of the child support goes directly to the household.

The impact of recent changes in the U.S. child support system on AFDC have been detectable but exceedingly modest. For example, Klawitter and Garfinkel (1992) estimate that over time, the routine use of the wage- withholding mechanism for child support will result in AFDC participation being 4 percent to 11 percent lower than it would be otherwise.

Two factors constrain the ability of child support payments to reduce the AFDC rolls and improve the economic well-being of these families. The first is that relatively few children born to unmarried mothers have their paternity legally established (less than one-third in 1990), and establishing paternity is a prerequisite for obtaining a child support order. Given that unmarried mothers and their children represent a significant portion of the AFDC caseload, it should not be surprising that only about 16 percent of all AFDC families received support payments in 1992 (Committee on Ways and Means, 1993). Second, the fathers of AFDC children frequently have very low incomes themselves, which translates into very low child support awards or no award at all (Bartfeld & Meyer, 1994; Garfinkel & Oellerich, 1992). These outcome are especially likely when the father is a teenager (Pirog-Good & Good, 1994). Indeed, the legal establishment of paternity for teenage fathers is a rare event in any case (Danziger & Nichols-Casebolt, 1988).

Is it possible to increase paternity establishment rates and the amounts paid by fathers so that child support can affect a much greater percentage of the AFDC population and perhaps even replace AFDC to a large extent? Where paternity is concerned, the existence of substantial interstate and intrastate variation in paternity establishment rates suggests that considerable improvement is indeed possible (Committee on Ways and Means, 1993; McLanahan, Brown, & Monson, 1992). In cases where parents are inclined to cooperate with paternity establishment, a variety of administrative procedures are available that, if adopted, can raise rates significantly (Adams, Landsbergen, & Cobler, 1992; McLanahan et al., 1992). It also appears that providing fathers with *multiple* opportunities to consent to paternity can increase the rates (Committee on Ways and Means, 1993).

Consistent noncooperators pose more of a problem (Adams et al., 1992).

Interestingly, the source of noncooperation is often the custodial mother. In some cases she may fear that enforced child support would jeopardize her current (or future) relationship with the father. In others, she might view child support as obligating her and/or her child to maintain a certain level of contact with the father, which she wishes to avoid. In still other instances the mother may believe that she is protecting the father from certain adverse consequences (e.g., medical expenses) by not revealing his identity (Wattenberg, 1987). Establishing paternity could also result in a financial *loss* for an AFDC mother who had previously received more than $50 a month "under the table" from the father, since AFDC regulations do not permit her to keep more than that amount. Finally, qualitative data suggest that misunderstanding of how the child support system works is common among low-income mothers and fathers and that many members of both groups harbor strong negative feelings toward the system based on their experiences with it (Furstenberg, Sherwood, & Sullivan, 1992).

In theory, a mother who refuses to cooperate with the paternity establishment process can be denied her AFDC benefits, and her children's benefits may be sent as a protective payment to someone other than herself. It is unclear to what extent these sanctions are applied in practice, but it is apparently quite infrequent. Of course, the obligation-oriented climate of current reform efforts may reduce the reluctance of welfare administrators to use existing sanctions or the federal government to develop new ones (e.g., requiring welfare mothers to identify their children's fathers in hospital delivery rooms). Whether such measures would have a demonstrable impact on rates of paternity establishment is an open question.

Once paternity is established, increasing the amount of child support collected from fathers can be accomplished through two major mechanisms: setting higher award amounts and doing a better job of collecting those amounts. In terms of the former, the guidelines most states use for establishing awards reflect the assumption that "the noncustodial parent should spend as much on the child as he or she would have spent had the family remained intact" (Bassi & Barnow, 1993, 495). Although alternative ethical principles could be used to generate child support awards, some of which would result in higher awards than currently prevailing guidelines suggest (e.g., Betson et al., 1992; Garfinkel & Melli, 1992), public sentiment does not seem to be strongly in favor of such a shift. It should be noted, however, that Garfinkel and Oellerich (1992) estimate that *as a group*, noncustodial fathers have the ability to pay significantly more in child support than they currently do.

A more promising avenue for increasing the size of awards is the periodic updating of child support orders to reflect changes in the father's income, a procedure mandated by the 1988 Family Support Act. Although the income of the father is typically very low when the child is born, there is frequently significant improvement in his economic circumstances during the following years (Meyer, 1993; Phillips & Garfinkel, 1993; Pirog-Good & Good, 1994). To the extent that updated awards reflect these changed circumstances, the awards will increase.[2]

Finally, there is substantial public support for taking steps to increase the compliance of fathers with child support orders. This domain is especially relevant to AFDC because low-income fathers are more likely than higher-income ones not to comply (Bartfeld & Meyer, 1994). It is clear that routine wage withholding has a significant impact on collections (Bartfeld & Meyer, 1994; Garfinkel & Klawitter, 1990; Garfinkel & Robins, 1993). Implementing wage withholding can be logistically difficult, however, so that it does not always occur even though it is legally mandated (Meyer & Bartfeld, 1992). Consequently, proposals that address some of these administrative obstacles (e.g., establishing a national child support clearinghouse with registries of parents who owe support) would, if adopted, yield additional gains in support collections (e.g., Garfinkel & Robins, 1993).

Overall child support reform probably holds more promise as a vehicle for shifting the cost of AFDC from the government to noncustodial fathers than as a means of substantially enhancing the economic well-being of poor mothers and their children or of moving large numbers of them off the welfare rolls.[3] Nevertheless, some increase in well-being and decrease in the AFDC caseload is likely to occur (Garfinkel & McLanahan, 1994), and the importance of these gains should not be dismissed.

AFDC Family Caps

One of the most publicized and controversial initiatives in the obligation-oriented arena involves the assistance payments made to AFDC households where additional children are borne by the mother. Several states (e.g., New Jersey) are now experimenting with a policy of *not* raising benefit levels when children are born into a family already on AFDC. The attention that this policy has received, despite the fact that very few states have adopted it, is testimony to the deeply held values and beliefs that it touches upon in the society at large. A key value is that women should not have children they cannot afford to raise. In other words, women on AFDC are seen as having an *obligation* not to bear additional children as long as they are receiving assistance. And a crucial belief is that AFDC has traditionally provided an economic incentive to women and teenagers to have children out of wedlock.

The empirical evidence on the latter issue is mixed. AFDC does have a positive impact on the incidence of nonmarital births, with estimates of the size of this impact ranging from minor to moderate (e.g., Acs, 1993; Fossett & Kiecolt, 1993; Moffitt, 1992; Murray, 1993; Robins & Frostin, 1993). On the other hand, the decision of AFDC mothers to have *additional* children has not been found to be related to the size of the benefit increases associated with having them (Acs, 1993; Robins & Fronstin, 1993).[4] Given this finding, it will be intriguing to see whether significant, sustained reductions in the fertility rates of AFDC mothers will occur in states adopting the family-cap policy. Sharply and abruptly reducing the AFDC benefits provided for the *first* child would probably have a more pronounced effect on the AFDC caseload, in view of the research evidence. Nevertheless, as long as the public views an initial out-of-wedlock birth as less objectionable than subsequent ones, such a measure is unlikely to receive the popular support needed for adoption.

From a policy-making perspective, manipulating benefits to reduce AFDC birthrates has the advantage of simplicity; implementation of such a charge is fairly mechanistic and easy to bureaucratize. It is important to recognize, however, that economic considerations represent just one factor influencing the decision of young, low-income females to bear children out of wedlock. Qualitative studies have convincingly documented the complex and powerful cluster of psychological, social, and subcultural forces that interact in the lives of these teenagers and women and serve to make unwed motherhood a status they find desirable in many cases, especially when compared with their perceived alternatives (e.g., Anderson, 1991; Musick, 1993; Quint & Musick, 1994). Designing interventions that effectively target these forces is a challenging task, to put it mildly, and the programs that result tend to be far from mechanistic and bureaucratic (e.g., Quint, Fink, & Rowser, 1991; Ruch-Ross, Jones, & Musick, 1992; Schorr, 1988).

Time-Limited Welfare

At first glance the imposition of time limits on AFDC receipt would seem to represent the most draconian of all the obligation-oriented proposals for welfare reform (e.g., Haveman & Scholz, 1994; Jencks, 1992a). And it would be, if the proposers were indeed recommending that after a certain period recipients simply be dropped from the rolls and "obligated" to fend for themselves in the free-for-all of the labor market and private charity. Virtually no one has suggested such a scenario, however. Rather, what is typically proposed is a system in which recipients would be offered a guaranteed public-service job after two years or so on welfare (e.g., Ellwood, 1988). Alternatively, recipients might be required to engage in unpaid work experience in order to receive continued assistance.

The second option is, for all practical purposes, the same as the work requirement discussed earlier in this chapter. The first option, on the other hand, appears quite different on the surface. In terms of its relationship to the dimension of self-sufficiency versus government support, however, it closely resembles work experience. In the case of both strategies, it is the government that provides support; in one instance it is through assured welfare benefits that must be "worked off" (work experience), and in the other it is through assured wages that must be "worked for" (guaranteed jobs).

To the extent that guaranteed jobs represent a form of guaranteed income support, the self-sufficiency appeal of time-limited welfare is more symbolic than substantive. Of course, policy makers and the public may prefer that government support be offered through employment rather than welfare for ideological reasons, but skepticism abounds concerning the ability of the government to fund and administer large-scale job programs. When these doubts are viewed together with the logistical challenges associated with expanding unpaid work experience to a national level (Brock et al., 1993), the fate of proposals for time-limited welfare would seem to be uncertain at best.

Mixed Approaches

As their name implies, mixed strategies attempt to foster self-sufficiency by offering, *in a balanced fashion*, rewards for desired behavior as well as punishments for undesired actions. As logical as this approach may seem, there are relatively few interventions in the welfare reform arena which incorporate this principle as an explicit feature in their design. An excellent example of such a program is LEAP (Learning, Earning, and Parenting), a demonstration project in Ohio that focuses on teenage custodial parents and pregnant teenagers who are receiving AFDC and do not have a high school diploma or GED. The monthly welfare checks of LEAP participants are increased by a specific amount when they regularly attend high school or an educational program leading to a GED but are decreased by the same amount if they fail to attend regularly. Each teenager in the program is assigned a case manager to help her overcome barriers to school attendance, and all participants are eligible for child care and transportation assistance.

The assumption underlying LEAP, one that is supported by research, is that high school graduates are less likely to become long-term welfare recipients than those who drop out. At this point, the interim findings for LEAP indicate that it does have a significant positive impact on school enrollment: Of those in the study who were in school when LEAP began, LEAP participants were more likely than control-group members to remain in school. Among those who were dropouts at the beginning of the program, LEAP participants were more likely than nonparticipants to return to school. Whether this impact will eventually result in higher rates of school *completion* remains to be seen, but preliminary findings are positive in this regard (Bloom et al., 1993).

To be sure, the ultimate criterion for judging LEAP's success will be its impact on welfare receipt among its target population, an issue that can be addressed only by long-term research. To the extent that these investigations continue to yield positive findings for LEAP, policy makers should consider making more extensive use of mixed approaches in welfare reform efforts.

OPPORTUNITY-ORIENTED APPROACHES

Opportunity-oriented approaches are based on the recognition that contextual factors play a crucial role in determining whether increases in ability and/or motivation can generate corresponding increases in economic self-sufficiency. For example, the labor market must be able to provide employment for those who have been trained; schools need to offer quality educational experiences so that those who are motivated to graduate actually have some skills when they finish. Thus, opportunity-oriented approaches attempt to establish an environment that supports the efforts of motivational and ability-focused interventions.

As might be expected, the arena for opportunity-oriented approaches encompasses many of the core institutions and policy domains in American society, such as employment, housing, education, and healthcare.[5] Exploring these areas in any detail is well beyond the scope of this chapter, even though their relevance to the ultimate success of welfare reform cannot be denied. Ironically, as important as these contextual factors are, they have received relatively little attention in recent public discussion of welfare reform, which has been dominated by motivational concerns and references to the obligations *recipients* incur under a "social contract" model of public assistance.

From a self-sufficiency perspective, the opportunity-oriented proposals that most frequently appear in analyses of welfare reform focus on child care and health insurance. Qualitative data clearly indicate that low-income, single mothers view the lack of high-quality child care as a serious obstacle to their being employed outside of the home (Pavetti, 1993), although research that rigorously demonstrates that increasing access to such care will raise employment levels among these women is limited (Polit & O'Hara, 1989). In part, this result may be due to the fact that many mothers prefer to make informal arrangements for child care with friends and relatives. Thus, when they participate in a work or training program that provides assistance in purchasing child care in a formal setting, these mothers may expend considerable effort in securing informal, unsubsidized care in which they have greater confidence. The intuitive appeal of the connection between child-care assistance and employment is sufficiently powerful, however, that mandatory welfare-to-work programs and proposals now include provisions for child-care assistance that extend *beyond* the time of the recipients' departure from the welfare rolls (Hagen & Lurie, 1993).[6]

A roughly similar situation exists in healthcare. Welfare mothers report that they are extremely reluctant to take jobs that do not offer medical coverage comparable to that of Medicaid, which is available to all AFDC recipients (Pavetti, 1993). Consequently, states are now required to guarantee such coverage for a transitional period after recipients leave AFDC due to employment. Low-skilled jobs frequently offer little or nothing in the way of healthcare benefits, however, a circumstance that puts former AFDC recipients at risk when the transitional period ends, and represents an incentive for them to return to welfare. Thus, movement in the direction of universal coverage as part of healthcare reform can serve to reduce this incentive.

Unfortunately, controlled studies that document the impact of extended Medicaid benefits on employment levels and welfare dependency are few and unclear in their implications (Polit & O'Hara, 1989). At a more general level, the evidence is unambiguous that the availability of private health insurance has a strong negative impact on the probability of receiving AFDC and a strong positive impact on the probability of being employed (Moffitt & Wolfe, 1992).

Overall, it seems reasonable to expect that increasing the availability of high-quality child care and medical coverage to AFDC mothers who wish to work would have at least a modest effect on their short- and long-term self-sufficiency. Although expectations are no substitute for data, the "face validity" of these interventions (not to mention their humaneness) is such that they deserve continued attention and experimentation.

CONCLUSIONS

In 1973 economist Henry Aaron authored a slim volume entitled *Why Is Welfare So Hard to Reform?* More than two decades have passed, and the policy-making challenge of bringing about substantive change in the welfare system has yet to be successfully addressed (Chilman, 1992; Reischauer, 1989). To be sure, many of the interventions reviewed in this chapter can have, and do have, beneficial impacts. As has been seen, however, these impacts are typically quite modest in terms of the levels of self-sufficiency and economic well-being attained by the target population. Those who are helped by these interventions are not usually able to put much economic distance between themselves and an AFDC standard of living. Frequently, the only upward mobility they experience is the short journey from the ranks of the nonworking, welfare poor to those of the working, nonwelfare, not-quite-as-poor.

Most policy makers and taxpayers want welfare reform to accomplish much more than this. They would like reform to transform the welfare system into one that enables recipients to achieve a level of self-sufficiency that is comfortably above the poverty line, "within hailing distance of the American mainstream," as Burtless (1989, 140) puts it.

Can ability-oriented, motivational, and opportunity-focused strategies be strengthened to the point where these lofty goals for welfare reform are within reach? Simply put, the answer is that we don't know. In some cases we don't know because the cost of fully implementing an intervention exceeds the resources that have been made available for it (e.g., education and training); in others we don't know because it is unclear whether it is possible to overcome, *on a national scale*, logistical obstacles to policy implementation (e.g., problems in establishing paternity for child support purposes or in enforcing work and training requirements for AFDC mothers). In still other cases, policies have not been in place long enough for their sustained impact to be accurately assessed (e.g., family-size caps on AFDC benefits). Indeed, if it is true that the most important long-term effect of obligation-oriented policies will be to change subcultural values regarding work and childbearing in low-income communities, it could take a generation or more for the impacts on self-sufficiency to manifest themselves fully.

To the extent that self-sufficiency strategies cannot live up to the high expectations that are held for them—and the record thus far certainly provides support for skepticism—a long-standing value dilemma in American society is intensified. It is the question of whether dependency reduction or poverty reduction should be assigned a higher priority in the formulation of social policy (Ellwoood, 1989; Morris & Williamson, 1987). Self-sufficiency strategies emphasize dependency reduction, although supporters of this approach certainly hope that significant poverty reduction will accompany lessened dependency. But what if dependency reduction strategies are not potent enough to accomplish this secondary goal and, indeed, demonstrate limited success at achieving their primary objective? Should poverty reduction be addressed more directly, even if it means *increasing* the level of dependency within society? Policy makers in the United States have traditionally been very reluctant to take this step with respect to the able-bodied poor. Proposals for guaranteed jobs (e.g., Ellwood, 1988), children's allowances, and government-insured minimum child support benefits (Garfinkel, 1992; National Commission on Children, 1991), for example, have not gathered much momentum in recent discussions of welfare reform.

As long as this strong cultural preference for dependency reduction over poverty reduction shapes the reform agenda, the accomplishments of reform are likely to be very constrained, although they will not be negligible. Female-headed families in the United States will probably continue to be less well-off economically than their counterparts in many other Western industrialized nations, nations that are not as averse to using social policy to directly provide economic security to their citizens (e.g., Wong, Garfinkel, & McLanahan, 1993).

The available evidence suggests that the United States possesses the economic resources to go much further in providing such security than it currently does (Burtless, 1994). Policy makers have chosen not to, and this decision is rooted less in scientific evidence than it is in the values they have brought to the decision-making process. As Burtless (1989) has observed, "In the final analysis, the decision of policy makers to adopt or reject a particular set of reforms will not hinge on the exact behavioral consequences of reform, even if these were known with certainty" (pp. 139-140). It may be that self-sufficiency, a value so highly prized in the United States, represents a check that our social policy bank account cannot fully cover, at least where welfare reform is concerned. To the degree that the current debate over the welfare system brings about a greater awareness of this possibility, it will have served a highly useful purpose, regardless of whatever else it may achieve.

NOTES

1. With permission from the federal government, however, a number of states have continued to experiment with various aspects of the benefit reduction formula (see Wiseman, 1993).

2. In this context it should be noted that a major demonstration project is currently under way, dubbed "Parents' Fair Share," which attempts to increase the employment and earning levels of noncustodial parents of children on welfare (Bloom & Sherwood, 1994).

3. Meyer's (1993) research on divorced mothers, however, indicates that child support can help them avoid returning to AFDC once they have left.

4. Robins and Frostin (1993) did find a positive relationship for mothers who were high school dropouts, however.

5. Popkin, Rosenbaum, and Meaden (1993), for example, found that low-income black mothers who moved to middle-class suburbs as part of a housing program were more likely to be subsequently employed than a comparable group of mothers in the same program who moved to new locations in the city.

6. The obstacle to employment represented by child-care expenses could also be reduced by altering income tax policy to make the existing child-care tax credit refundable; this change would enable low-income parents, who frequently pay no taxes, to benefit from the credit (National Commission on Children, 1991).

6

Poverty, Politics, and Policy

Alfred Baumeister
Franklin D. Kupstas
Pamela Woodley-Zanthos

By whichever index—education, health, or security—one chooses to gauge the present well-being of our children, there is little reason to be sanguine about recent trends. In view of current political and economic developments the future portends more of the same. A myriad of indicators derived from demographic and social patterns, income disparities, epidemiologic factors, morbidity and mortality data, health and social support systems, surveillance reports, and policy initiatives have been analyzed and scrutinized by many private and public agencies and professional groups (e.g., Baumeister, Kupstas, & Zanthos, 1993; Carnegie Foundation, 1994; Children's Defense Fund, 1994). The collective conclusion is clear and inescapable: In all significant health domains U.S. children are severely compromised and inexorably becoming more vulnerable.

Although numerous political and policy twists may be placed on the data, such as cause and effect in the guise of nature versus nurture, without exception prime indicators show that public commitment to the needs of children is sorely tested. Not only have trends over the past fifteen years revealed a distinct and pronounced erosion of the well-being and welfare of ethnic and racial subgroups, but the general condition of the conventional "middle class" is increasingly compromised as well. When viewed from an international perspective, the United States has assumed the unenviable, alarming position of sacrificing children in favor of other competing interests or dependent segments, such as the elderly (Baumeister & Kupstas, 1990).

To be sure, there is ample rhetoric by politicians, assertively fueled by advocates, in recognition of the problems and special needs of children. Everyone seems to be "for the children." Indeed, certain policy initiatives, such as the 1989 and 1990 amendments to the Social Security Act that provide health insurance to poor and near-poor children and the Family and Medical Leave Act of 1993, have been undertaken in recognition of the unequivocal fact that an entire generation has been failed and placed in such risk and jeopardy as to demand urgent and substantial action.

Grand declarations of alarm, expressed devotion to traditional American values, together with a steadily increasing stream of well-publicized, blue-ribbon reports describing and decrying the plight of children have not been translated into a coherent, comprehensive and continuous public policy that addresses the ever-growing constellation of risks for disease, disability, and death among children, particularly those who are impoverished or left adrift at the margins. Recent acrimonious and unproductive debates over healthcare reform have revealed just how deeply fault lines of contention run, divisions that are threatening to tear asunder an already precarious system of health-related services for poor children and their families.

As for the recent federal legislation amending Title XIX and expanding medical coverage to all poor and near-poor children, data from the Health Care Finance Administration show that not a single state is in compliance with the law. Most are not even close. Whereas health reform was the overriding political issue two years ago, now the vagaries of political fortune have turned attention to welfare reform, including threats to Medicaid provisions.

The stark reality is that millions of children are in crisis. But this crisis does not elicit enduring public outrage and commitment that forces politicians and policy makers to contend in a comprehensive manner with the practical day-to-day realities of children living in poverty - and what that means for our society as a whole. A major handicap for children is that they do not vote. In the face of the evidence we cannot deny that the effects of poverty on children are pervasive and enduring.

POVERTY IS NOT GOOD FOR CHILDREN

Despite a modest upturn in the nation's economic health following the 1990-1991 recession, child poverty rates continued to edge upward. According to data recently released by the Census Bureau, at the end of 1993 about 15 million children (or about one in four) in the United States were living in or near poverty, more than at any time in the past thirty years. The U.S. Bureau of the Census has reported that over the last five years, poverty rates for individuals under eighteen years of age have increased-from 19.6 percent in 1989 to 22.7 percent in 1993.

More detailed examination of these bleak numbers reveals that children living in female-headed households are most likely to be impoverished (54 percent in 1992). In addition, the youngest are hit the hardest. Approximately one in every four children (26.2 percent) under six is poor. Of all children younger than three, a disproportionate 27 percent lived in poverty in 1992. It is this group to whom services are not consistently or adequately available and yet are most essential.

Another less well publicized but extremely significant feature to the child poverty picture is that the length of time in poverty is increasing as well (Baumeister et al., 1993). Chronic poverty, as contrasted with acute poverty, is a potent predictor of outcome. This means that access to services, opportunities, and resources is delayed or denied during the crucial developmental period of maximum vulnerability. As one example, a study by the U.S. Department of Education showed that every year in poverty adds two percentage points to the risk that the child will fall behind in school (Kennedy et al., 1986).

Racial and/or ethnic resource disparities not only continue but are on the increase. For children under six years of age poverty rates in 1991 were 14 percent for whites, 44 percent for Latinos, and 51 percent for African-Americans. Although white children experienced the steepest rise among all three groups between 1973 and 1992, it is important to emphasize that minorities, who represent only one-third of all children under six, still account for over 60 percent of poor children. The poverty rate for African-American children under six years of age is the highest since the Census Bureau began reporting this information. Figure 6.1 shows poverty trends over time for children under age six. These data are based on the official family poverty level and do not include the near poor.

Figure 6.1
Yearly Poverty Trends

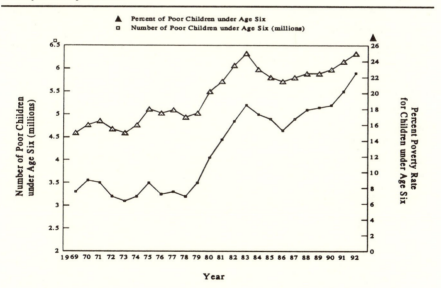

Technically, it is not children, but families who are poor. When we consider family income and poverty rates for children in young families between 1973 and 1992 and compare these figures among different racial groups, the disparities become even more compelling. For all groups, median income for young families (i.e, adults under thirty years of age) dropped by over 34 percent during this period. Overall child poverty rates increased by 110 percent. Among young white families, the median income dropped by 19.7 percent and the child poverty rate rose by a staggering 142 percent. For Latino families, the median income decreased by 24.6 percent and the child poverty rate rose by 48 percent. Finally, for young black families, median income fell by 50.4 percent, the worst of all groups.

The consequences of poverty are not simply a static condition that affects the individual child in a specific and short-lived way. Rather, chronic and concentrated poverty is an insidious long-acting often intergenerational process, the consequences of which compromise health, educational success, and social well-being. Numerous surveillance studies demonstrate that a disproportionate number become mentally and/or physically hurt, some seriously and permanently (Baumeister et al., 1993). For instance, family income is a more potent predictor of children's IQs at age five than maternal education, ethnicity, or membership in a single-parent family (Duncan, Brooks-Gunn, & Klebanov, 1994).

The multifaceted adverse impact of poverty can be observed in various ways over the lifespan of the individual. Poverty is usually not a unidimensional or direct cause of health and social impairments. Instead, it stands as a proxy for many other adverse conditions that act directly upon the individual. By now it is well understood that environments in which economically disadvantaged children develop are less conducive to optimal physical and mental growth than are environments of children who are raised in more advantageous settings (Baumeister et al., 1993; Institute of Medicine, 1985; Starfield, 1989). These adverse effects begin at the most basic level of development, namely, prenatally or even preconceptually.

Poor mothers are much more likely to be less healthy before conception and, on becoming pregnant, less likely to receive prenatal care. Consequently their babies are more frequently delivered under substandard conditions. The result is that these infants are often born too early and too small, suffer more frequent, persistent, and severe illnesses throughout their infancy, are less apt to be fully and appropriately immunized, are at greater peril for a higher rate of accidents, face greater risk of abuse and neglect, and have a higher mortality rate than are children born to mothers in better circumstances. In addition, for many of these poor children, nutrition tends to be inadequate, child care substandard, cognitive and emotional stimulation minimal, school attendance erratic, and housing substandard.

Findings from the 1988 National Health Interview Survey of Child Health (Adams & Hardy, 1989) show that the percentage of children under seventeen years of age exhibiting developmental disabilities, learning disabilities, and emotional problems is inversely related to family income. The National Center for Health Statistics (1991) reported that individuals under eighteen years of age who lived in families with annual incomes under $10,000 were three times as likely to be in poor health when compared with children whose families earned $35,000 or more per year. Youths three through seventeen rated in poor to fair health were seven times more frequent among lower- income groups.

Obviously, given the increasing number of families caught in an economic squeeze, in terms of current dollars, a great many more children today must be rated in poor health medically and behaviorally. Again, there is a continuing racial disparity in regard to health indices such as low birthweight and infant mortality, with more than twice as many African-American children born small and dying before their first birthday compared with white children (Children's Defense Fund, 1994).

Measured in human terms, the costs are enormous. The economic costs are substantial as well. Data from the National Medical Care Utilization and Expenditure Survey indicate that in 1988 healthcare costs for all children exceeded $40.5 billion. Approximately $4.4 billion was spent on those with chronic disabling conditions, an average of $1,406 per child as compared with an average of $487 for other children. Expressed in current dollars, expenditures for treating chronic health and developmental problems are much greater because of escalating medical care costs. In addition, studies of national costs underestimate out-of-pocket expenditures and typically do not take into account expenditures for related social and education services.

Houk and Thacker (1989) introduced a measure-"Disability Years"-that represents the number of years people survive with disabilities. This provides an index of the public health impact and associated costs of disability. About 20 percent of children between birth and fifteen years of age experience one or more disabilities. Their average survival is fifty years, translating into 280 million years of disability for this age cohort.

THE NEW MORBIDITY

During the mid-1970s the incidence of many of the so-called dread diseases was greatly reduced by the implementation of public health measures, including immunizations and medical interventions. However, at the same time a new phenomenon was emerging, what we have termed the *New Morbidity*, that includes a constellation of environmental, behavioral, and biological risks profoundly affecting the health and welfare of a large segment of the nation's children. In addition, increasing poverty, forced fiscal constraints at federal, state, and local levels, ballooning health and social services costs, and political and/or policy changes have accelerated risks of diseases and disabilities.

The New Morbidity is an expression of the interaction of environmental, behavioral, and biological factors that place children in jeopardy for a myriad of health and developmental problems. These interactions may occur at any time during the individual's life but are particularly deleterious in the prenatal-perinatal period and through early childhood. Although most of the conditions falling under the rubric of the New Morbidity are not "new" in an absolute sense (with certain notable exceptions such as pediatric HIV/AIDS), we are nevertheless confronting a dramatic and serious increase in the numbers of children who are experiencing chronic health, developmental, and social problems, including mental retardation, learning disabilities, emotional disturbance, diseases of the central nervous system, failure to thrive, substance abuse, suicide, and crime.

Paramount to this New Morbidity is the undeniable fact that the vast majority of these children are found in lower socioeconomic strata. Numerous empirical studies show a strong connection between social and/or economic disadvantage and the increased incidence of New Morbidity problems. Take, for example, the incidence of psychosocial and psychosomatic disorders encountered in primary care. Starfield and others (1980) observed that the number of children in seven primary care facilities who exhibited behavioral, educational, or social problems was much higher than generally assumed by the pediatric community, ranging between 5 percent and 15 percent. Of thirty-six types of childhood disorders recently diagnosed in major medical centers, 66 percent were psychosocial in nature and clearly linked to economic disadvantage (Starfield, 1989). Not only was the overall number of children affected higher than expected but, it was also observed, prevalence of these various problems was highest among children from the least affluent families. These findings have been repeatedly confirmed by more recent studies (Baumeister, Kupstas, & Klindworth, 1991).

Results from a well-known, classic longitudinal study of lower-middle-class and upper-class infants diagnosed at eight months of age with developmental delays are especially revealing as to the importance of environmental factors in dictating the developmental course. An early report by Willesman, Broman, and Fiedler (1970) found that when these same children were assessed at four years of age, 13 percent of the lower-class children had measured IQ scores of 79 or less, whereas only 7 percent of the middle-class children were found to be mentally retarded. For the upper-class children, the figure was lower yet, only 2 percent. It appears that the association between early developmental delay and later IQ deficit are linked to poverty and the various conditions (poor health, inadequate housing, high stress, poor nutrition, etc.) that are inextricably linked with it. The interaction of various social, behavioral, environmental, and biological variables tends to place the individual at increased risk for later adverse developmental sequelae (Broman, Nichols, Shaughnessy, & Kennedy, 1987).

Although adverse social and economic factors may not necessarily be the direct cause of brain disorders, they certainly must be considered predisposing. Moreover, by their interaction with innate characteristics, they modulate the effects of brain disorders.

Avery (1985) has identified three mechanisms through which these interactions are expressed:

1. By virtue of life circumstances, the child before or after birth may be placed in harm's way and thus have an increased exposure to high-risk conditions, which in turn may lead with greater frequency to brain disorders.
2. In an unfavorable environment, a child with brain injury may also develop in a maladaptive way. Because of this double jeopardy, a child may perform worse than expected due to either brain injury or social, cultural, and economic factors alone.
3. Lack of timely and effective rehabilitative services may maximize central nervous system injury and compromise learning during a critical developmental period.

Adversity begets adversity. Evidence conclusively demonstrates that already vulnerable infants reared under adverse environmental conditions are at increased risk for poor cognitive development. A group of premature infants from a neonatal intensive care unit who had displayed significant illness during the neonatal period, and who were also predominantly poor and nonwhite, were followed from birth to 3.5 years. After completing assessments of their cognitive and psychosocial development, Escalona (1982) found that "environmental deficits and stresses impair early cognitive and psychosocial development for both full-term and premature infants, but the latter group is more vulnerable to environmental insufficiencies than are full-term babies" (p. 679).

A very critical study of the connection between adverse environmental circumstances, premature low birthweight, and long-term outcome was reported by R.S. Wilson (1985). The importance of his study lies in the perfect genetic control in which monozygotic twins were compared. Of particular interest were concordant pairs of twins, one of whom was born significantly smaller than the other. By age six, the low-birthweight twin had recovered from relative developmental cognitive delay associated with low birthweight. Prematurity was a powerful initial suppressor, but the child returned to his natural trajectory. On the other hand, cognitive delay was strongly associated with family status, particularly maternal education. Wilson concluded that prematurity or low birthweight, aside from the extremes where there are likely to be significant neurological sequelae, does not explain decrements in IQ. Rather, premature low birthweight is a *symptom* of a broader constellation of interrelated circumstances.

Clearly the chain of bioecological events is complex. Factors that predispose a child to poor outcomes involve environmental conditions, social conditions, and genetic risk factors (Starfield, 1992). On the basis of a multivariate analysis done separately for black and white children, McGauhey, Starfield, Alexander, and Ensminger (1991) analyzed the impact of social environment on various health outcomes. Six components of adverse social environment were used, including low family income, family with mother as the only adult, maternal education less than high school, maternal self-perception of health as fair or poor, five or more children in the family, and crowding in the home. Each component was divided into low-risk, moderate-risk, and high-risk states. The values were then summed to obtain a social conditions score for each child. It was found that low-birthweight children in high-risk social environments, but not those in moderate-risk or low-risk environments, were at increased risk for poor health outcomes compared with comparable normal-birthweight children. In addition, it was observed that this disadvantage is not outgrown during childhood - it was evident in both preschool as well as schoolage children.

McGauhey and others (1991) concluded that the effects of low family income are more direct on white children than on black children. For the latter, such factors as low maternal education, poor maternal health, and crowded living conditions are strongly correlated with poor health. Generalizations observed with one racial or ethnic group should be very cautiously applied to the other.

Given the ample evidence illustrating the importance of social, behavioral, biological, and environmental influences both singly and in combination on adverse health and developmental outcome, the search for protective influences and the ways in which they actuate developmental resilience in children is critical to an understanding of how risk factors operate. Although causal relationships are often difficult to establish when attempting to clarify the interaction of various complex processes, strong inferences are nonetheless possible from these and other studies. Baumeister, Dokecki, and Kupstas (1991) describe these processes as being "both subtle and complex in character, with environmental contingencies tending to exacerbate biological vulnerability, creating a synergistic effect in which the combination is more influential than the sum of the individual factors" (p. 11).

Because individuals and their environments represent an integral symbiotic process, it is imperative that an understanding of this process include assessment of single variables and their interactions. A univariate clinical approach, embedded in traditional medical and psychological service systems, is neither an adequate nor a sufficient basis on which to predicate public health initiatives to effectively confront the complex constellation of causes and effects that arise when social adversity meets biological vulnerability.

Piecemeal and patchwork efforts to address the health crisis faced by millions of marginalized children are doomed to failure. The New Morbidity model aids in this understanding by providing a bioecological framework in which to describe and analyze systematically, both singly and in combination, a wide array of variable categories that govern the individual's developmental experience.

THE NEW MORBIDITY MODEL

The New Morbidity model is explicitly designed to avoid exclusive reliance on a disease orientation to understanding and preventing health and developmental problems. Rather, it is based on a population-based epidemiological concept of prevention that includes the etiology, range and type of impairment, the functional nature of the disability, and extent and effects of the handicaps. By and large, evaluation of the impact of low income on health outcomes, along with assessment of measures designed to alleviate these effects, have been based on a disease- by-disease clinical approach. However, from a public health perspective the goal is not merely to change incidence of one condition at a time but, rather, to generate a coherent strategy that addresses the developmental needs of children, not just their diseases and disabilities. To draw an analogy with the perpetual arguments over the nature of intelligence, health should be regarded as a general factor, *not* as specific factors.

In addition to including the basic concepts identified above, the model relies heavily on the premise that prevention of handicap or disability depends not only on control of personal characteristics but equally on the broader context of social and physical environments. In the New Morbidity model, "absolute" disability is of such a debilitating nature that it would be evident in practically every environment. More importantly, most prevention efforts are conceived in "relative" (i.e., less severe disabilities defined by prevailing standards of "normal" behavior) terms of the demands, constraints, and opportunities of variable socioeconomic contexts. Culture or environment defines competence. Therefore, risk factors, indicators of child health, and current or potential quality of life assume great prominence in the New Morbidity model. To summarize: The New Morbidity concept is designed to move from descriptive studies of socio-economic status-health relationships (of which there are ample numbers) to analytic strategies with a view toward understanding the mechanisms, the matrix of causes, and the moderators to determine how these can be altered to produce healthy children.

The New Morbidity model is used to organize the ecology of the individual under five categorical variable classes: (1) predisposing, (2) catalytic, (3) resource, (4) proximal, and (5) outcome. The purpose of these variable-class headings is to identify how various factors interact to place children at risk by maintaining or exacerbating already existing conditions and to use the findings as a guide in making decisions regarding possible points of preventive intervention. In addition, these variable-class headings are organized into a hierarchical scheme in terms of temporal occurrence to outcome, from proximal to distal.

This temporal ordering is important when attempting to target prevention programs at particular population groups according to established risk factors. For example, some general prevention initiatives such as prenatal care, cessation of smoking, and adequate nutrition should be applied to the entire population. Other prevention efforts, however, should be applied selectively and at specific times to particular groups known to be at elevated risk, such as drug-exposed pregnant women. The summary model is presented in Figure 6.2. The New Morbidity model is primarily oriented to poverty and prenatal-perinatal factors, although many other variables are implicated. Some of the more salient variables that influence occurrence of subsequent morbidity are described within the model. However, it is important to emphasize that only through an understanding of their interactions will we be able to determine which children and families are at elevated risk.

Figure 6.2
New Morbidity Model

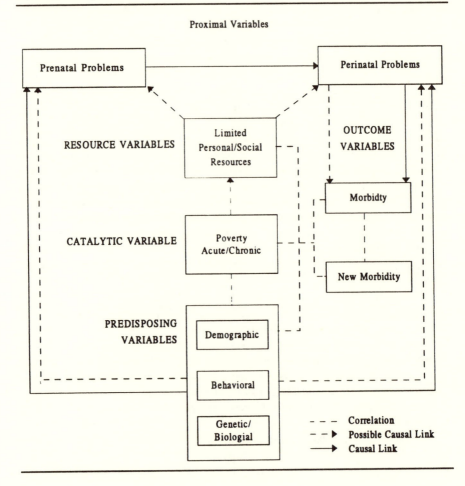

In the model a public health perspective is adopted that emphasizes *sensitivity* and *specificity*. Sensitivity refers to the correct identification of those at risk for some condition (e.g., mental retardation) and who will benefit from a particular intervention (true positives). Specificity is an index of either those who are not at risk for the condition or those who will not profit from that intervention (true negatives). Not only of great importance in planning for public health initiatives, these measures also permit an analysis of benefits and costs.

It should be noted that the New Morbidity model is flexible in its ability to accommodate numerous variables within its framework and to juxtapose these variables as the phenomenon under study changes. These general variable-class categories will be explained for the purpose of illustrating the multidimensional nature of the model and the transactional process that takes place within and between each variable class.

1. *Predisposing variables* are the most obvious targets for primary prevention efforts. This variable class is further divided into three subcategories: (1) demographic characteristics such as race, education, and socioeconomic status; (2) behavioral factors such as personal habits and cultural beliefs; and (3) genetic-biologic factors. Predisposing influences play a major role in conditioning children's development. All predisposing variables, whether demographic, behavioral, or genetic, are known to have possible causal links to pre- and perinatal health and developmental problems. Again, these variables do not act in isolation and can have the effect of constraining or catalyzing the operation of other classes of variables.

2. *Catalytic variables* serve as a link between predisposing variables and resource variables. Catalytic variables include acute and/or chronic poverty, along with adverse living conditions that are a direct result of inadequate financial supports and economic disadvantage. These include factors such as poor nutrition, substandard housing, and limited access to various social networks that empower individuals, enhance physical and mental health and development, and improve overall family and community living conditions. The effects of poverty, whether acute or chronic, pervade intellectual, emotional, and physical development. Poverty makes the home environment less conducive to optimal development in children, whether from poor nutrition, inadequate medical care, reduced intellectual stimulation, or overall family stress.

   Disadvantage, whether economic, educational, or biologic, occurs across time, each generation passing on to the next the unfortunate and cumulative consequences of its own experience. It is important to view poverty not as an isolated or singular condition but as a multidimensional process that can affect children's health and development in subtle and profound ways, both directly and indirectly. Although poverty may be correlated with other classes of variables, there is little doubt that one of the major negative results stemming from economic disadvantage is the strong dependence upon, and oftentimes lack of access to, various public resources and programs for poor individuals and families to enhance health and well-being. Catalytic variables are inextricably linked with resource variables and act as a catalyst to initiate or limit the operation of other variables.

3. *Resource variables* are those support systems that include educational, medical, social, and political services such as counseling for sexually active adolescents; classes in child care, parenting skills, and nutrition; prenatal care; supplementary nutrition programs; quality daycare; vocational skills training; child and adolescent mental health services; and case management. These services link the individual and family to the greater community and can serve to attenuate the negative effects of various ongoing insults to health and development.

   When available or accessible, these resources enhance the physical, intellectual, economic, and emotional development of at-risk children and their families and empower them to take responsibility for major decisions affecting their health and welfare. Resource deficits, on the other hand, are exemplified by poor primary and preventive healthcare availability and are often an influential factor in creating health problems related to poverty. For example, adequate and timely prenatal care, particularly for women known to be at risk, enables us to identify and treat a variety of potentially harmful influences, such as poor maternal nutrition, infection, and stress. When various resources necessary to maintain proper health are not available or accessed, the results are often manifested in serious and costly proximal conditions.

4. *Proximal variables* are influenced by predisposing, catalytic, and resource variables and are most directly related to prenatal health factors and perinatal problems. Proximal conditions are most immediately reflected in the well-being of newborns. They place the child at increased risk for subsequent long-term morbidity. Prenatal factors include biological and behavioral influences that can have adverse consequences for both the pregnant mother and her developing fetus. These potentially serious problems can include poor maternal weight gain, hypotension, hypertension, preeclampsia, toxemia, infections, and placental problems. Perinatal problems are most easily identified with the well-being of the newborn infant regarding such factors as low birthweight, preterm birth, and intrauterine growth retardation.

   The occurrence of any one of these conditions can lead to serious consequences for the child, including a wide range of morbidities and high incidence of mortality. Low birthweight associated with prematurity is the most significant socially linked proximal factor associated with New-Morbidity-related outcomes in children.

5. *Outcome variables* include a vast array of long-term and short-term adverse health and developmental conditions. Although these conditions can be viewed as final common pathways of the transactions occurring within and between all other variable classes, they can also be seen as catalysts that increase the likelihood of other high-risk conditions. These outcomes include adverse conditions such as developmental disabilities, educational disadvantage, chronic health problems, and various psychological and emotional disturbances. Outcomes may differ in their specific manifestations, but the New Morbidity model suggests they share some common origins.

   There is little doubt of the relatively high risk for New Morbidity outcomes among certain groups of children. This disproportionate risk can be viewed as a transactional process in which some children are behaviorally and biologically vulnerable to environmental and psychosocial influences that in turn predispose them to an array of disabling health and developmental conditions. The connection between poverty and these deleterious conditions is not necessarily direct; yet it is nonetheless a major influence, particularly when mediated by various proximal and distal variables. Although our knowledge of the precise nature of these correlations, causes, and effects is not complete, there are data to support these conclusions.

The range of topics embraced within the New Morbidity model is considerable, focusing as it does on primary prevention of many behavioral and medical disorders. Certain general topics are immediately relevant to this discussion, not only because of their centrality but because of their timeliness.

Health Insurance

In 1992 more than 8 million children had no health insurance during the entire year. In addition, millions of other children were uninsured during some part of the year or had coverage that failed to pay for key preventive care or preexisting conditions. Comparing children's access to healthcare between 1988 and 1992, the Children's Defense Fund (1994) reports that although there were 3.1 million more children younger than eighteen in 1992 when compared with 1988, close to a million fewer children were covered by employment-related insurance. This was true even though 91 percent of these children lived in families where one member worked at least part time, and 73 percent lived in families where at least one member worked full time over the course of the entire year.

By far the most important national health insurance program for poor and near-poor children and their mothers is Title XIX of the Social Security Act - well known as Medicaid. In recognition of the direct relationships between low income and accelerated risk of health disorders, in 1989 and 1990 Congress amended children's healthcare provisions to ensure universal healthcare and medical assistance for all those under twenty-one years of age who are in poor and lower-income families.

More specifically, eligibility for children's healthcare is now expanded and is separated from cash assistance. Of particular relevance is the Early and Periodic Screening, Diagnosis, and Treatment (EPSDT) program. Now all eligible children are to be identified by the states and must be furnished with regular comprehensive screens and examinations (e.g., six during the first year), all medically necessary healthcare, and case management to obtain educational, social, psychological, and other services (such as early education). Services not only include routine examinations but follow-up diagnosis and testing as necessary, immunizations, lead blood screening, hearing and vision assessment, dental services, rehabilitation, physical therapy, behavioral interventions, and any other "necessary" services. Congressional intent in expanding and defining medical assistance under these amendments is to provide "the nation's largest preventive health program for children."

However, the intent of the law has not been matched by state action. Requirements and provisions under Title XIX have largely not been implemented. The states have failed in their obligations under the law, and the Health Care Finance Administration, charged with monitoring compliance, has failed in its responsibility.

Predictably, judicial redress has been sought. The first federal court case (*Scott et al. v. Snider et al.*) to secure full implementation was brought in November 1991 in Pennsylvania. Three years of litigation were concluded in October 1994 under a Stipulation of Settlement in which infants, children, and adolescents in low-income and low-wage families are to be provided prompt, continuous, and complete healthcare in complete accordance with federal law. The New Morbidity prevention model was an important feature of the plaintiffs' presentation. This landmark class action suit will undoubtedly be pursued throughout the country.

Prenatal Care

Primary prevention obviously means that intervention methods should be implemented as early as possible, consistent with measures of sensitivity and specificity. According to the Institute of Medicine the single most important factor, after socioeconomic status, in predicting birth outcome is prenatal care. Although there is inconsistency in the empirically-based literature regarding the benefits of prenatal care, especially in uncomplicated pregnancies (Baumeister et al., 1993), certain medical and demographic indicators strongly suggest that timely and adequate prenatal care can avert adverse pregnancy outcomes, including infant mortality.

If children are lacking health insurance, in all likelihood many were born to mothers who were also underinsured or uninsured throughout their pregnancies. A major consequence is lack of adequate and timely prenatal care. The results are reflected in increases in morbidity and mortality rates for high-risk infants and children. According to government figures released by the U.S. Department of Health and Human Services in 1992, the percent of babies born to mothers who received late or no prenatal care in 1991 was 5.8 percent, the lowest in five years. However, if we look at the trend since 1980, this figure has actually increased to 13.7 percent. For white mothers over this time period the increase has been to 9.3 percent and for black mothers the increase has amounted to 21.6 percent.

Pregnant teenagers are much less likely than older mothers to obtain adequate prenatal care (i.e., during the first trimester) or to receive no prenatal care at all. Natality statistics collected by the Department of Health and Human

Services reveal that in 1989 48 percent of adolescent mothers failed to obtain early prenatal care and that in about 4 percent of births no prenatal care was obtained at all. Adolescent Caucasian mothers were significantly better off in this regard than adolescent African-American or Hispanic mothers (Merkel-Holguin & Sobel, 1993). Figure 6.3 presents percentages of mothers receiving late or no prenatal care by race or ethnic groups, age, and education. Although these data are from 1988 final natality statistics, provisional data indicate no reason to believe that the current situation is any better; indeed, they suggest it is probably worse in the sense of population disparities.

Figure 6.3
1988 Natality Statistics

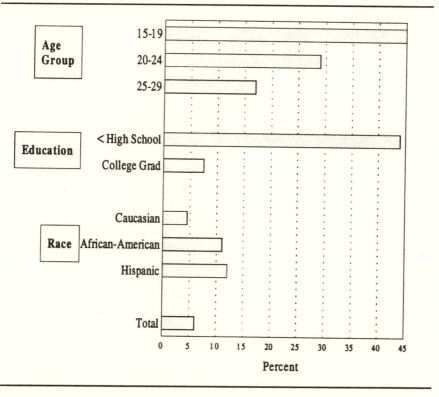

Low Birthweight and Infant Mortality

Low birthweight and infant mortality have become points of departure for understanding mechanisms and altering their effects because low birthweight is a prime indicator of infant mortality and morbidity.

In 1991 the nation's low-birthweight rate (<2500 grams) was 7.1 percent, higher than any year since 1976. Again, there is a significant racial disparity. Incidence of low birthweight for blacks is over twice that of whites: 13.6 percent and 5.6 percent, respectively.

Comparisons of low-birthweight rates among different subpopulations help to illustrate disparities that exist in factors such as education, socioeconomic status, access to healthcare, and nutrition. All these considerations have an impact on the health of mothers and on ante- and postnatal development. A well-established fact is that low-birthweight infants are at increased risk for immediate physical and developmental problems which can, in turn, lead to long-term disabilities.

Low-birthweight infants present with neurodevelopmental handicaps at three times the rate of normal birthweight babies. These handicaps include enduring disabilities such as cerebral palsy, autism, mental retardation, developmental delays, hearing impairments, and mental disorders, with risk increasing as birthweight decreases. We are quite capable of saving more and more of these small infants, but we do so at considerable long term costs, both in economic and human terms.

Compared to normal-birthweight infants, low-birthweight infants are forty times more likely to die during the neonatal period (birth through twenty-eight days). Risk of death is elevated five times through the first year of life. For those infants born at very low birthweight (<1500 grams), the risk of death during the neonatal period is about 200 times greater when compared to normal-weight infants.

The first prospective study of babies weighing less than 1,000 grams has demonstrated how subtle, serious and enduring low-birthweight sequelae can be (Halsey, Collin, & Anderson, 1993). At age four, about 75 percent of these babies exhibited generalized performance lags on cognitive and motor measures. Moreover, these effects appeared to be related to disturbance of fetal brain organogenesis rather than to blatant intracranial hemorrhage or other documented neurological events.

In light of these facts, the falling incidence of infant mortality should be regarded as salutatory. The current overall rate of 8.9 percent is the lowest in history. The decline in overall infant mortality stems primarily from the increased use of neonatal intensive care units, progress in the application of sophisticated life-saving technologies, and more aggressive medical interventions for these infants. However, this positive trend must be tempered with the understanding that it comes with a price. Those saved are typically low-birthweight infants who are at highly elevated risk for subsequent morbidity.

Although there has been an overall decrease in infant mortality, black infants are still more than twice as likely to die within the first year of life (16.5 percent) when compared with white infants (7.5 percent). Also, death among poor babies one year of age and younger is approximately twice that of nonpoor children. One likely reason for these differences may be that healthcare interventions, particularly prenatal and neonatal care, are differentially available and accessible across socioeconomic groups. At the same time, race and income are not entirely isomorphic in that whereas the odds ratios associated with low birthweight are equal for poor white and black infants, among the nonpoor rates are higher for blacks than for whites (Starfield et al., 1991).

The Starfield et al. (1991) study also shows that poverty is directly connected to risk of low birthweight among white babies. The study was longitudinal and presented the opportunity to compare reproductive outcomes for those women poor at the time of one pregnancy but not another. For instance, a shift in poverty level reduced the risks of low birthweight 8.2 percent and 8.9 percent, depending on the direction of the shift. For black infants, risks remained high regardless of a shift in poverty level. Clearly, poverty status does not have the same meaning across racial groups. An intergenerational effect may be implicated (Baumeister et al., 1993).

Adolescent Pregnancy and Childbearing

Each year approximately a million adolescents become pregnant in the United States, the highest rate among industrialized nations. About half of these pregnancies are not carried to term. According to recent data from the National Center for Health Statistics, the teen birthrate rose for the fifth consecutive year in 1991, reaching 62.1 births per 1,000 girls. This figure amounts to over half a million babies born to teen mothers between the ages of fifteen and nineteen. Also, more than two-thirds of these births were to unmarried mothers, a trend that continues to grow. This trend is important because there is a strong association between poverty and marital status directly affecting children in these households. For the years 1973, 1989, and 1992, the poverty rates for children in young, married two parent families was 7.9 percent, 16.5 percent, and 21.4 percent, respectively. For female-headed homes, however, the poverty rates for the same years were 67.9 percent, 71.2 percent, and 74.3 percent showing a dramatic difference when compared to married couple families (Children's Defense Fund, 1994).

Teen birthrates again show a strong racial component, with approximately twice as many black teen girls giving birth when compared with white or Hispanic girls. In addition to initial support to provide for the immediate health needs of the newborn infant and young child, is required ongoing support to ensure optimal development in all facets of the child's life. Such factors as parents' marital status, employment opportunities, education, and healthcare resources are all important indicators of whether or not this ongoing care will be afforded the child. Because a majority of teen births are to unmarried women, one of the most important variables affecting the future course of both mother and child, especially in the areas of financial and occupational opportunity, is the mother's educational attainment.

A strong correlation exists between the age of an adolescent mother at the time of her first pregnancy and probability of her not completing high school. For those girls who were seventeen years old at the time of giving birth to their first child, approximately 53 percent completed school or earned a GED. Only 29 percent of girls fifteen years of age giving birth for the first time completed their education. The pattern also holds true for teenage fathers when compared with their nonparent peers. The former have a 40 percent higher high school dropout rate (Mott & Marsiglio, 1985).

There is ample evidence to suggest that adolescent pregnancy and childbirth is strongly associated with subsequent poverty, often long term and multigenerational. Half of all women who had their first births between the ages of fifteen and seventeen subsequently had incomes below 150 percent of the poverty level when they reached their mid-twenties (Baumeister et al., 1993). For those women younger than fifteen at the time their first child was born, this percentage increased to 78 percent. It appears not only that adolescent childbearing does influence the probability of subsequent poverty and educational underattainment but that the reverse is also true-poverty and school dropout are strongly correlated with a higher probability of adolescent pregnancy and childbearing.

The National Longitudinal Survey of Young Adults (Sum, 1986) showed that adolescents who were raised in families below the poverty level were 3.5 times more likely to become adolescent mothers than were teens who were raised in more advantageous circumstances. Finally, Polit and Kahn (1986) reported that two-thirds of pregnant adolescents, along with adolescent mothers under the age of eighteen, who were raised in Aid for Families with Dependent Children (AFDC) households were themselves born to adolescent mothers. Only 25 percent of these mothers were reared in a two-parent household and only 30 percent graduated from high school.

A common message that runs through all these and more recent reports suggests that economic and social factors are strong catalysts in the shaping of attitudes of young people in regard to reproductive behavior. Many young women who are the recipients of intergenerational poverty either are in reality or perceive themselves to be unable to attain gainful employment for any number of reasons. It appears that when financial and/or employment opportunity is out of reach and the future is bleak, many will opt for immediate gratification, which, for many young girls includes pregnancy and childbearing. Regrettably it also often means, ultimately, a life of dependency and despair for them and their children.

POLICY ISSUES

There can be no doubt that children by the millions have suffered the malevolent effects of significant social changes, alterations in family life, and economic travail. Environmental instability, stress, changing societal values, and exposure to old and new threats increasingly compromise their health and well-being. Hardest hit are those children and their families who are severely and chronically impoverished. The result has been a marked increase in risks for disease, disabilities, and even death. These are problems inextricably linked to changing economic factors and value systems.

Public policies designed to create a better outlook for children have historically been anchored in a peculiarly American contradiction of value: self-reliance versus the need to secure the common purpose. In a perhaps unwitting but mean way children who are born into impoverished families are pitted against their parents. That is, while we have always professed a national commitment to "save" the children, yet at the same time we have an ingrained traditional abhorrence of "welfare." Today welfare reform is driving the political debate and as surely as many continue to live in the shadows of life, policy will be devised to reduce the burden-but for whom?

A valuable lesson is to be learned from the War on Poverty of the 1960s. During that heady period of new social policy, many initiatives were enacted in a broad-based effort to correct social and economic imbalances and inequities-Head Start, Medicaid, Medicare, and food subsidies among them. But without addressing the fundamental issue of redistribution of wealth, a concept abhorrent to the American ethos, the war was not only extremely costly but certain to be lost. The truth is that few people, of any political stripe, are fond of welfare programs such as AFDC. That includes the recipients, for the most part. The fragility of piecemeal programs that marginalize by class and caste should be readily apparent in light of today's political realities. The patchwork system of welfare supports and entitlements only creates greater disparities, disillusionment, and disadvantage.

There are many promising solutions, as demonstrated by numerous model, good practice programs. But these programs have not and will not be replicated and take root broadly without major systems changes because they are fundamentally incompatible with a categorical funding philosophy and with bureaucratic structures that fragment rather than coordinate services. Public services are bound up in rigid rules and are not judged by hard outcome measures. There is no quick fix. At the same we must recognize that the national interest is at stake and that profound system changes will be necessary to protect our collective best interests. This is where policy and politics meet because the decisions to change are value laden.

The fundamental clash of values is starkly reflected in the controversy surrounding the recent book, *The Bell Curve*, by Herrnstein and Murray (1994). The essence of their position is that distribution of intelligence has a huge genetic component and that in advanced societies variations in intelligence, as measured by IQ tests, produce class distinctions. A particularly volatile aspect of their analysis is the raising once again of the genetic explanation for the fifteen-point average IQ difference between black and white "ethnic" groups (their word choice).

The debate over the relative contribution of heredity and environment to individual and group differences in intelligence is hardly new. Plato adopted the genetic determination in *The Republic, Book V*, where he observed: "One man will acquire a thing easily, another with great difficulty; a little learning will lead the one to discover a great deal; whereas the other, after much study and application, no sooner learns than he forgets;...would these not the sort of differences that distinguish the gifted by nature from one who is ungifted?" Each iteration of the eugenics concept inevitably insinuates itself into policy discussions and decisions of whatever era with which it happens to coincide (though the meetings can hardly be called coincidental). The "marriage" can be especially volatile during a cycle when domestic and social issues are at the forefront of the public and political forum.

Perhaps more directly than anyone else, Herrnstein and Murray have extrapolated their analyses to question the wisdom of current welfare and other social and economic policies. In brief, they question whether social programs can have any real effect in addressing and adjusting class disparities. They conclude that we are entering an age-generally, the so-called information age in which the talents of the more cognitively sophisticated will be in greater demand, with a concomitant decrease in the usefulness of skilled and unskilled labor-in which class structure will be driven more than ever by intelligence differentials.

The policy implications of this debate are enormous. For example, a policy maker facing a constituency angry about crime, welfare, and taxes can readily exploit scholarly positions that genetic factors are causally implicated in racial IQ differences, that this biological disposition cannot be overridden, and that social programs designed to do so (such as Headstart) are therefore costly, ineffective, and should be downsized if not discontinued. Political and policy determinations ineluctably follow from the expression of societal values. Scientific data do not drive policy as a rule; rather, they are used selectively to defend positions that are rooted in attitudes, values, and even prejudices. There are those in positions of influence who not only are comfortable with the idea of genetic predispositions but use these arguments to bolster policy determinations.

Not all scholars, of course, adopt the conclusions reached by Herrnstein and Murray. In fact, examination of the same data have led many to draw very different conclusions. The arguments have become heated, acrimonious, and sometimes ad hominem. There is a great deal at stake because underlying "truths" that mold public policy are ultimately a moral test rooted in public attitude. This method of formulating public policy is not inherently bad, especially if it stimulates debate in which signal can be clearly discerned from noise.

Variability is inherent in nature, human or otherwise. It ill serves us to ignore this most basic biological and social truth. Group differences, whether they arise primarily from genetic or environmental factors, will never be obliterated. But the claim has been made and documented here that poverty is closely connected to adverse and costly developmental outcomes for children, regardless of why they are impoverished. Health and behavior disorders of poor children, only touched upon here, must be addressed within a comprehensive, flexible, and integrated program that has as its primary objective the prevention of conditions that place many at a competitive disadvantage—call it "Even Start."

7

Government, Business, and Community:
Toward an Integration of Politician, Executive, and Citizen

Chris E. Stout

This chapter uses an integrative approach in linking the mandating and regulatory power of governmental bodies with the economic and profit-making skills that private business and industry hold in order to achieve beneficial change within a local community level. Governments and private enterprises have their individual short-comings, yet a collaborative relationship allows for exploiting the best of both while minimizing their respective weaknesses. As with most important situations compromise will play a great role in any of the proposed issues of change herein. Hofmann (1993) states, "Compromise is an intrinsic and inevitable part of the political process" (p. 25). Governmental involvement may have various intrinsic problems, such as marked bureaucracy, duplication of effort, diffusion of responsibility, dependence on multiple forms and paperwork, poor management, and lack of a focus on outcomes. This is where the efficiency of well-managed business can play a pivotal role. Governments may mandate yet not achieve the desired goal of the mandate. In certain circumstances, governments may instead choose to empower competent businesses to carryout training efficiently, to support wages and benefits fiscally, and to provide concomitant, fair, and ethical benefits for the business (e.g., tax breaks, low-interest loans).

Governments may certainly promote options for businesses, community groups, or citizens to develop their own productive, practical solutions or alternatives (similar to Deming's model of empowerment). This also provides the beneficial artifact of countering the common phenomenon experienced by citizens who are disenfranchised and politically impotent, who may turn to more aggressive, less adaptive means of gaining governmental attention or who simply feel helpless and alienated. No humane government or society would choose either option for their peoples.

In terms of paradigm shifts or changes in mindset, we need to move away from dichotomous perceptions between effective business practices and governmental service delivery. There are no such dichotomies between the problems of illiteracy, poor healthcare, violence and crime, and poverty. They seem quite integrated and synergetic, but in a negative direction. Why cannot the steps toward their solution be integrative and synergistic, also?   An examination of some specific areas may be illuminating.

MILITARIZATION VERSUS SUSTAINABLE DEVELOPMENT

As the United States begins to downsize its military, many complain that doing so will negatively affect the U.S. economy through the associated job and contract losses. Although this may be true at initial phases, it need not be the case for developed countries nor should it be viewed as a potential loss for developing countries. National pride and jingoism may indeed be sensitive for a while, but common sense and societal good should be the focus of hyperfunding shifts to other areas.

From a humanitarian perspective, the statistics are striking. Jordan (1992) notes that "the 142 million deaths caused by war since 1500 equals an average of 793 deaths per day (to 1990). In 1990, the number of deaths due to wars was 7211 per day. That is 300 per hour, or 5 per minute, or one every 12 seconds" (footnote, 9). World military expenditures for 1990 were about $880 billion. Some may think that such death tolls are unavoidable (but that is an argument for another venue). Some also feel that such monies spent act to aid their economies. In reality, such spending actually has the opposite effect. Eisenhower recognized this in the late 1950s. He said, "Every gun that is made, every warship launched, every rocket fired, represents, in the final analysis, a theft from those who are hungry and are not fed, who are cold and are not clothed" (cited in McKenzie-Mohr & Winter, 1992). Although some beneficial new technologies have been developed as a result of military research and development, such benefits do not translate into actual aid for the economy. In contrast, such spending instead fuels inflation and increases unemployment (McKenzie-Mohr & Winter, 1992).

But how can this be true? Some may argue that a key aspect of military spending is job creation. Actually, when military spending is compared to the relative amounts spent for the civilian sector, this is not the case. "Military spending is highly capital intensive and, as a result, produces relatively few jobs compared to the more labor intensive civilian sector" (McKenzie-Mohr & Winter, 1992, 9). It has been noted that equivalent military dollars spent in the civilian sector would yield two to four times as many jobs (Regeher & Watkins, 1983).

In Third World countries in particular, this economic impact is amplified in the loss of civic expenditure for military economies. For example, between 1960 and 1990 total military costs were "two trillion dollars more than public expenditures for all levels of education, six trillion dollars more than expenditures for the health care of a rapidly growing, largely underserved, population. The Third World, with three-fourths of the world's population, accounted for less than 10 percent of global education expenditures [and] for no more than 5 percent of world health expenditures" (Sivard, 1991, 10).

Concern exists additionally with the involvement of industrialized countries in "arming" Third World countries. "The largest market for arms transfers is the Third World in general and the Middle East in particular. Third World countries under military control have three times as many [wars] as the rest of the Third World; and an incredible number of deaths in wars, a total of 14,141,000 deaths since 1960, 19 times as many as in other Third World countries" (Sivard, 1991, cited in McKenzie-Mohr & Winter, 1992, 10). Moving away from dollars spent on military activities could provide the following: In terms of "what the world spends on the military in half a minute, approximately $1 million, would build 1000 classrooms in the Third World. What we spend in 12 minutes on militarization, approximately $12 million, would establish 40,000 pharmacies in the Third World, while what we spend in 6 hours, approximately $700 million, would save the lives of 5 million children a year who die of diarrhea" (McKenzie-Mohr & Winter, 1992, 9). Vis-à-vis education spending, for the cost of one ballistic submarine ($1.5 billion), eighteen poor countries could double their entire annual education budget (Sivard, 1991).

SOCIETAL AGGRESSION AND VIOLENCE

Military actions hold a primarily political genesis, but societal organized and nonorganized violence is also a key issue for cultural survival and productivity and for psychological inquiry. Although "external" factors such as economic inequality (class differences) or high stress levels may lead to violence, Staub (1992) believes, "these conditions tend to powerfully activate basic needs in people, like the need for physical, material security; the need to defend one's self-concept, values, and customary way of life; the need for a new comprehension of reality, as social disorganization and change make people's world views ineffective in understanding the world and their place in it; and the need for connection to and support by other people, as connection is disrupted by people focusing on their own needs" (p. 12).

The response to societal aggression takes the form of intervention by outside groups, that is, by those not directly involved in the aggression or the responses to it (e.g., other nations, or the United Nations). Such outside groups should hold "great potential to influence events and inhibit the progression along a continuum of destruction. Their active opposition can reactivate the perpetrators' moral values, cause concern about retaliation, or make harm doing costly" (Staub, 1992, 12). Behavioral psychologists would view this as a "response cost" paradigm. Passivity is politically tantamount to choosing to allow a behavior to continue, thus reinforcing it, not extinguishing it. A specific example of the application of this paradigm was in the nonviolent, nonmilitary economic boycotting of South Africa.

POVERTY

Military action and impoverished countries seem to go hand - in - hand. Clark (1989) notes: "If we look at a map of the world and ask-Where is armed conflict going on? Where are populations growing fastest? (and) Where is the greatest poverty?-we discover the maps coincide. Of the 120 armed conflicts taking place in 1987, all but four were in the so-called developing countries of the Third World. Likewise, the highest rates of population growth are located in those same countries, and there are also found the lowest rates of literacy, of per capita income and nutrition, and the highest levels of infant mortality and epidemic disease. . . . The triple threat of exploding population, continuing poverty, and access to modern weapons makes these peoples-by far the majority of the human race-a powder keg, ready for ignition at any moment" (pp. 365-366).

POPULATION CONTROL AND ENVIRONMENTAL STABILITY

Beyond deforestation, pollution, and other such environmental threats via development and production is the key issue of population overexpansion. It is estimated that by 2025 the current world's population of 5.3 billion will double. Attempts at provision of contraceptive devices do not work well as evidenced by India's linkage of a behavioral reward (gaining a major appliance of a family's choosing) with sterilization. And China's strict prohibition against more than one child, while effective, is seen as too totalitarian by most other countries and peoples. For many, social status, masculinity and femininity, and government subsidy is contingent upon having children-at early ages and with multiple offspring.

VALUES, SOCIETY AS REFLECTED IN THE MICROCOSM OF THE FAMILY, AND WELFARE

If there is one area the United States has not shown great intellectual or practical leadership in it is welfare. Magnet (1992) sums up the American paradox thus: "After all, only [in America could] a culture [be] both sexually permissive and cavalier about the traditional family [and] create a welfare system that makes no distinction between legitimate and out-of-wedlock children, and that virtually on demand gives an income with more buying power than a minimum wage job to unwed teenage girls who have a baby before even finishing high school. And only in a culture that both vibrates with the celebration of sexual thrills and also has removed the stigma from having out-of-wedlock children will significant numbers of women permit themselves to get enmeshed in that system" (p. 45). It is also the same system in which current political tides wish to compound the problem by reversing the availability of abortion.

CONCLUSIONS AND RECOMMENDATIONS

Governmental intervention in addressing societal needs must permit psychology must play a greater role in terms of behavior modification and reinforcement theory. Any changes that result must be balanced with a basic ethic of humanitarianism. For "The 'culture of poverty' is no social-scientific fiction or racist canard. Welfare and chronic unemployment are undeniably associated with [poor education] delinquency, and crime. And it is fear-realistic fear-of crime that keeps potentially class-mixing institutions like parks, squares, stores, movie theaters, restaurants, subways, and most important, schools, and neighborhoods, class-stratified" (Scialabba, 1992, 3).

Improved education also yields some helpful, not readily observable positive side - effects. For example, Kendal (1979) found a negative correlation with female literacy and population growth in countries of the Third World. Education's role in world advancement is manifold. Beyond its good in decreasing social isolation and political oppression, education and literacy aid business, which then improves productivity, which then aids the economy, which then aids the society, which then aids the individual, and the cycle repeats. Illiteracy, however, is not endemic to Third World countries. In the United States today, businesses spend more than $40 billion per year to provide remedial education to their employee workforce (Manion, 1992).

Education beyond basic skills of mathematics and literacy should include values training and technology education. Using the United States as a model of what not to do provides an ironic education itself. Regardless of the culture, country, or religious beliefs, there are some basic, fundamental values that are pancultural: responsibility, altruism, growth and development, sanctity of life, justice, honesty and truth, and the like. Such could be "taught" in the educational environment in any country. Such instruction could be intended to supplement and support similar training from parents and the home.

Work has value not simply in meeting the Maslovian needs of food and shelter. People are social beings; we gain self-esteem from task completion, we enjoy social contact with individuals of like ilk, and most of us feel hope in simply looking forward to something - even if it is work in which we feel competent. Thus, to provide capitol to people in need reinforces in them a limiting dependency and teaches them that they lack control over their destinies - neither of which aids to instill a hope for the future, enhance self-esteem or self-worth, or provide any other type of psychological or emotional benefit.

Kaus (1992) recommends that all nonworkers, including mothers with children, *not* be provided cash support of any kind; instead, the government should develop jobs and training at subminimum wages along with provision of daycare if need be (in the United States, an extension of the Earned Income Tax Credit would allow for such working individuals to rise above the poverty line). Businesses involvement through the provision of wage incentives based upon good job performance, attendance, demonstrable attainment of appropriate personal goals, improved academic skills, completion of high school or college education, improved job skills, and expansion of job expertise would create a win-win situation for both employer and employee. Training, counseling, and necessary social services could be provided as well. For to stop economic support without sustainable skills would be shortsighted and inhumane.

The concept of civic liberalism may play a key behavior reinforcement role in that it "would 'use the public sphere to incubate and spread an egalitarian culture' of common interests, sentiments, and experiences" (Scialabba, 1992, 3). In theory, this concept holds pancultural promise.

Key psychological principles of motivation also come into play. Behaviorally speaking, although loss of income or loss of a benefit may influence behavior, it is a contingency that is quite state or situation dependent although it may widely vary between individuals thereby perhaps becoming trait-dependent. We need to exercise caution not to become punitive or lapse into the all-too-easy paradigm of blaming the victim. For example, cutting benefits to a family who fails to gain immunizations for their children does little to get the children immunized and could actually worsen their situation because the cutbacks now "punish" the family. Such punishment loses sight of the true goal, which is to influence parents to immunize their children and to provide opportunity for cultivating healthier families that will then have fewer future healthcare needs, thereby cutting costs and reducing the governmental burden. Humanitarianly, this improves the quality of life; economically, it is simply less expensive.

Money is not always a central or a sufficient factor in explaining social behavior and motivation. Thus motivation and status need to be explored vis-à-vis the people and cultural norms involved. Nevertheless, there is likely merit to shaping behaviors toward healthy outcomes and away from a system that iatrogenically creates learned helplessness in recipients. A psychologist with the

U.S. House Ways and Means Committee questioned, "What are the psychological implications of creating a system in which people can be irresponsible?" Developing such a system does take some integrated forethought and development. Making benefits contingent upon immunizations, for example, but not having the clinics nearby, or not providing a means of transportation to the clinics, or having hours that are inconvenient, or not providing home health services, all act to penalize those in need and trying to comply. Basic behavioral principles demonstrate that rewarding "good" (wanted) behaviors yields better results than punishing "bad" (unwanted) behaviors.

Similarly, requiring school attendance in schools that are unsafe, unclean, and poorly staffed is a paradox, not a reasonable expectation. Again, a holistic, systemic examination of motivation in tandem with the context of the goal behavior must not be ignored if failure is to be avoided.

Hofman (1993) and Sullivan (1992) offer several guidelines:

- Re-evaluate priorities.
- Require any new system must to be as simple, coherent, responsive, cost-effective, and outcome oriented as possible.
- Make any new system publicly accountable and ensure broad community involvement and participation.
- Evaluate outcomes and impacts of programs and redirect as need be.
- Develop multiple collaborations among government, business, and community leaders.

However, cautions in guarding against stereotyping and scapegoating must be taken in this area. It is quite easy for outsiders to blame victims as being lazy, uncaring, and so forth. Blaming only adds to distancing, poorer understanding, and anger.

Many critics today believe competition in the business world often yields more problems than solutions. Collaboration among relevant parties in almost all venues produces greater desired results. Some may argue that the timing for such a collaborative effort may not be right for some countries or governments. This may very well be the case, but we must remember, "If not now, when?" We can also learn from our own history "that the most comprehensive social legislation was passed at the height of the Great Depression. This may very well be, then, the very time to judge crisis as the opportunity for change in resolving our social problems" (Sullivan, 1992, 523).

The complex realities that face all countries in dealing with Third World issues cannot be dealt with as simply or as rapidly as we would wish. However, we should begin to accept that the idea of the world is evolving toward a greater interdependence. The application of psychological conceptualizations and principles may bode well in aiding the achievement of this goal.

—— ◆ ——

Healthcare Issues

—— ◆ ——

Community-based
Mental Health Systems

Donna R. Kemp

This chapter examines community-based mental health systems through a review of their history, an examination of their current status, an assessment of their successes and failures, and an exploration of their future.

THE HISTORY OF COMMUNITY-BASED MENTAL HEALTH SYSTEMS

Concern with mental illness has occurred throughout recorded history. Even in ancient times attempts were made to help people with emotional problems. Problems of living such as rejection in love, disobedience of children, and unhappiness were dealt with by elders and priests. One of the twelve tables of Roman law in the fifth century B.C., for example, referred to the disposition of a man's goods if he was found "raving mad" (Eaton, 1980). The history of community mental health is traceable to before 400 B.C., when traditional Chinese medicine addressed mental function and disorders.

The history of mental health policy is not the same in all countries. Culture, religion, and politics affect how mental health problems are addressed in different countries, specifically in the development of policy and the provision and organization of services.

Before the fifteenth century mental illness was largely ignored. Treatment mostly consisted of benign neglect. Bizarre behavior was seen as culturally deviant, but not requiring confinement. Few references to people with such behaviors are found. Mental healthcare was originally largely left to the family, and in some countries, such as India, this is still the primary system of care for even persons with serious mental illness. In Europe mental health services often developed from individual charity and government aid to the poor. Religion sometimes played a role in the development of community services. In some

European medieval monasteries, for example, the mentally ill were housed and humanely treated, and in Ghell, Belgium, for over 600 years the community has cared for persons with mental illness and mental retardation without ever using mental hospitals.

In a few Arab countries asylums were established as early as the eighth century in Baghdad, the ninth century in Damascus, and the fourteenth century in Granada, Moorish Spain. In Europe during the Middle Ages, mentally disturbed people were often accused of witchcraft, and increasingly the community sought the confinement of deviant people. In 1665 the Great Confinement resulted in imprisonment of perhaps 1 percent of the population of Paris in the Hospital General when beggars, lunatics, and vagrants were rounded up. Even then some humanists viewed these people as sick with mental problems. These humanists (Vives, 1492-1500; Weyer, 1515-1588; Pinel, 1745-1826; Dix, 1802-1887; and Charcot, 1825-1893) believed such people should be protected (Zilboorg & Henry, 1941).

In the United States during the colonial period, community care was provided primarily by the family and the parish. Persons with mental illness who were not cared for within the family were provided for by individual charity or under the Elizabethan poor relief laws. At this time religion played an important role in the definition of mental illness, as persons with mental illness were perceived to be possessed by the devil. People with severe emotional problems that involved rages against family members, theft or destruction of property, or attacks on people were sometimes chased away, locked up, or even killed. Increasingly, persons with mental illness were appearing in facilities such as poorhouses and jails at the local level.

In the United States general hospitals were founded in the late eighteenth century, becoming a possible new facility for care. In the eighteenth century the Pennsylvania Hospital became the first hospital in the United States to admit mental patients. Their status as patients may have been reflected by the fact that they were treated in the basement of the hospital, beginning a two-tiered approach to healthcare that continues today, with mental healthcare consistently in the lower tier, the poor stepchild of general healthcare. The first hospital established only for persons with mental illness opened in Williamsburg, Virginia, in 1776, soon to be followed by the establishment of a psychiatric hospital in Pennsylvania and other states (Grob, 1973).

In the late eighteenth century Dr. Phillippe Pinel took charge of two Parisian insane asylums and with a humanitarian and accepting approach, began a mode of treatment to be referred to as "moral treatment." This approach called for a sympathetic and supportive environment. In England William Tuke started the York Retreat based on Quaker permissiveness and kindness. Small enough to maintain a link to the community, early mental hospitals in the United States followed the concept of moral treatment based on transcendentalist philosophy (see Bockoven, 1963; Grob, 1973, 1983; Rothman, 1971; Rothman & Rothman,

1980). Many people, however, continued to be placed in urban alms houses and jails. In response to these conditions, Dorothea Dix worked to develop the spread and growth of state mental institutions. She advocated the establishment of state hospitals to remove the insane poor from the poorhouses and jails, and Horace Mann in 1828 put forward a philosophy of public welfare calling for the insane to be made wards of the state (Eaton, 1980). For financial reasons, the alms houses and jails gladly and quickly released the mentally ill from their control and turned them over to the new state hospitals. In the 1800s states developed systems of farm-based institutions devoted to moral treatment based on concepts of compassionate care.

Rapid urbanization and increased immigration rapidly led to the state mental health systems' being overwhelmed. Many people with organic-based dementia from syphilis and elderly persons with other unrecognized dementias, later to be identified as Alzheimer's disease, and brain damage from small strokes became patients who remained in the institutions for the rest of their lives. Also, people who seemed different or who had no one to care for them in an urban environment were placed in the mental institutions, including many people with mental retardation, epilepsy, or substance abuse problems. As legislative funding decreased, institutions became overcrowded, conditions deteriorated, and treatment gave way to custodial care. By the late nineteenth century the state hospitals were places of last resort with long-term chronic patients, and institutionalization increased following periods of economic difficulty (Brennen, 1973).

Clifford Beers founded the national Committee for Mental Hygiene in 1909 and encouraged citizen involvement, prevention of hospitalization, and aftercare. But with the fears of the eugenics movement in the early twentieth century, there was not much support for community care. By the 1920s and 1930s a few psychiatrists were affiliated with child guidance community clinics. The U.S. Public Health Service's Division of Mental Hygiene was created in 1930, but it dealt only with narcotics addiction. State hospitals continued to grow during the Great Depression and World War II but were faced with fewer resources. Some hospitals had 10,000 to 15,000 patients. On the eve of World War II mental health policy appeared stable with a system of public mental hospitals. In 1940 public hospitals cared for 98 percent of all institutionalized patients. There were 410,000 patients in state facilities and 59,000 patients in veterans', city, and county institutions. A substantial percentage of state budgets went to institutional care. It was World War II that brought an emphasis for short-term and community-based treatment. This was encouraged by the military's interest in psychological testing, the high numbers of men rejected from the draft for mental health reasons, and the large number of combat-related stress disorders that needed to be treated quickly to return soldiers to combat or to the community.

By the late 1940s more than two-thirds of the members of the American

Psychiatric Association (APA) still practiced in public institutions (Grob, 1987). The enactment of the National Mental Health Act of 1946 ended a period of federal inactivity and brought the federal government into mental health policy in a significant way. The act focused on research, training professional personnel in psychiatry, and making grants available to states to establish clinics and treatment centers and to fund demonstration studies on prevention, diagnosis, and treatment. Funding for institutional care and treatment was specifically excluded.

The depletion of resources during the Great Depression and World War II contributed to the deterioration of the mental hospital systems. After the war a series of exposés were made on the scandalous conditions in state mental hospitals. Slowly services were growing in the community, and after 1945 community clinics that had largely been serving children and delinquents began to serve an adult population. Grob (1987) did an extensive analysis of the factors that brought about the changes in mental health policy that occurred after 1945. Factors he identified included:

1. the change in the composition of the patient population since 1890, from acute cases largely institutionalized for less than twelve months to long-term chronic patients, many of whom were over sixty-five and suffering from conditions associated with aging, to patients exhibiting other conditions with behavioral symptoms probably of unknown somatic origins, to dependent persons in custodial care;
2. a growing division between modern psychiatry, which began to see mental illness as preventable through early treatment in community facilities, and the traditional mental hospital;
3. a new psychiatric epidemiology, an extensive broadening of psychiatric boundaries, and a rejection of the traditional distinction between mental health and mental abnormality;
4. the growing importance of scientists and academics in the formulation and implementation of policy;
5. the New Deal expansion of the role of the national government;
6. the decline of eugenics and hereditary viewpoints and the growth in environmental ideologies and social activism;
7. the development of the "Young Turks" and reorganization and activism of the APA;
8. the growth of a coalition of medical and social activists who brought the federal government into health policy through the Hill-Burton Act of 1946 for hospital construction and other legislation;
9. a series of exposés by A. Deutsch (1948), M. Gorman (1948), A.Z. Maisel (1948), and F.L. Wright (1947) and the best-selling novel, *The Snake Pit* (Ward, 1946);
10. the growing rhetoric of community care and treatment by the Council of State Governments, the Milbank Fund, and others;
11. experimentation with new policy initiatives in California and New York;
12. and establishment of a biomedical lobby.

In 1949 the Governors' Conference began to seek new ways to deal with mental health programs. The conference report detailed many problems in the public institutions, including obsolete commitment procedures; shortages of and poorly trained staffs; large elderly populations; inadequate space, equipment, and therapeutic programs; lack of effective state agency responsibility for supervision and coordination; irrational division of responsibility between state and local jurisdictions; fiscal arrangements damaging to residents; and lack of resources for research (Grob, 1987). In 1949 the National Institute of Mental Health (NIMH) was established. In 1954 a special Governors' Conference on Mental Health adopted a program calling for expansion of community services, treatment, rehabilitation, and aftercare. There was also a growing antipsychiatry movement based on the writings of Ronald D. Laing, Thomas Szasz, and others who did not believe in mental illness but saw its definition and treatment as related to social control.

Major deinstitutionalization of hospitals began in the mid-1950s. The introduction of psychotropic medicines to reduce and to control psychiatric symptoms created optimism that some mental illnesses could be cured and others would be modified sufficiently to allow the mentally ill to function outside institutions. The psychosocial concept of a therapeutic community became widespread with the hope that cures could be obtained through an environmental milieu therapy.

Institutional care was becoming increasingly expensive. As the federal government increased support for the mentally disabled in the community, the states became anxious to transfer the costs to the federal government's welfare system (Williams, Bellis, & Wellington, 1980). The negative aspects of institutionalization were also increasingly recognized with growing pressure for reform by mental health professionals and the public (Goffman, 1961; Scheerenberger, 1983).

During the 1950s the states pursued both institutional care and expansion of community services. In 1955 the Mental Health Study Act led to the establishment of the Joint Commission on Mental Illness and Health, which prepared a survey and made recommendations for a national program to improve methods and facilities for the diagnosis, treatment, and care of the mentally ill and to promote mental health. The commission recommended the establishment of community mental health centers and smaller mental hospitals. Many progressive recommendations were made in the eight volumes published between 1958 and 1962. These included a focus on socialization, relearning, group living, and rehabilitation that encouraged a social treatment model. The commission also advocated prevention. The work of the commission was to lay the groundwork for the Community Mental Health Centers Act of 1963.

Ideas developed throughout the 1950s and 1960s began to coalesce into legislation (Levine, 1981). In 1960 the election of John F. Kennedy raised hope for an expanded federal role. Kennedy was favorably disposed to mental health issues because he had a sister who suffered from mental retardation and mental illness. Also supportive were key White House assistants and officials in the Bureau of the Budget. A lengthy and complex process occurred in the development of mental health policy from the recommendations of task forces and panels that endorsed a policy of deinstitutionalization and the passage of the Mental Retardation Facilities and Community Mental Health Centers Construction Act of 1963. Kennedy put the weight and prestige of his office behind the advocates of a community- based program that largely bypassed the states.

Grob (1987) believes "rhetoric rather than reality carried the day" in passage of the 1963 law (p. 455). During the remainder of the decade, the civil rights movement and public interest law strengthened mental health policy that focused on decreasing the role of mental hospitals. Open door policies, informal admissions, psychotropic drugs, and preparation of patients for early release reinforced the policy of community treatment.

The passage in 1965 of Medicaid and Medicare stimulated the growth of skilled nursing homes and later, intermediate care facilities; it also opened the way for what became known as the transinstitutionalization movement of many hospitalized mentally ill and mentally retarded persons to nursing homes and other community institutional-like settings. By placing these people in the community, state officials could shift costs to the federal government. The expansion of inpatient and outpatient psychiatric services in acute general hospitals was stimulated by increased third-party reimbursement by the government and by the insurance companies. Although much change occurred, no coherent overall policy was developed. The community mental health centers were to be the major component of the new system, not the state hospitals, but there were problems with defining their roles and even greater problems with resourcing them. This was to result in a high price to be paid by many severely mentally ill persons and their families as many people with chronic mental illness drifted into the homeless population.

After 1965 hospital populations declined rapidly, and in the late 1960s and early 1970s numerous institutions throughout the United States were reduced in size or closed. Resident populations in state and county mental hospitals declined from 521,000 in 1950 to 215,000 in 1974. From 1965 to 1969 only $260 million was authorized for community mental health centers. During the Nixon administration mental health center funds were impounded, and from 1970 to 1973 only $50.5 million was appropriated. Residents were released from the institutions, but community-based facilities designed to replace them did not appear in sufficient numbers. This opened the door for private profit - makers who "bid" for the former residents and their state and federal benefits. Many of these private profit - makers provided only minimal and low-quality care.

In 1971 Title XIX of the Social Security Act (Medicaid) was amended to require institutional reform and the meeting of accreditation standards by facilities in order to receive federal dollars. To qualify for Medicaid, an individual was required to be disabled, as determined under the Supplemental Security Income (SSI) program, and had to meet state income and resource standards. Persons with mental illness could qualify for services in an Intermediate Care Facility/Psychiatric Rehabilitation (ICF/PR). Generally, for individuals who resided at home, the income and resources of parents were deemed available to them for purposes of determining eligibility for Medicaid. The income and resources of parents were not deemed available to individuals in institutions or facilities such as ICFs/PR. However, states could, at their option, cover individuals in the community who would be eligible if they were in an institution and were receiving services under a 2176 waiver. States had discretion in setting payment rates for community-based services, but payments had to be consistent with "efficiency, economy, and quality of care" (Committee on Energy and Commerce, 1988). In 1975 Congress required community mental health centers to provide aftercare services, like those already developed by mental retardation professionals, and mandated linkages between community mental health centers and state hospitals to ensure continuity of care. Also in 1975, the passage of PL 94-142 mandated that a free and appropriate education be available to all handicapped children from three to twenty-one years of age, including those residing in public institutions. Those handicaps could include emotional or behavioral problems if they had an impact upon a child's ability to learn. Earlier such problems were most often thought to be the province of mental health professionals working in other settings. Although full implementation did not occur until 1980, the new legislation put the focus on educational settings and on early intervention.

In 1979 parents of persons with metal illness founded the National Alliance for the Mentally Ill (NAMI). In the same year the President's Commission on Mental Health recommended several measures: Local communities should be allowed the flexibility to provide only the services needed; medical and mental services should be integrated through more consultation between agencies and caseworkers; new financial resources should be made available for mental health services; and the needs of underserved groups such as children, the elderly, and people in rural areas should be met. Many of the recommendations were incorporated in the proposed Mental Health Systems Act (PL 96-398), which became law in October 1980. The new legislation required statewide plans for mental health systems, but there was no real opportunity for the new act to become operational. In 1981 the Omnibus Budget Reconciliation Act of the Reagan administration revamped the legislation. Twenty-one categorical health grants were lumped into four block grants, including one for mental health and substance abuse that defined twelve services. The mental health and substance abuse categorical grants, which had gone directly to local agencies, were now consolidated and were distributed by the state governments. Excluding capital and District of Columbia expenditures, expenditures for the alcohol, drug abuse, and mental health administration went from $1,105,477 billion in 1979 to $761,007 million in 1982 (Hudson, 1993).

During the 1950s, 1960s, and 1970s various commissions and reports along with court cases stimulated the deinstitutionalization movement. The focus became community treatment, integrated services, and treatment in the least restrictive setting.

THE CURRENT COMMUNITY MENTAL HEALTH SYSTEM

Kiesler (1982) has seen mental health policy in the United States as a "nonfield" or at best as undeveloped. He defines national mental health policy as: "the defacto or dejure aggregate of laws, practices, social structures, or actions occurring within our society, the intent of which is improved mental health of individuals or groups."

The National Comorbidity Survey published in January 1994 reported that 30 percent of all Americans experience a psychiatric disorder (Torrey, 1994). The National Institute of Mental Health has estimated that between 4 and 5 million adults, or 2.1 to 2.6 percent of the population, have some form of serious mental illness. There are 3.3 million persons eighteen years of age or older in the noninstitutionalized civilian population that have had some kind of serious mental illness within the past twelve months. Thus, for every 1,000 persons in the United States, 18.2 have displayed a serious mental illness (U.S. Department of Health and Human Services, 1992).

In 1990 mental health treatment accounted for 10 percent of all U.S. health spending $67 billion), with only one in five persons with mental illness treated (Carlson & Castro, 1993). Also in 1990, NIMH conservatively estimated the cost of treating mental illness at $148 billion: $67 billion for direct treatment and $81 billion for indirect costs such as social welfare and disability, morbidity and mortality connected to mental disorders, and costs on family caregivers. Federal funding largely comes from the Department of Health and Human Services (DHHS), where mental health programs were reorganized in 1992 into the Substance Abuse and Mental Health Services Administration (SAMHSA), consisting of the Center for Mental Health Services, the Center for Substance Abuse Prevention, and the Center for Treatment Improvement. The institutes on mental health, drug abuse, and alcohol and alcohol abuse are now in the National Institutes of Health and focus only on promotion of research in mental health and substance abuse. The Veterans Administration (VA) and the Bureau of Indian Affairs (BIA) provide community mental health services directly in a number of locations. The fifty states provide community mental health services through a variety of ways, including directly through regional mental health centers or through grants or contracts to local governments, nonprofit organizations, or profitmaking organizations. This complex intergovernmental array of organizations makes coordination difficult.

Mental health care remains focused on inpatient care, but the site of that care has shifted from state institutions to the general acute care hospital in the community as the most frequent inpatient site (Kiesler & Sibulkin, 1987). Many people are also seen in psychiatric units in general hospitals and in short-term public or private community inpatient facilities; children may receive services in special residential treatment centers for children. Although the cost of inpatient care has risen at all sites and most sharply in general hospitals, total costs have been held in check because the length of stay has decreased. Most of that decrease has occurred in state mental hospitals and VA facilities even though those facilities still have the longest stays (Kiesler & Sibulkin, 1987). Since the states have become responsible for the distribution of the federal grant funds for mental health, many funds have been shifted from the community mental health centers to community mental health services more sympathetic with the needs of the seriously mentally ill (Hudson, 1983).

Community inpatient services are complemented by community outpatient services such as private practices of mental health professionals, family services agencies, community mental health centers, day hospitals, social clubs, halfway houses, group homes, assisted housing, and foster care. Agency models are diversifying, and there is a trend toward greater specialization. Specialized services such as special education for the emotionally disturbed children in the school system and forensic programs in the criminal justice system are also available. Community mental health services involve 2,965 organizations providing services to 3.0 million people or 1.22 percent of the population (NIMH, 1992).

Funding issues have remained critical. In an intergovernmental system each level of government has tried to place more costs on another level of government. Many mentally disabled have, in effect, been transinstitutionalized into nursing homes and large group homes. States have sought ways to receive federal funds for these facilities, particularly through Medicaid which looked to contain costs by defining who was eligible for reimbursement in facilities. Federal law and Medicaid regulations by the Health Care Financing Administration (HCFA) (1986) did not allow payment for services to people under sixty-five years of age in a skilled nursing facility that was an institution for mental disorders, defined as an institution for mental retardation or senile and presenile organic psychotic disorders. Patients with a diagnosis of senility or organic brain syndrome were considered mentally disordered in a facility with a treatment plan for mental disorders but were not considered mentally disordered in a facility with only general nursing care. Alcohol and chemical dependency were also considered mental disorders if psychological or psychosocial treatments were involved.

A 1980 HCFA audit in California concluded that skilled nursing facilities with special disability services were institutes for mental disorders, and in 1985 the Supreme Court upheld the ruling that a skilled nursing facility may be an institute for mental disorders. A similar situation occurred in some other states, resulting in the movement of people with mental illness from nursing homes, creating a second deinstitutionalization of people previously transinstitutionalized from the state institutions. This movement was promoted primarily for funding reasons. The U.S. Omnibus Reconciliation Act of 1987 required screening of new and current nursing home patients for mental illness. Further, Medicaid funding has increased for mental health clinics, and because Medicaid standards are more flexible than the funding standards for the old community mental health centers, many social service agencies now operate mental health clinics that resemble the traditional single-service psychiatric outpatient clinic of a general hospital.

The disease model with a focus on finding and treating the cause of the emotional and behavioral dysfunction, with an approach based on diagnosis, treatment, and cure, continues to be of significance for people with serious mental illness. The focus is short-term inpatient care with the emphasis on medication and intrapersonal needs and with limited resources for interpersonal and environmental needs with a psychosocial focus. In 1986, the State Comprehensive Mental Health Services Plan Act (PL 99-660) required the states to provide case management as a condition of receiving federal funding; it also mandated the development of state mental health plans. Various coordinating mechanisms have been put in place to develop a wider base of service and support systems for the chronically mentally ill, including case management, multidisciplinary treatment teams, community support systems, integrated services, substate mental health authorities, and funding through pooling of resources or capitation (Dill & Rochefort, 1989). Advocacy systems to protect the rights of persons with mental illness have also been put in place. Consumer groups for persons with mental illness continue to grow, playing an increasingly important role in lobbying for funding and for changes in the mental health system. However, the approaches used and their availability vary community by community under a fragmented intergovernmental system.

The mental health approach to people with less serious emotional disorders is focused on outpatient treatment with modalities such as psychotherapy and employee assistance programs that have a community, nonmedical, interpersonal, and environmental approach. Active in this area are a variety of professionals, including psychologists, clinical social workers, and family counselors. The orientation of many of these professionals is away from the medical model, although they may pay at least lip service to that model when third-party payors require diagnosis using the Diagnostic Statistical Manual, fourth edition (DSM-IV), for reimbursement.

Stigmatization of people with mental illness continues to create problems. Stigmatization involves being perceived as significantly different in a negative way. This can be seen in the resistance of neighborhoods to the establishment of group homes - the "not-in-my-backyard" phenomenon.

Those seeking funding for care for persons with mental illness may also have to compete against other disability groups such as mental retardation and substance abuse. In some states, such as California, residential care homes for persons with mental retardation receive better financial reimbursements than residential care homes for people with mental illness. Mental retardation is viewed more sympathetically as an accident of nature involving people who are not usually dangerous or beyond control. Mental retardation is also associated with children rather than adults, even though most persons with mental retardation are adults. Mental illness and substance abuse are seen as volitional and are sometimes associated with violence. Both are also perceived to be associated with adults who are seen as responsible for their actions even though many children and adolescents are diagnosed as mentally ill, as substance abusing, or both.

SUCCESS OR FAILURE?

There has been extensive criticism of deinstitutionalization and the lack of sufficient development of community services. The original plan for the community mental health centers called for the establishment of 1,500 sites, with each center serving between 75,000 and 200,000 residents providing a multitude of services. The centers were never adequately funded, and only about 700 were established by 1980 while state hospital populations decreased from 560,000 in 1955 to 125,000 in 1981. Between 1970 and 1973 thirteen hospitals closed in eight states. Community mental health center outpatient episodes rose from 379,000 in 1955 to 4.6 million in 1975 (Shadish, Lurigio, & Lewis, 1989). There was a failure of coordination between most centers and their state mental institution systems. Only 3.6 percent to 6.5 percent of admissions were discharged mentally ill patients referred by state institutions (Torrey, 1988). Dr. Richard Cravens, former branch chief of the program acknowledged in an interview in 1989 that the system could not handle the needs of the severely mentally ill because the centers were not equipped to deal with the whole array of services such people require they could provide neither income support nor vocational training, nor housing (Issac & Armat, 1990). Underfunding and mismanagement aggravated the situation (Issac & Armat, 1990). The passage of Medicare and Medicaid in the mid-1960s played a primary role in the deinstitutionalization of state and county mental hospitals by encouraging transinstitutionalization into nursing homes (Gronfein, 1985). This has been only part of a continuing cycle in which each level of government and each government program has tried to minimize its expenditure by passing costs on to others. Growing legal rights and advocacy that narrowed the grounds for psychiatric commitment encouraged the release and retention of people with mental illness in the community. Although rights the mentally ill sorely needed, they faced a serous consequence of this advocacy when they were unable to recognize their own illness and the family and community were unable to get them to accept treatment.

In 1979, during the Carter administration, First Lady Rosalyn Carter chaired the President's Commission on Mental Health. In her opening statement before the Subcommittee on Health and Scientific Research (1979), the First Lady declared: "I believe the problems of the chronically mentally ill point up the critical weakness in our present systems of care: the lack of adequate planning; poor coordination between federal, state, and local governments; blurred lines of responsibility and accountability in the government entities; and treatment programs that are dictated by reimbursement mechanisms rather than by patients needs."   Before the same committee, Val Halamandaris, legal counsel to the House Committee on Aging, observed: "Any pretext that deinstitutionalization has stemmed from concern for people is absurd....It has stemmed from the desire to save money"; and Frank Lanterman, a former California lieutenant governor, commented: "I have devoted my life to taking care of the mentally ill, the handicapped, and the developmentally disabled. And now it is coming to a rather sad and confused conclusion" (Subcommittee on Health and Scientific Research, 1979).

Many professionals and researchers believe there is evidence of a "revolving door" cycle in community hospital psychiatric units, emergency rooms, and state hospitals, with recidivism rates from 14 to 40 percent within a six-month period. This would indicate that the deinstitutionalized and others, who would at an earlier time have received long-term care, are now involved in episodic county hospital visits. Kiesler and Sibulkin (1987), however, concluded that there was no "revolving door" because the national readmission rate to hospitals had not changed over the previous fifteen years. They found that most of the increase in the number of people and the rate of people hospitalized could be accounted for by the increased risk associated with the demographics of the baby boom cohort, who were in the age range of onset for many other disorders.

Kiesler (1982) concluded in the early 1980s that there were no studies showing hospitalization to have a "positive impact on the average patient which exceeded that of the alternative care." He found patients of alternative care were less likely to ever be hospitalized, and the best predictor of hospitalization was prior hospitalization. Kiesler and Sibulkin (1987) found alternative care outside of hospitals to be more effective and less costly; they also found that aftercare, in general, delayed rehospitalization. Paul and Lentz (1977) found the psychology of the attending physician had the greatest effect on the decision to hospitalize.

The deinstitutionalization movement occurred too quickly and with too great a focus on getting people out of the institutions without sufficient development of mental health and social services and residential facilities.   The implementation process was poorly handled with a lack of adequate planning. The people who were deinstitutionalized from mental hospitals are now relatively elderly and are no longer a major focus of community mental health care. It is the younger population of patients with personality disorders and psychoses, most of whom have not been in the state hospital systems and are often difficult to manage who raise concerns in the community. This population also is often dual-diagnosed for drug abuse and alcohol abuse. How the states have been able to deal with this has varied. The states that developed noteworthy systems are those that have considerably lower rates of poverty and mental illness, as well as more politically integrated service systems (Hudson, 1990).

With growing fiscal retrenchment in many states, several trends developed in the 1980s: a greater focus on the more severely disabled; an increase in the utilization of acute hospital care, residential treatment, day treatment, and case management services; and a decrease in traditional outpatient services. Although the severely mentally ill receive a higher priority for service, the service systems still do not meet their needs for long-term maintenance and support services (Surber, Shumway, Shadoan, & Hargreaves, 1986). Housing remains a significant problem in many areas. Many state mental health authorities have only recently begun to accept responsibility for residential facilities.

The availability of affordable housing and cuts in welfare payments compound the problems of persons with mental illness in the community. Urban renewal projects replaced low-income housing with higher-priced housing. A study of twelve cities showed that the poverty rates in those cities grew by 36 percent in the late 1970s and early 1980s when the low-income housing supply shrank by 30 percent (Wright, 1988). From 1980 to 1983, the budget for the Department of Housing and Urban Development was cut $30 billion (Johnson, 1990). A substantial portion of the homeless mentally ill are women and men who before deinstitutionalization would have been residents of state mental hospitals (Marcos, Cohen, Nardacci, & Brittain, 1990). A 1985-1996 study of homelessness in Chicago found approximately 20 to 30 percent of the homeless they interviewed showed signs of clinical depression or psychotic thinking (Rossi, 1989). Nearly one out of four reported being in a mental institution for a period of over forty-eight hours, a rate four times higher than for the general public. In addition, the population of county jails and state prisons includes a considerable number of people who are mentally ill.

In response to the fear of persons with mental illness wandering city streets and committing criminal acts, there has arisen an interest in methods to bring people with mental illness under care in the community. Outreach programs attempt to bring them into care, and crisis response teams try to provide emergency care on the streets. Many communities do not have these services, however, and many severely mentally ill persons refuse treatment. This has led to a search for alternatives to increase social control and to provide for treatment without consent through an increased reliance on legal guardianship, durable power of attorney, and outpatient commitment. In states such as Hawaii and North Carolina, state law allows a person with mental illness to be "committed" to a community treatment program or a mental health board (Korr, 1991). Yet as Paul Appelbaum (1994) shows, with the tide of reform ebbing, there has been less change than most people predicted even though over the past two decades many states have changed their laws regarding involuntary hospitalization, right to treatment, liability of professionals for violent acts committed by their patients, and the insanity defense. Applebaum (1994) concludes when the law gets in the way of the need to treat persons with serious mental illness, it is often put aside; an extra-legal process is established by family members, mental health professionals, lawyers, judges, and the general public. However, the reality remains that there are still families overburdened by trying to take care of family members with mental illness and there are still many persons with mental illness who fall between the cracks of the system.

THE FUTURE

Mechanic and Rochefort (1994) argue that practical solutions must be developed within existing political structures. They advocate developing assertive community treatment programs such as the one in Dane County, Wisconsin, the Program for Assertive Community Treatment (PACT), which uses a multidisciplinary, assertive, continuous care team that serves a designated group of patients with severe chronic mental illness and is concerned with all aspects of their lives and functioning; capitating mental health care through a system of providing for all defined services for a specified time period through a prepayment system tied to the care of a particular client, with the provider agreeing to be at risk for costs exceeding the capitation amount; developing local mental health authorities responsible for the range of services required by persons with mental illness need; and structuring reimbursement to encourage efficient use of resources.

In order to provide adequate community-based mental healthcare services, the most important issue to resolve is funding. Crucial to this issue of funding is to treat of mental health problems the same as physical health problems. Many who believe that mental health and physical health are interdependent support this view (Kemp, 1994). They also believe that paying for such treatments is cheaper than paying for the social services required for the untreated mentally ill (NAMI, 1995). This means that any healthcare reform in the United States needs to address the provision of mental health benefits equally with physical health benefits. However, if this occurs there is a need for safeguards to preserve the planning, monitoring, licensing, and other oversight functions of the state mental health authorities (Hudson, 1993). But not everyone agrees that mental health should be included in a national health policy. Kiesler

(1995) argues that mental health policy is already defective because it is dominated by general health policy that is focused on dealing with hospitals and physicians rather than on promoting appropriate treatments. Mental health policy is better developed separately with an emphasis on prevention, outpatient care, and attention to chronic mental health problems. An editorial in the *Wall Street Journal* (1995) argues that the definitions of mental illness are too broad and the costs of treating millions of people for less serious mental health conditions would be excessive. Instead, the *Journal* advocates a stable social order based on traditional values and families.

A poll by the David L. Bazelon Center for Mental Health Law found two-thirds of Americans favor including mental health coverage in any proposed national healthcare reform legislation and 75 percent of those want mental health problems covered to the same extent as physical illness (Goode, 1994). However, of the 1994 healthcare reform proposals, only three included mental health benefits, and in all those proposals mental health benefits were more restrictive than physical health benefits. The Clinton Health Care Plan had an inpatient mental health eligibility of thirty days per episode and sixty days per year and psychotherapy benefits up to thirty visits per year (Starr, 1994). Congress was concerned over the cost of providing mental health coverage (Rosenblatt, 1994). Although no healthcare reform will pass in 1994, with healthcare accounting for 14 percent of gross national product in 1994, within the next few years healthcare reform will have to be addressed, and it is essential for mental health policy that mental health receives equal footing with physical health in any reform.

Clinical Application, Policy, and Development of Behavioral Healthcare under Healthcare Reform

Jerry A. Theis

This chapter reviews the issues of clinical application and policy development within the behavioral healthcare delivery system under healthcare reform. The integration of psychological principles and policy development requires close analysis of current healthcare reform debates and trends affecting behavioral healthcare delivery. Important changes in several aspects of U.S. healthcare have major significance for behavioral healthcare and for the expectation of a broadened population of consumers. The 1990s have emerged as the decade of change in healthcare necessitated by the financial climate.

PARADIGM SHIFT

As a result of the paradigm shift to a preventative-oriented early intervention model, as opposed to the diseased-oriented illness model enforced by high-cost, highly technical procedures and interventions, healthcare consumers will begin to experience engagement in community-based primary care and services rather than acute hospital-based care and services. This approach is led by healthcare reforms, current public policy principles, which include cost containment mandates, reduction of inappropriate utilization of costly technology, a broadened demand for access to care, and a broadened benefit plan design, coupled with an increased public awareness and demand for quality assurance. This fundamental shift is not a simple rearrangement but a major shift in accountability from provider needs to consumer needs. This shift is a result of a trend toward increased economic responsibility to the consumer. The sharing of healthcare costs will result in a consumer demand for knowledge about the fundamentals of behavioral healthcare service delivery. This basic psychological principal will require practitioners to be orientated to consumer needs as a first line of response in their clinical application of services. This model for reform offers customization to the end purchaser. The services are equivalent in cost and outcome yet the packaging of this services is tailored to customers needs.

MANAGED CARE

Healthcare today is increasingly managed. Direct expenditures on behavioral healthcare is now estimated at over $100 billion per year. Employers and purchasing groups and the government are seeking managed care strategies or are developing various models that can demonstrate and produce cost-effective, quality care (Greenberg et al., 1990). Healthcare policy development will need to entail a wide range of strategies and mechanisms to create a balance between access, quality, cost, and satisfaction.

Healthcare reform's vehicle may be fueled by the need to make healthcare affordable, but public approval for reform solutions may be slowed unless there are effective strategies that demonstrate the above. Economic risk will shift from the payors to the customers and the providers of care. This economic risk shift will have implications for policy development within this dynamic behavioral healthcare environment. Many employers who choose to self- insure in order to maintain greater flexibility and more control over costs may migrate into these new delivery systems. Self-insured employer groups will begin to focus more on how to measure the value of what they are purchasing, as will the government; they will look beyond traditional utilization management thinking and become more focused on issues of access, availability, performance measurements, and treatment outcomes (E. Rooney, 1992).

PERFORMANCE-BASED MEASUREMENTS

Since consumers have the same enquirers about behavioral healthcare services that they have about general healthcare services, providers must be prepared to offer relevant data elements and standardized methods of data collection and sampling as a first line of response to consumer education and awareness. It will no longer be acceptable to justify the lack of data reporting by the consumer's inherent inability to comprehend data. Information varies in its value depending on the particular interest of consumer groups, and therefore providers must discern which issues are important to the particular consumer groups being served. Intuitively, group practices need to participate in quality performance measurement designs in the same way that managed behavioral healthcare companies do. Since behavioral healthcare no longer has the luxury of remaining hidden from accountability, it will be essential for group practices to establish means to measure the less illusive goal of quantifying quality and outcome. The data would cover five major domains:

- access to care
- cost-effective utilization of service
- clinical and administrative efficiencies
- patient satisfaction
- health promotion and preventative care

Considering a mental health service as a product with components allows mental healthcare providers to explore how to maximize those components that produce high customer satisfaction. The intent here is not just to describe specific sets of measurements but to underline their importance in the approach providers must take to describe how they will provide practical application of their clinical services. Relevant product components may include ease of use, time consumed, convenience, or transferability. For example, practitioners will need to demonstrate their knowledge and competency, professional manner, and skill, particularly during the initial phase of intervention. Consumers will be protected with such standards as informed consent and treatment planning as well as confidentiality protection in patient rights. They will need to be guaranteed excellence in services, which will be measured by global rating scales or report cards.

Patient retention, for example, may be an indicator of quality. Good patient service and the ability to meet patients' expectations consistently can be measured by the extent to which services help the patients achieve their goals, by the extent to which individuals were satisfied or dissatisfied, with their services, and by the overall rates of patients' level of functioning (occupational, academic, social, etc.). To retain patients who may be assigned by purchasers, either independent or pooled, practitioners must devote themselves to meeting patients' expectations. Patient retention will create a long-term relationship not only with the patient but with the purchaser, and the provider will gain as a result of meeting the purchaser's expectations. When customers define the care they receive as quality care, they will be retained; their retention through satisfaction with care will likely result in a positive clinical outcome and the *durability* of the product will exist. Whether or not purchasers use performance-based measurements in their contracting decisions, providers and specialty managed care companies must learn to utilize these indicators and their results for useful reporting and for managing clinical operations. As direct capitation with practice groups emerges, internal monitoring of quality performance-based indicators can lower operating costs, improve quality, and sustain growth. Report cards, once endorsed by all stakeholders, will provide the marketplace with inventories of information beyond cost. As healthcare reform resurfaces as a major issue throughout the United States, a reliable set of information must be available. The development of agreed-upon methods of comparing healthcare plans and the provision of sets of indicators consumers' can use to make the comparisons will emerge to assist in the decision-making process. This will reduce the variance of reporting techniques and, therefore, increase data integrity for the future consumer purchasers. Whether through the use of report cards or new technologies, consumers can then take a more active role in their healthcare decisions.

INFORMATION TECHNOLOGY

Information technology will be required to enable the measurement of administrative efficiencies through state-of-the-art telecommunication applications, thereby offering the ability to parallel industrial standards. Specific quality performance indicators and standards will allow for linguistic and cultural diversity and particularity; in times of crisis they will provide the customer with immediate access to appropriate care and service (AMBHA, 1994). The administrative and clinical efficiency made possible through the application of information technology will ensure that necessary services are received, so that the patient is efficiently directed through the full continuum of care as case managers, particularly in the social work field, further refine their case management functions. This intervention will require data to be efficiently reported and monitored. The ability to demonstrate access to care at appropriate levels of services will be essential. The product will serve as a patient advocacy function necessary to achieve patient retention and improve outcomes.

Similar to the private sector, community health planning, and federal and state regulatory bodies, including Medicaid and Medicare, will use data information as a central component for policy development. Since healthcare data capabilities vary with most managed care organizations and provider groups, it may take several years and significant resources to achieve the desired data reporting. Providers need to understand that data and information format provided to the purchasers can set the stage for dialogue in a relationship building toward mutually agreed upon goals and expectations. Cost of specific episodes of care, age-specific and diagnostic specific utilization of care, evidence of patients receiving appropriate follow-up care, preventative health services, functional outcome assessment and measurement improvement, and so on, are examples of these kinds of data reporting that will be required.

FUTURE DELIVERY SYSTEMS

Future provider networks will be able to demonstrate the utilization of the full continuum of care and the ability to effectively direct patients' flow to the targeted appropriate levels of care. As providers respond quickly to reform initiatives and become a component within an integrated delivery system, the full continuum of healthcare will be achieved. Opportunities will exist when policy development includes benefit plan designs that recognize these alternative levels of service. As direct capitation arrangements with provider networks become increasingly sought, providers who are flexible and offer individualized outcome-driven treatment services will likely succeed.

Any sponsored benefit plan design that encourages the use of a provider network must maintain an oversight role to ensure that the ongoing quality of the network, and its maintenance (credentialing and recredentialing) are well documented and fully implemented. Payors will inherently be more responsible in monitoring the provider network's overall performance. Those payors who pay for their own healthcare benefits are arguably more exposed as a result of their direct imposition of financial disincentives based on benefit plan design, which can affect their healthcare decision when seeking services. Ironically, the stronger the penalty, the greater the liability for the contracted parties.

MEDICAL COST OFFSET THEORY

Concern over the cost and overutilization of behavioral healthcare resources will bring forth innovative effort within newly structured, integrated delivery models. These efforts will offer full-service healthcare with an emphasis on behavioral health. This insight will be reinforced by the heightened awareness of the medical cost offset theory and its implications under direct capitation.

Affective disorders, particularly depression, are among the most frequently occurring psychiatric disorders. Up to 5 percent of the population may suffer from depression at any one time, and up to 30 percent of the population may develop marked depression, as compared to 1-2 percent who develop a bipolar depressive disorder (Kesler, 1994). Of most concern is that symptoms of depression are frequently not recognized by practitioners, and only 31 percent of those diagnosed receive treatment of any kind (Borus, Howes, & Devins, 1988). One such psychological policy application may be to increase the proportion of people with major depressive disorders who receive treatment.

Medical cost savings, that is, the money saved in medical expenditures due to the referral of a patient in need of behavioral health services by a specialist, is a phenomenon recently receiving attention in this emerging industry. Medical cost savings, the reduced cost of medical and/or surgical services that are attributed to the use of nonmedical or behavioral healthcare interventions, are based on the premise that appropriate and effective treatment of psychiatric and chemical dependency disorders reduces healthcare costs for the individual, the payor, and the capitated provider. There is evidence that psychotherapy in general, with targeted and brief solution-focused interventions in particular, has been effective in producing these medical cost savings (Cummings & Follette, 1968; Follette & Cummings, 1967). Glazer (Glazer & Bell, 1993) reviewed the medical cost offset literature and found that major offset effects come from decreased inpatient medical and/or surgical utilization of specific diagnostic groups.

Medical cost offset is best achieved in integrated, organized systems of care, where there is immediate availability of a behavioral health specialist within the confines of the primary care physician's office setting. When medical care providers identify patients who are particularly high utilizers of medical services and refer them to a behavioral health specialist, referrals and interventions will be less costly and will enhance the effectiveness of the medical and/or surgical and behavioral health treatment being provided (Glazer & Bell, 1993).

CONTINUOUS QUALITY IMPROVEMENT

Payors will have heightened expectations and will therefore focus not only on their behavioral healthcare expenditures, but on their assessment of direct and indirect costs as a value-added expense. Healthcare purchasers will enter into these partnerships with provider networks structured to achieve better value for the cost of their services. These partnerships, with the support of data, will lead to *quality initiatives* between purchasers and providers that will perpetuate continuous quality improvement. Both parties will gain a better understanding of the complexities of the provisions of behavioral healthcare.

This new generation of managed care will represent value-driven service, with specific performance measures that will supply the necessary information on a delivery system's efficiencies. Furthermore, outcome measurements will be necessary and essential in order to meet high standards and further the competitive advantage. Evidence of reduced readmission rates, quality oversights, and adverse occurrence monitoring will be an ongoing focus of review.

Outcome management data can facilitate clinical practice guidelines that can assist providers in the establishment of more effective, proactive patterns of good care. This new data will enhance the ability of healthcare delivery systems to identify problematic system needs and to encourage and support policy development of new programs to enhance the quality of care and access of needed clinical services. Health outcome research has clearly been recognized for its emerging importance for healthcare decision making and policy development. The current environment of healthcare reform will emphasize increased rational use of limited healthcare benefits with particular focus on technology, sound clinical assessment, and analysis of the cost-effectiveness of treatment interventions and strategies.

Emerging management of care and the movement toward treatment matching will empirically determine the clinical care models; this will be a complex task requiring outcome-driven data that demonstrate the effectiveness of services. Performance standards, such as symptom reduction and increased level of functioning, will require organized systems of care to focus their efforts toward a continuous quality improvement process. This continuous quality improvement process will then form the feedback flow that will create mechanisms for improved behavioral healthcare. Empirically based treatment protocols will continue to substitute for nonempirically based treatment supported by clinical care models that integrate both operationally and clinically.

Healthcare reform will require payors to make a fundamental shift of attention, from measuring utilization of services to measuring what is accomplished. Making outcome the primary factor in the reformed healthcare system is essential in determining specific outcomes. As behavioral healthcare services integrate with medical and/or surgical healthcare, the approach to outcome measurement must be consistent. There needs to be a strong relationship, as well as, distinction between individual treatment outcomes and systemic outcomes, for example, measuring improvement in patient health status as a variable that results from a specific behavioral healthcare intervention.

Date collection systems can supply legislatures with accurate, specific information on the utilization and availability of healthcare services. This information can then be used in development of policy, healthcare plan design, actuarial planning, and establishment of effective regulatory mechanisms. Current state-level reform activities continue to reflect the need and expectations for detailed healthcare data. In addition, state policy makers who view this attempt as a cost-effective measure will be required to integrate clinical practice parameters into actual clinical practice.

Healthcare reform, quality initiatives, advances in technology, and the movement toward computerization of healthcare information and practice together provide the setting and opportunity for further evolution in outcome measurement approaches. With common data sets, methods, and technical factors that will accelerate the electronic methodologies, integration with clinical information systems, clinically-based terminals for entry involving episodes of care "Smart Cards" are now being discussed in their architectural designs (Gaus, 1994).

CONCLUSION

Enormous inefficiencies characterize the healthcare delivery system in the United States. The internal and external forces of the market and the overall dynamic healthcare environment have preceded the current debate on healthcare policy development and reform. This ever-changing marketplace has realigned the behavioral healthcare industry in several ways, emphasizing accountability, access, quality, cost, and satisfaction. The continued formation of integrated, well-managed provider networks capable of assuming economic risk offers major implications for policy development in the industry. The response to these policy developments will be the creation of innovative and responsive delivery systems that can accommodate linguistic and cultural diversity, provide access to care, and address the healthcare needs of different populations and different geographic regions.

This refined delivery system will serve patients in a customer-oriented way through the provision of appropriate care at the optimal time and in the most cost-effective way. Its emphasis will be on outcome measurements and performance-based contracting. These organized systems of care will be able to demonstrate continuous quality improvement to the payors in an equitable and consistent manner, unlike the current delivery system. Thus, the goals that the management of healthcare through outcome measurements and quality initiatives seeks to achieve are precisely the goals that underlie the movement of healthcare reform.

Overall, this shift will have a substantial impact on the direct and indirect costs of healthcare and as a result of improved efficiencies and quality of care, will affect the broader economy. This data and new delivery system will actually direct the way healthcare delivery systems conduct its business and positively influence quality of care provided to patients.

Healthcare Payment and Delivery Redesign: New Relationships and Behaviors

Wanda Jones

Healthcare, in the latter part of the twentieth century, is in the midst of a vast reconstruction. A few key shifts are rippling through the industry leaving no component—or participant—unchanged. As with any other societal new wave, it is easy to get caught up in the eddies and lose sight of the wave itself. Healthcare professionals, like everyone else, tend to think of life in terms of the world that existed at the start of their careers. Adaptation to a new set of conditions is easiest when the change takes decades; today, change occurs in months or weeks. People are in both economic and psychological disarray.

Ideally, this condition would be welcomed by healthcare professionals as offering new pathways for experiences, new opportunities for creativity. Unfortunately, they are too often responding with negative behaviors instead. The four typical responses are attempts to insulate themselves from unwanted change, attempts to control the behavior of others; attempts to exploit the changes for financial gain; or to do the least that can be tolerated without risk of loss of position, money, or reputation, regardless of long-term consequences.

Policy makers tend, at least in the healthcare field, to be naive about the potential reactions of healthcare professionals to public policy measures. Too often these unconsidered outcomes cause more pain than the problems that inspired them in the first place. For example, when policy makers lowered Medicaid compensation to physicians so that the program could cover more people, many physicians ceased accepting Medicaid patients. For the many Medicaid patients cut off from access to physicians through normal means, emergency rooms then become the main source of primary care. The policy had achieved the very opposite of the effect intended.

Solutions to healthcare policy and delivery problems are intellectually discoverable, but the psychologies of the main players and their subsequent behaviors are seldom faced realistically. Every business dealing is also a social contract whose psychological implications must be understood if the players are to avoid entering into arrangements that are fundamentally flawed. In healthcare this includes physicians, healthcare executives, payment plan executives, buyers (businesses and government), nurses and other professionals, and patients; in policy making it includes advocacy organizations, legislators, academic professionals, consultants, and the media. If policy makers seek to create beneficial results with minimal problems, they must combine a historian's long view with a psychologist's motivational view of how people behave and interact with each other.

The players' psychologies are best understood by choosing a construct or conceptual framework through which to view behavior, then seeing how it might apply to the individual or group under consideration. Following is a look at the major changes taking place in healthcare and their effects. Changes for physicians will be addressed in more depth than for other players, since healthcare reform affects them most profoundly.

PARADIGM SHIFTS

Why do people keep talking about a paradigm shift in healthcare, and what is it? In fact, several paradigm shifts are underway simultaneously. Paradigm shifts in medical science include movements from invasive to noninvasive, large-scale to small-scale, and organ system-based to total organism-based and molecular medicine. A physician no longer has to make a major incision to do many surgical procedures but uses miniaturized surgical tools through a laparoscope. The surgery can be done on an outpatient basis, and the patient recovers more quickly and has fewer complications. Other specialists are finding their knowledge capital becoming obsolete as a result of molecular medicine, psychoneuroimmunology, brain chemistry, and other developments on the frontiers of medicine. These changes affect all surgical or procedural specialists; fewer procedures are being done, fewer specialists are needed, and their income reflects the lower fees for reduced services and ambulatory care. For the first time, some specialties are becoming not only surplus but obsolete.

Paradigm shifts in healthcare economics include fee-for-service medicine to capitated care. Instead of being rewarded for each procedure or service, hospitals and doctors with managed care contracts are being paid a fixed amount per case, or per person per day or per month. This is creating an incentive to give less care and is causing a massive surplus of both hospitals and medical specialists, along with a new demand and respect for primary care physicians. In healthcare reform states, consumers can choose among more health plans and levels of deductibles so that they really are the direct source of payment for their initial care. The usual medical pecking order is upset, making specialists feel quite vulnerable in their traditional referral relationships. As hospitals empty, they can no longer underwrite expensive programs such as trauma, neonatal intensive care unit, and organ transplants. Physicians associated with those high-end programs - once the source of considerable prestige and income - are now finding themselves completely surplus to the market.

Paradigm shifts in power from the medical profession to the payer-buyer also exist. As a profession whose style of operation was set in medieval times, medicine has long had the freedom to operate independently, but within the limits of professional ethics and common practice. Currently, however, power has shifted to the payers, who can determine which physicians a patient may see, approve the services a physician may prescribe, limit the drugs that may be offered, and set the fees that may be charged. General public policy has, by accretion of many small actions, determined that the healthcare system should move from one based on the professional guild or entrepreneurship of physicians to one based on publicly-set and business set expectations and economic constraints, administered through agents such as payers, purchasing cooperatives, and regulatory authorities.

The profession was long able to resist corporate competition and corporate control by virtue of its collective organization, authority, and strategic position in mediating the relation of patients to hospitals, pharmaceutical companies, and the use of third-party payment. Today, physicians still hold authority and strategic position, but these have eroded. Specialization has diminished the scope of relations between doctors and patients. Although patients who have established satisfactory relationships with private physicians are less likely to enroll in HMOs (health maintenance organizations), HMOs have been developing more rapidly than before partly because ties between doctors and patients are so much weaker. (The rise in malpractice suits against private physicians has the same cause.) Employers and the government have become critical intermediaries in the system because of their financial role, and they are using their power to reorient the system. (Starr, 1982, 454)

A paradigm shift in patient expectations is noted by the upswing of self-care education. Educated patients, part of the TV generations of the last four decades, take more responsibility for their own health than did their parents. They demand more of physicians and are more open to alternative therapies. Many know more about nutrition than their doctors. Acupuncture's value was appreciated by consumers long before the medical profession saw it as more than quackery. A vast array of consumer-friendly alternative healthcare services now form a popular and competitive parallel universe to traditional healthcare. More importantly, educated patients are not afraid to ask questions and are more likely to treat the physician as just another source of consumer service. In attempting to respond to this new consumer awareness, providers are adopting themes such as "Patient-Focused Care," "seamless delivery system," and "one-stop shopping." Many physicians find this more organized consumer-style care galling.

A change in access to medical knowledge has also been observed. Under the guild system, the medical profession controlled access to and use of its professional body of knowledge. Physicians dominated the licensing boards for nurses and other healthcare professionals, and they feuded with any who tried to encroach on what physicians considered their own territory, such as nurse-anesthetists and nurse midwives. All this has changed dramatically. Patients now have access to previously unavailable medical information through a National Cancer Institute hotline, a nurse-based call-in system, and various health resource libraries. Patients can even obtain copies of their own medical records. The health-obsessed media give consumers frequent early news of each medical advance.

Paradigm paralysis is, unfortunately, an easy disease to get and is often fatal. More than a few organizations, which were dominant in their prime, have succumbed and died of it. It is a "hardening of the categories," so to speak. It grows from a situation of power. We all have our paradigms, but when one is successful and in power, there is a temptation to take our paradigm and convert it into the paradigm. After all, isn't it what made us successful? Once we have THE paradigm in place, any suggested alternative has to be wrong. "That's not the way we do things around here." This problem can occur at all levels, in all organizations, and will, in the long run, throttle new ideas. (A.J. Barker, 1993, 254)

The medical profession is faced, for the first time in history, with educated, aware patients who expect to participate in making informed choices about their own care. The one thing that once distinguished a guild-based professional from laypersons - a body of carefully controlled knowledge - is becoming permeable at the edges, leaving a smaller center over which only procedural specialists preside.

SPEED OF CHANGE

These paradigm shifts are inexorable. They were not planned and initiated as conscious policy but are the result of larger social forces, technological trends, and the effects of many incremental decisions by people tightly connected in an imitative industry.

The recession of the 1980s drastically accelerated changes in the healthcare universe. Buyers could not afford double-digit increases in premiums, nor were they willing to pay what amounted to half of a minimum-wage worker's annual salary for insurance. Buyer price resistance was strengthened by the formation of buyer cooperatives such as CalPers, the bargaining agent for government employees and retirees in California; CalPers was able to go from double-digit premium increases in 1990 to *negative* 6 percent, for some, in 1994. Constraints on private sector payment contracts meant that cost shifting no longer worked to buffer the sagging payments from Medicare and Medicaid. Hospitals went from a small bottom line to zero profits, and from there to accessing cash reserves in order to stay in business. At this writing, various researchers are estimating that with full managed care, only one-third of current hospital capacity will be needed. By extension, there are probably at least twice as many specialists than will be needed with full managed care. An entire profession is finding many of its members redundant in their career lifetimes.

Even this brief summary of the scale of revolution in healthcare economics shows how frightened health professionals can - or should - be. Any one of these changes would be hard for a physician to accept; collectively they present an enormous threat.

ALTERED RELATIONSHIPS

These sweeping changes, and the speed at which they are occurring, are manifested in increasingly conflicted relationships. In this period of adjustment, new relationships are being formed and tested. When times are tough, people seek security. If former relationships no longer offer security, they are jettisoned. As healthcare relationships are realigned, all parties are affected and the changing relationships are reflected in changes in individual behaviors. Most relationships are sets of nested boxes, existing at several levels, so each individual change, in turn, influences others. A ripple effect is generated.

Reversed Buyer-Seller Relationships

The seller of services—the health professional or hospital or other institutional provider—is in surplus. Buyers can pick and choose, set prices, and approve or disapprove services, pre-empting what once were the key prerogatives of the seller. Much of this shift derives from the monopsonistic behavior of Medicare (market dominance by the buyer, not the seller). Medicare accounts for such a large share of income that few providers can do as they once would have and simply terminate an unhealthy business relationship. The rules have turned; sellers are now dependent on buyer acceptance, rendering them vulnerable, worried, contemptuous of the buyers, and conflicted between loyalty and concern for the patient and the need to satisfy the buyer. Providers must constantly ask, "Is this service (treatment, medication, procedure) covered?" and "If not, will I give (prescribe, perform) it anyway?"

The payers' monetary control gives them so much power that they may become contemptuous of the providers' opinions. Instead of being governed by what is best for the patient, payers can use a series of decision-rules to deny as much care as feasible. Payers see these controls as necessary in the fee-for-service environment with its incentive to give more care than is needed.

The underlying difficulty is the uncertainty of medicine, the extraordinary range of practice variations, and the frequent absence of an objective standard to sustain a specific practice decision. Under such circumstances errors occur in providing both "too much" and "too little" care, and each type of error may be exaggerated depending on whether fee-for-service or capitation-like incentives are operative. It is important that patients understand in a general way the incentives that are likely to affect their physicians' behavior under uncertainty, but it would be ludicrous for physicians to reveal all of the uncertainties and possible options that affect the decision-making calculus, even if they could articulate and explain them. In contract, physicians have an affirmative obligation to protect their patients from harm, and to inform them if, in their judgement, the constraints imposed by a healthcare plan are injurious to their health. (Mechanic & Trust, 1994, 219)

Worse still, with competitive contracting, there is a further realignment of interests wherein both payer and provider share an incentive to give as little care as possible to the patient. (Lest this be doubted, it is only necessary to compare the extent and elaborateness of prior controls against overtreatment with the current lack of controls against undertreatment.)

Patients have little influence in this struggle. In theory, they might take their business to another health plan and another physician, but few enjoy such flexibility. Or they can wait until the problem becomes patently unbearable, at which time their only recourse lies in the courts.

Organizational Power

As vulnerable sellers fall behind in the economic war, they band together for protection and strength in the marketplace. Hospitals are merging into regional healthcare systems, and physicians are moving from solo to group practices.

Physicians who once felt that they knew the healthcare people they were dealing with-their colleagues, their patients, the chief executive officer (CEO) of their local hospital - now find their futures are affected by strangers -executives of health plans whom they have never met, bureaucrats in HCFA (Health Care Financing Administration-Medicare and Medicaid), and functionaries in various regulatory and accrediting agencies. A sense of powerlessness is produced, fueled by actual war stories of interactions that did not work. Differences among providers that once made a difference in their incomes-their skills, experience, and talent with patients- now make no difference. A less capable doctor is paid the same as the best doctor. If best doctors become cynical, they may begin to work closer to the average.

For physicians to band together defensively, then, is understandable. But doing so resolves little, and it creates other tensions that will, in their turn, further affect the healthcare industry. "Paranoia" is the term used most often by people describing physicians who are meeting in groups; it is fear and mistrust of those in perceived power positions. Memories are long. Anecdotes about services disallowed and its consequences grow into horror sagas: "What they did." Even the most intelligent, well-adjusted physician can begin to feel victimized, and many are rightly angry about what these experiences mean to their patients.

Economic Considerations

Economic considerations are corrupting relationships in all directions, including the relationships between doctor and patient, professional and colleague, and provider and payer. The very existence of insurance tends to remove a sense of responsibility for costs from both providers and patients. It is easy for patients to think that if "the insurance covers it," that's the same as being free. As consumers, they feel little responsibility for excessive prices or for unnecessary or excessive services. For their part, physicians are aware that patients neither know nor care what the insurance company pays, so some may feel free to manipulate the coding system to maximize billing to the insurer.

Worker compensation programs are rife with fraud in which the patient and the physician conspire to escalate a simple case into a world-class claim. Corruption of this kind makes it difficult for an industry to police itself, as the medical profession believes it should be left alone to do, since so many of its own members are culpable. Policy makers, in turn, with ample evidence of such corruption, have the excuse they need in order to justify imposing more and new forms of control. More controls, of course, invite more new evasions of them, leading to more fraud and corruption. The forces of professional ethics and altruism are not strong enough to balance the forces that lead to corruption. When these influences are seriously out of balance, the result can be self-contempt, which leads to isolation; mutual contempt, which limits interest in collaboration; and contempt from others, which leads to various forms of avoidance or control.

Economic Transactions

As the scale of economic transactions moves to levels ever more remote from direct patient care, relationships among the players become more remote from reality, more resistant to mutual influence, and more isolated from the medical or social consequence of economic actions.

The widespread frustration felt within the healthcare industry draws much of its energy from a sense of loss of community, of common purpose, as well as from a sense of mutual benefit. When bureaucrats in a utilization-review organization tell physicians their patient care is improper, physicians feel not only wronged but helpless to do anything about it. Resentment is stored up, ready to explode in rages about any subsequent apparent injustice. Physicians lose awareness of and tolerance for the trade-off decisions that a regulatory agency or health plan must make between the interests of the buyer and the interests of the provider.

While physicians may be obliged to adjust to income expectations trimmed by future realities, the ease and affability of that adjustment will depend in no small measure on the administrative simplicity or complexity of whatever new arrangements are instituted under health care reform. Much of the frustration voiced by physicians today has to do not with a tempered take-home pay but rather with the frustrations of securing those payments - the barrage of bureaucratic forms and processes, transient rejections of legitimate claims for payment in ways that appear primarily to delay cash flow; criticisms of care rendered, backed by refusals to pay which—in essence—restrict the exercise of that professional autonomy which may be the most exquisite privilege as well as the most meaningful responsibility of being a physician. (Rother, 1992, 126)

Because the interactions are around money, a dependency is created that leads to parent-child interactions rather than adult-adult interactions. The psychology of this is that children respond to unwanted parental control by lashing out and becoming resistant to reason. That feeling can be perceived in any audience of physicians who are discussing matters that involve the new business relationships, even those which might benefit them, such as the formation of new medical groups or mergers of hospitals.

The relative size of the parties also affects the dynamic and outcome. Large payers and regional healthcare systems tend to look for relationships at their same scale, rather than learning to seek out and improve the relationships with smaller, more local elements of their own networks. That is, payers will interact with medical societies about medical policy but ignore the medical staffs of contracting hospitals. Statewide or multi-state hospital systems will attempt to interact with professional associations or with large medical groups with whom they co-contract, rather than with the physicians who actually admit to the programs offered by their hospitals, feeling that this is the job of the local units. Although this is natural, it further diminishes physicians' sense of belonging to an organization that cares for their individual welfare and success. Even the military, with its hierarchy, frequent moves, dull jobs, and physical risks manages to produce fierce loyalties. In healthcare, loyalties are to one's specific professional niche first, and only secondarily, if at all, to the organizations with whom one shares responsibility for the health of the community.

Relationships once based on a sense of mutual competency are being undermined.

Norman Rockwell's doctor is long gone. The August 1990 cover of Healthcare Financial Management reflects the change. A male physician, dressed in a blue smock, viewed from the back, stands beside a male hospital administrator wearing a business suit. They smile at each other and each scratches the other's back with a long back scratcher. No patient is present. Instead, the doctor engages in a financial give and take with the hospital that is pleasing to both. (Bodwin, 1993, 6)

The new scale of operations in healthcare has magnified beyond the ability of most people to comprehend the situation, create a plan for the future, and lead people to accomplish it. If it is difficult to manage a group practice of under 25, how much more difficult to manage one of 200 or 2,000 physicians? If it is difficult to manage a 200-bed hospital, how much more difficult to manage a regional system of 20 hospitals, or a national system of 200 hospitals?

Mergers of hospitals have been common events in most urban states since the 1980s. Previously, when two or more hospitals merged, the original hospital administrators were usually left in place. Rarely did any have experience in managing a multi-hospital system; most simply continued operating the merged system as though it were just a collection of separate hospitals. The stress created by merging hospitals, each with its own history and culture, usually results in tension between local autonomy and central direction. Preoccupied by this tension, administrators focus their attention internally, rather than externally toward market success. The result can be that the merged hospitals fare less well in the market than they had as independent facilities. A paralysis can grip the entire organization—board, management, medical staff, and employees. Early success could have reassured all elements that the merger was the right step, but the very fears brought about by the merger prevent the progress that might ease them.

This organizational immersion in self-defeating and dysfunctional behavior is crippling, coming as it does during a period when the industry is under challenge from payers and buyers. Just when leadership and advocacy from the health profession in improving the healthcare delivery system is most needed, internal stresses make that leadership impossible. Thus, a sense of fatalism and resignation creeps into conversations about the future of healthcare. "What is the government going to do?" becomes the question, when a profession that felt empowered would be asking, "What are we going to do?" Another consequence of these stresses is that those affected, particularly physicians, tend to discuss healthcare issues only when their own incomes are threatened, making others discount their suggestions as self-serving.

To act effectively in new scale of healthcare delivery, physicians and hospitals need to band together. Ironically, as soon as either element forms organizations with potential power, individual members often challenge the very people they selected to lead them.

Science Advances

A new paradigm in medical science takes from fifteen years to centuries to adopt widely in community hospitals. A new technique or knowledge base is developed in research centers; young physicians learn it, go into practice, request support of the hospital to fund the necessary equipment, space, and staff, and then begin to let the medical community know that a new technique is available. This method works well when the technique is something that only one physician has to learn for it to be adoptable. When the new knowledge affects many diseases and specialties, the medical field is extremely resistant to early adoption. Physicians have an investment in their original knowledge base, and the hospital has an investment in its resources.

Having physicians now in practice admit that their tools and methods are obsolete, elect to go back to school for more training, and then replace one infrastructure with another has been done occasionally, but only when it is apt to produce massive increases in personal income, as the advent of angioplasty did for cardiologists. For a new science that may not produce massive income enhancement, the chance is nil that the transformation will be early unless deliberately planned by an entrepreneurial entity.

Why is this important to consider now? The paradigm shift currently under way at the clinical trials stage is toward molecular medicine, that is, the use of altered genes for diagnosis and treatment. In cancer, it will supplant surgery, radiation, and chemotherapy for some cancers or make treatable others that were once fatal. In heart disease, it will identify people prone to heart disease very early in the disease process. In mental illness, it will help determine whether patients are suffering from a functional illness or an organic syndrome, based on inherited mental illness. Its broadest potential cannot be even guessed at this time.

The importance of this issue to policymakers is threefold. If new paradigms are adopted slowly, additional investment will be made in old technologies during the slow adoption time. Patients who could have been cured will be high users of healthcare in and out of the system. Furthermore, the new industry will remain infantile and costly because the volume of activity does not arise to spread the cost of new resources.

Just as the country is making an investment in the "information highway," it is important to recognize the value of innovations coming from the life sciences industry and to facilitate their adoption against the double disincentives of high investment in past technology and declining income, which make adoption of any innovation problematic. How do existing physicians respond? Will they attempt to learn this new science or stonewall to the end of their careers, fighting any newly-trained practitioners who offer a more effective modality to "their" patients one, however, that in its early stages will have a high per care cost?

Many years ago I asked an executive responsible for the future development of a very large corporation, "What do you worry about most on your job?" His answer was startling. "I worry most about what my people don't know that they don't know. What they know that they don't know, they're able to work on and find the answers to. But they can't do that if they don't know that they don't know. (Davis, 1987, 221)

Weakening Healthcare Community Roots

Hospitals were once built by country-of-origin groups, usually European immigrants, by religious organizations, or by a total community. Healthcare professionals were drawn from those same groups, as were most of the employees. This coherence no longer exists. European migrations have been supplanted by Asian and Southern Hemisphere migrations, and the more recently-arrived groups have not brought health professionals proportional to their numbers, nor have they built culturally-distinct hospitals. Providers in some states are from totally different backgrounds than the people they serve, as in southern California, where it is not unusual to have a predominance of physicians from India and Asia, a Filipino nursing staff, and a Mexican-American constituency. White males run the payment plans and the hospital. The security, mutual trust, and mutual commitment that came from shared community roots is no longer there, but many providers are still playing out a mission to a cultural group, such as Jews, Swedish Lutherans, Germans, or Episcopalians, who have long since diffused into the community. For providers, learning to serve the replacement groups that now occupy the neighborhoods is like going on a foreign mission. Under these circumstances, it is not uncommon for the hospital to remain, but for the physicians to follow their patients to the suburbs. When there was cohesion, there was the comfort of knowing that one's contribution was appreciated, that there was support. The ties no longer bind except in a rare few unchanged communities.

Gender Power Shifts

Perhaps the most fundamentally unstable relationship in healthcare is that between men and women, as reflected in the collapse of the traditional, extremely rigid demarcation between the medical profession and nursing. About half of many medical school classes are now female. Men are entering nursing at a notable rate and when they do, often gain top jobs faster than women with comparable experience and training. Many women are becoming successful hospital administrators.

Not only are women physicians becoming more prevalent, but nurses are operating more independently, taking more responsibility for the patient's welfare while in the hospital, with extended roles in the community and in the home. "Ninety percent of services a family practitioner performs can be done under appropriate supervision by a trained nurse practitioner or physician's assistant" (Goldstein, 1995, 31). Women are learning to come out of the passive handmaiden role, or victim-of-discrimination mode, to take their place as professional colleagues, expecting respect from as well as giving respect to men. Women physicians tend to adopt the mores of their male colleagues, even to the extent of adopting their opinions of nurses, thus losing the potential benefits of merging female power at both key levels of the health professions.

Compound these shifts with the growing involvement of minority professionals in any of these categories and you have a recipe for personal interaction problems on a daily basis. Changes in traditional gender roles in healthcare is only beginning. After the present wave of female medical students enters practice, their sheer numbers will tend to tilt the profession toward more complete recognition of women's abilities and leadership potential. The effect on male physicians of the rebalance of power toward women will be interesting to observe in the decades to come.

Individual Autonomy

The new mode of operation for modern provider organizations is team care, with the physician as a member of a team that also includes a nurse, a social worker, an educator, and a case manager.

Some physicians have a difficult time in shared responsibility groups. The hegemony of the physician is narrowing to the actual diagnosis of the patient's problem or to invasive procedures. Care supervision, patient counseling, interaction with the patient's family, carrying out of treatment plans, all of these may fall within the skill areas of other professionals. The physician may take to this pattern like a duck to water, especially if he or she has been in a teaching environment. If accustomed to independent action in a solo practice setting, however, the physician may find the team approach to care maddeningly slow, often irritating with its demand for a coaching approach to dealing with colleagues.

Power Exchanges

Power exchanges are symbolized by content of funds flow. Money, the centerpiece of most managed care contracts, is actually a symbol for desired levels of power and control. When a hospital signs a managed care contract with a for-profit payer, it transfers the "power" to make the profit represented by the 30 percent withhold. In exchange, the payer enables the hospital to have a protected piece of market share within a shrinking market, which allows it to stay in business. On the other hand, in the case of a capitated contract, the problem on the table is how to divide the cap rate between the hospital and physicians. Because this discussion is too often seen as a power negotiation, physician groups will demand 50 percent of the cap rate, even though financial information will demonstrate that physician services should require no more than 30 percent. Hospital services are inherently more expensive per event of care and for the standby costs of high end services.

Administrators who claim to need more than 50 percent of the cap rate are seen as attempting to control doctors, to limit their power, to limit their incomes, and to limit the number of physicians who participate in the funds flow. One administrator antagonized his entire organized medical staff when he said, "Within two years, most of you will be working for me."

Physicians who come to capitation late in their careers have not had the seasoning in large-scale business arrangements of their mature group practice siblings. As a result, they may approach capitation negotiations with a risky combination of ignorance and paranoia. Hospital administrators observing colleagues who have participated in a managed care conversion cycle or lost their jobs because of it are twice shy. They are likely to exercise less leadership and avoid confrontations with dissident physician groups. What this can mean to policy-makers is uneven progress across the country, uneven success, much trial and error, and a continuing compulsion for oversight and control of a process meant to be based on free-market principles.

Professional, Citizen, and Government

The interests of the health profession and the interest of the public, as expressed through elected officials, are moving apart. These relationship changes are largely ignored or discounted by those who observe or attempt to influence the health field. Public policy makers, in particular, seem to have little insight into the fact that if changes are made in the context in which a professional operates, there will be consequences, usually protective and resistive. As a result, the healthcare profession has come to have such a contempt for policy-makers that they are seen as separate from the voters who elected them. Policy makers are perceived as operating on their own agenda, and not in the public interest at all.

This partly explains why the health profession was so slow to deal with the problem of high costs. Some physicians and hospitals may say to themselves and each other, "Don't those in (Washington, Sacramento, Chicago,...) know that by cutting payments to us they are lowering quality of care?" And they would mean it with all the fervor of those who believe they are looking out for the patient's interest. Of course, they also may not see that a second MRI scan done in a single inpatient stay "to rule out any changes" is excessive, or that a C-section rate of 27 percent is due, perhaps, more to compensation factors and physician convenience than to an increase in high-risk pregnancies.

If a state's legislators presumed to tell bridge-building engineers that no bridge could have more than one ton of steel per linear foot, howls of rage would be heard. Everyone knows—even the legislators themselves—that few legislators understand how to build bridges. In healthcare, however, every legislator is a patient, a family member of a patient, or a friend of a patient, and each has his or her own physicians, insurers, favorite pharmacy, and friends with medical stories. Legislators are, they believe, capable of understanding what people mean when they say, "I don't believe it is right that I am turned away from an emergency room just because I don't have insurance," or "I should have guaranteed health insurance even though I have lost my job," or "I want to have the reasons explained to me be before I undergo a mastectomy," or "I don't want to have any test of any of my body fluids for any reason without my consent, unless it is for public safety." But while legislating in the public interest in these areas, lawmakers can step over the line into controls that do not make sense to everyone, and they may lose respect and credibility. For example, requiring every primary care center contracting with Medicaid to stock both adult- and child-size catheters, even though children are seen in a different location is micromanagement to an absurd extent (personal interview, 1994). Yet licensure laws and government payment programs are rife with such rules. Medical professionals' resentment of trivia grows daily; this fund of resentment looms large just when legislators want the medical profession to embrace a new definition of the public interest, such as converting to risk-based contracts for healthcare, particularly for the poor, or moving from aggressive treatment of the dying to humane non-intervention support for terminal illness.

These long-held and growing resentments are creating a chasm between medical professionals and policy makers. Some legislators generally discount what the organized medical profession says, and the medical profession resists to the last inch the proposals of legislators with whom they disagree. This atmosphere of distrust may lead to new, unprecedented controls. An excellent example is legislative imposition of fee schedules for Medicare and Medicaid, when the medical profession had been forbidden from adopting its own fee schedule as a violation of the Sherman Anti-trust Act. Other examples are plentiful, such as naming consumers to medical licensure boards and requiring relicensure.

The apogee of legislative incursion into the healthcare system has been the Clinton-era attempt at national healthcare reform. In formulating the bill, the medical profession and hospitals had little input. Drafters of the bill seemed oblivious or indifferent to the inevitability that the proposed reforms would profoundly affect healthcare delivery and were ignorant of obvious externalities. They made little or no attempt to think through the consequences to the people to be served to their needs and service requirements; it seemed that their only concern was how those services should be paid. Designing a workable delivery system would have required listening to both the public and the providers; this the Clinton administration was unwilling to do or else it believed that the delivery system was unproblematic, that only the payment element of the health system needed reform.

An indication of the developing gap between the health profession and the public interest is the public's anger when any healthcare professional steps outside the medical guild role to work from the public's standpoint. There was a striking example in Oregon, where a physician, Marvin Kitzhaber, ran for the legislature, then introduced a bill to prioritize services available to Medicaid patients so that the funds could cover all who were eligible. The vilification that Kitzhaber received from his colleagues for the so-called "rationing" bill expressed the rage of a profession that felt betrayed by one of its own. In a long tradition of the profession, Kitzhaber became a martyr for the public in ways it could hardly appreciate. Only recently has he been raised to the level of prophet and elevated to the governorship.

As these paradigm shifts and healthcare reforms continue, it is to be hoped that legislatures and healthcare professionals learn to adapt; that they discover a new framework for productive exchange that can heal the wounds of mutual recrimination and distrust. If we are to build a healthcare system for the next century, there must be a true collaboration. Unfortunately, the immediacy of present pain makes it difficult for either party to see very far ahead or to defer present gratification for a future good.

UNDERSTANDING THE PSYCHOLOGY OF THE HEALTHCARE PROFESSIONS

In the previous section the focus was on changes in relationships as a consequence and as a substrate for public policy development. In considering the psychology of the healthcare industry, it is useful to examine the constructs or concepts that explain behavior to consider and the settings in which behavior takes place. Following are several constructs and concepts that are particularly valuable: Maslow's hierarchy of needs; sins and virtues; professionalism; entrepreneurial scale and market share; specialty and age; collegiality; incentive; and competition.

Although these constructs or concepts will not clarify every potential reaction of providers to changes in healthcare policy, having these conceptual tools in one's mental kit may reduce surprise and dismay when change brings unexpected—and unpleasant—reactions.

This section focuses on physicians, but much also applies to hospital administrators, nurses, and other allied health professionals.

Basic Emotions

Maslow's hierarchy of needs starts with safety and security, ending with self-actualization. At best, physicians act from altruism and at the same time are self-actualizing, doing what they are trained for and love. At worst, physicians are fearful and suffer from a deep sense of insecurity. As we have seen earlier, declining utilization and/or income can lead to this worst case result. Fear leads to rage; free-floating rage is most often expressed in groups, where the group provides a cloak of apparent support, or where many share the same feelings and same sense of insecurity.

These feelings are aggravated by small events—an insurer declines to approve a surgery for a single patient, for example, and by big ones—one insurer cancels a contract, eliminating 500 procedures per year. Or the feelings can be triggered by other groups appearing to move ahead in market share, or by a hospital CEO appearing to favor one physician group over another, or by a colleague leaving to join another group.

When physicians live in a state of fear and insecurity, their behavior is often perceived as exaggerated in relation to the immediate cause. The reason is that the immediate cause is the last straw, only the most recent blow of many. An accumulation of injustices has made the physician impervious to reason.

The state of fear and rage is inherently unstable, as the organism attempts to right itself. Adjustment approaches may include

1. checking out, so that the physician no longer comes to meetings where bad news might be heard
2. dropping out of a plan or program, to eliminate one source of dropping income
3. attempting to form a break-away group
4. litigation

A physician may "do a geographic," that is, go to another hospital's medical staff or take a salaried job. At the extreme, he or she may try to pressure the hospital CEO to pay him or her to "manage" a program in exchange for a fixed income—with the implied threat that if such an arrangement is not made, the physician may take his or her patients elsewhere. Until recently, a favored strategy was participating in joint ventures with hospitals for expensive medical technology.

Policy-makers who expect hospitals and their medical staffs to be a cohesive unit should understand that hold-out physicians fear the power of hospitals to change their referral patterns and income. They disdain healthcare executives for their perceived lack of understanding of medical practice, and they have a good deal of unresolved rage at insurance companies, even while doing whatever it takes to get paid. Physicians who stand to lose their homes and their practices are not mollified by the notion that somehow health insurance rates will be lower because of it. If policy makers want change, they might find it happens faster with positive reinforcement for desirable behaviors rather than with negative measures on the profession at large to prevent the worst actions of a few.

Sins and Virtues

As with emotions, so with character. Physicians and other health professionals are mortal, with the same mixture of sins and virtues as any other human being. The mix may actually be skewed toward more virtuous character and fewer sins. However, when a few doctors sin, the entire profession appears guilty. Currently, the sin that most concerns policy-makers is greed—or perceived greed. What doctors see as just compensation for a fifteen year training cycle, horrible hours, and superior skill is seen by civilians as an outrageous multiple of the average household income of people being served.

Should an orthopedist in a small town in southern California make $1.5 million per year while declining to cover the ER, see MediCal patients, or serve on medical staff committees? What should a physician's income be? More to the point, what is it worth to a patient to have superior, dedicated medical services, and is it necessary to pay outrageous salaries to entice young people to endure the dreadful rite of passage through medical school? What will happen when salaries drastically decline, as they are doing now in highly competitive states, and many physicians leave practice? Suppose the present surplus disappears—are we willing to again encourage greed in order to reinvent the profession?

If policy makers want a result such as limiting physician income through setting salary caps, they should be prepared for the physician to drop the amount of labor provided for that salary. If one wants a total all-out work effort, then piecework payment, with unlimited income potential is the way to get it. Finding the balance without providing disincentives for entering the profession is a delicate task, not yet learned.

Professionalism and Income

A profession is defined by the terms of its work, its self-policing, and the way it closes ranks against those who would challenge its dominance. Today the professionalism of medicine is reflected in state licensure laws, corporate practice of medicine acts, limitations on the rights of other practitioners to perform in areas physicians consider their own in ethical standards organized medical staff structures, accreditation standards, practice guidelines, legal precedent, acculturation and group norms that operate through medical societies, or any grouping of physicians. In nursing, the effect is similar.

Professionalism used to include the right to set one's own fees and to be paid by those being served. Neither is now a universal condition, since physicians are paid by third parties who often set the fees to be paid. In effect, third parties are controlling physician income. With managed care, payers are in a position to channel patients-enrollees to a selected set of physicians, who thus gain in income while others lose.

Unfortunately, those with comfortable incomes appear to be insulated from the need to act on behalf of their own futures. In times of rapid contracting, awards tend to go first to the early, the aggressive, and the unprincipled -those who are not well paid now and who will grab at anything that promises improved market share and income. The slow, passive, and principled providers tend to wait for some time before they believe they must become involved in contracting. Inadvertently they find themselves in a backwater and closed out of networks.

Bad behaviors of the early group, unless the payer exercises more than usual due diligence, tend to bring on repression from payers, which feeds a sense of injustice and justifies further self-serving behaviors. Payers who go into a community to establish a foothold should be aware that they are at risk in two ways: If they contract with early signers, they may have picked the worst physicians. If they attempt to be selective, going with the best physicians, they will have to pay more and take longer to achieve market share.

Entrepreneurial Scale and Market Position

Every physician in solo practice is an entrepreneur or small business person. Although being competent at that level, he or she may not be competent at the next levels, in a single specialty group or multispecialty true group (not independent practice groups). Yet becoming part of a larger collection of doctors is usually the route to strong market position. Payers tend to favor aggregations of doctors that are self-managing. It is easier to contract with one 100-person group than with a hundred separate individuals. Physicians who are wise will "follow the money" to see where the dollars in healthcare are flowing and will position themselves to be part of that stream.

Payers and policy-makers must develop strategies that not only take advantage of the current surplus of medical manpower in many urban states but anticipate the quasi-monopolies that are now being created through the formation of megagroups.

Medical Specialty

Some who are deeply involved in healthcare believe that medical specialty may stereotypically equate with personality type. At the top of the ladder for aggressiveness are orthopedic surgeons. Brain surgeons and immunologists are the intellectuals. Obstetricians and pediatricians are nice guys. Internists are middle of the road. Cardiologists are bright, impatient, and need high income and status. Family practice physicians are nice, aggressive, and paranoid about other specialties. Radiologists are either phlegmatic and competent or martinets. Pathologists are isolates. Emergency room physicians are driven. Trauma surgeons are demanding and arrogant. Dermatologists are outside the pecking order, as are ear, nose, and throat specialists and allergists. Another way of classifying physicians is to distinguish between those who see sick patients and those who deal with machinery or specimens rather than the real patient in all his or her complexity. Medical specialty has been a general predictor of market success potential, income, likelihood of being in a group or being hospital-based, and potential for loss of income.

Age is another factor that determines how physicians will react to managed care. Older physicians tend to be resistant, hoping to wait out the trends before retirement. Middle-aged physicians note the most upset, as some may have created real income needs for themselves, do not want to retrain, and yet are too young to retire. They must keep working—but how and for whom? Younger physicians, in some states, come out of medical school knowing they will be practicing in a managed care environment and expect to be in a group or in salaried practice. In other states, it is as though the faculty has never heard of managed care and feels no obligation to prepare students for that eventuality.

Policy makers and payers who have a sense of the future might wish to signal their interests in a reconfigured medical manpower profile by disconnecting the links between medical school dependence on research, overhead payments, and the corresponding necessity for maintaining a large number of high-end specialists on the faculty, who in turn must train a given number of residents. Adding specialists to an already bloated manpower pool is counterproductive, yet medical schools are, for the most part, disengaged from the managed care revolution.

Practice Form and Location

Along with specialty and age, practice form and location account for the carrying rates of movement into managed care. Urban medical communities are usually oversupplied with specialists, and undersupplied with primary care physicians. Marketing in urban areas is attractive to insurers because they can reach large populations through a few key employers, with less need to deal with small business and individuals. Oversupply of doctors means that insurers can pick and choose among doctors who are vulnerable in the marketplace. It is notably difficult for an HMO insurer to go into referral areas that are undersupplied with physicians. The doctors can easily hold out from signing contracts for decades past the time when urban physicians have long since accepted preferred provider organization (PPO) or HMO contracts.

Practice form—solo, single-specialty, or multispecialty group; or hospital based—is also protective of early participation and success, with the market being attracted first to large multispecialty groups. These groups have the management stuff to deal with market and business issues, plus access to legal and financial help far superior to that available to individual physicians. The large groups have the infrastructure and capital for recruitment and distribution of physicians throughout the area, as well as the ability to install a clinical information system for patient care management.

Participants in mature groups are less apt to have the narrow outlook or "cabin fever" mentality of the solo practitioner, who does not have daily interaction with peers or a larger-scale viewpoint of his or her true place in the regional market.   Such solo physicians overvalue their own practices and underestimate the rate at which their patient base is being shifted to other physicians. It is a common story to have doctors say they did not understand the power of managed care until patients started requesting that their charts be sent to other doctors. Yet physicians in such small practices are among the most productive in the field. It would seem a good thing to bring them along easily into managed care, keeping the best and helping them function well until they mature as a component of a seamless delivery system.   Unfortunately, the enticements and support are not always available to counteract fear of the unknown.

Public policy thinkers will soon be faced with the blurring of traditionally separate organizations, as payers create networks, provider networks evolve that contain both hospitals and physicians, and as businesses become integral parts of these networks through long-term contracts. Suppliers, too, are accepting a shared risk by tying their compensation for supplies to the revenues of the provider. Regulation for one entity ripples through and becomes regulation of the whole health system. It is a paradox that the more complicated a structure, becomes the more likely it is to fail to work in all cases, thus needing more regulatory oversight, but the less likely that regulation will work with a system that is no longer standardized or stable or governed by a centralized ownership structure that can be held accountable.

Incentives

Managed care reverses incentives from encouraging doing more under fee-for-service to doing less under managed care. This particular incentive reversal is not yet appreciated in terms of its power. Currently, the incentive to do less is buffered by the oversupply of physicians and hospitals, the practice guidelines being put in place, and peer review processes. In addition, as long as there is a competing fee-for-service alternative, the patients who feel undertreated in an HMO setting can pay more and find the care they desire, if they can afford to. As the industry moves toward a higher proportion of managed care, this option will decline for most patients. What was once thought of as unacceptably low standards of care could become a new norm. When will the C-section rate be too low rather than too high? When will enough neonatal intensive care units close until low-birthweight babies cannot get referred to a hospital with such a unit because there is a waiting list? Which arthritis patients will be declined a total hip operation? "In the old paternalistic days, if a physician said "There's nothing more we can do" that was it; you started planning the funeral. Today, patients might respond, "Does the HMO give you a year end bonus if you come in under budget?" One of the sadder consequences of our monetarization of healthcare is that the public is much more aware of providers' economic motives and conflicts of interest. People thus become wary when told that further treatment is inadvisable" (E. Friedman, 1994, 10).

Presently there is a great deal of attention being paid to outcome studies and comparatives. A lot of bright people are working hard on such postfacto measures of quality of care. Unfortunately, many only evaluate care given and ignore care not given or not recorded. The seriousness of the problem calls for a serious approach, one that compares concurrent case management against a care plan for an entire episode of illness. Correcting this situation will require a deliberate effort to transform the role of the hospital system and its payer partners to that of advocates—not of the medical staff, but of the health needs of the community. "Since healthcare is heavily influenced by the social context in which people live and work, social factors might be expected to be an important component of physician-patient determinants, and there is no accepted method of categorizing social factors as there is for biological factors....Ideology determines the content of the discourse and how it leads physicians to avoid the social issues that cause illnesses and influence their course and response to treatment" (Starfield, 1992, 166).

The altruistic incentive to do something because it needs to be done, not because it is covered, seems to be diminishing. Can it be that the same public altruism that fosters healthcare reform produces a decline in private altruism? And is it the increase in need that has overwhelmed private altruism? The disappearance of the village aspect of society has made the healthcare provider just another service *in* the community, not a service *to* the community. "A resident, for example, recently turned to me and said "We've spent $100,000 on this patient. Isn't it time to quit?' The reality was that we had probably spent $100,000 on the patient, and indeed it was time to quit. What disturbed me was that the resident thought the two things were directly related'..that the woman had used up her "allotment' of healthcare resources" (Andreck, 1994, 32).

Competition

Capitalism works best when more than one player is competing for the same market. When a cartel or monopoly dominates, competition is absent. In the transition to managed care, price competition among payers requires them to select certain physicians to participate in contracts but to exclude others. This upsets the balance in a service area and can lead to rapid formation of competing contracting arrangements among the excluded physicians, which in turn allows other payers to come in. For policy-makers, this simple action-reaction model could make it possible to make changes more rapidly. It might be possible, for example, to create matching grants in the spirit of the old Hill-Burton program, which funded the development of hospitals, to aid in formation of groups. It would be important, however, that the first stage be considered experimental, and not expect a group to look and act maturely immediately. Action-reaction would speed up the creation process in such a case.

Unfortunately, competition also creates efficiencies that throw surplus capacity into sharp relief. There are many surplus hospitals today, trying to stay alive at low occupancy - and their physicians are trying to stay alive with them. As these hospitals begin to close, specialty physicians will leave those areas and reaffiliate with remaining hospitals, aggravating the competitive situation. Whereas one can close a surplus hospital, it is not possible to shut down surplus physicians. The surplus will increase the fear level, the search for remunerative activities, the litigiousness of the disenfranchised, and the moat-and-drawbridge style of negotiation.

Surpluses will trigger excesses of protectionism, as is now happening in many states faced with medical society demands for "any willing provider" legislation. Some physicians stayed out of HMO development as long as they could, yet finding it a powerful market force, they and other licensed health providers are now demanding legislation that would allow them to participate in contracts even if they are not needed. By rewarding such demands, policy-makers may negate much HMO progress. Removing the lowest performers from the list would bring untold new overhead costs. The psychological qualities need in this situation are courage on the part of the policy-maker and moral honesty on the part of the provider. Unfortunately, the nation may have to live through the opposite of these instead.

These are just some of the constructs or lenses through which to view the healthcare participants' psychological positioning and reactions as they live through the next few decades. Many permutations will be seen. Exceptions will abound. But the student of anthropology, social science, political science, and psychology will find much case material in the health sector transition to its future forms. One can only wonder if our public policy framework is similarly capable of renewal, or capable of examining its own world views and biases.

PSYCHOLOGY IN PUBLIC POLICY

Since most legislators are lawyers, and since their instinct is to address every problem as though it had a legal solution, there is bound to be cognitive dissonance between the psychology of physicians or healthcare executives and the psychology of policy-makers. Having outlined some of those psychological constructs, it is worth asking whether there is any avenue for an "East Berlin-West Berlin" type of accommodation. Some suggested solutions include the following:

- Instead of public hearings with prepared statements from association executives, hold direct interviews with affected providers to search for a wider range of alternatives and to help increase awareness of natural evolutions already underway that do not require a legislative ruling, but merely a financial incentive.

- Hold committee meetings in healthcare settings, with tours and presentations of changes in process, problems, conditions, potentials, and so on, so that committee members, not just staff or consultants, can have a direct view of the system they are regulating.
- Ask provider systems to present their reports and plans in ways that enhance understanding rather than obscuring it. One excellent method would use videos, not just paper plans, to show to all the affected physicians, community organizations, payers, and policy groups. Even local TV presentation of excerpts from these plans would give exposure that would stimulate the provider systems to do a much better job than they now do, and they would lead to greater speed in improving healthcare. Present reporting formats are so indirect that providers know the public will never see the documents, nor understand such things as how much surplus capacity overhead is being charged for in health insurance premiums.
- Announce a "Reverse Hill-Burton program" to buy and close unneeded hospitals. This would prevent unnecessary investments in infrastructure, allow consolidation of community service programs for greater cost-benefit, decrease the fraud and abuse that accompanies a dying facility, stimulate the reformation of the medical community into true groups, attract higher-level executives into the health field, remove obsolescent boards of trustees that cannot cope with the managed care transition, and release trained staff to be redirected into home care and outpatient services. This is one of those leverage decisions that causes much beneficial change. Its very scale and import makes it politically explosive however, and any coalition that sponsored it would have to be free of self-interest.
- Then, at the microlevel of policy development, it might help to include in staff reports not only a financial analysis, a political analysis, and a legal precedent analysis but an assessment of the overt and hidden incentives in the proposed legislation, the likely reaction of the main players, and the countermeasures that should be included in the legislation. Needless to say, this analysis should not come from official industry representatives.

Before the 1990s, the very idea of writing about the psychological aspects of public policy in healthcare would have been considered absurd. But unpredictability of behavior is on the rise. Attempts to channel physicians' behavior calls for skill in assessing the reality, discounting the rhetoric, and presenting compelling alternatives to their present pain. Such thinking is important now because the stakes are higher, change is at a much larger scale, and mistakes are being made that have far-ranging effects. Laws once passed are difficult to undo. And despite the mixed experience with Medicare and Medicaid, some still cling to the innocent hope that healthcare reform can be engineered with only positive outcomes. Policy makers who propose legislation tend to address healthcare payment reform as though no negative effects were to be expected, and they do not see its inexorable connection with healthcare delivery. That, in turn, practically assures that negative effects will occur.

Perhaps the most crucial truth to be understood at this point is that no change happens in isolation. All change triggers other changes. Somewhere the "early adopters," those with personal psychological health and vision, are not resisting, not fighting, but are acting creatively and proactively. Behind the problems in the healthcare system and the psychological barriers in its members a ferment is brewing, and the emergence of new goals is stirring new ideas about how to meet them.

———— ♦ ————

11

Decision Support Technology in Managed Mental Healthcare

John S. Lyons
Michelle Shasha
Nina J. Christopher
John T. Vessey

Increasingly, managed care initiatives are securing larger market roles in the financing and administration of mental health services in both the private and public sectors. Regardless of the ongoing process of healthcare reform in the United States, managed care will continue to exert considerable influence on the mental health services sector.

Managed mental healthcare developed out of a need to contain escalating costs of services. When managed care organizations assume the risk for overutilization, corporate profits and survival rest on careful management of resources. In the first generation of managed mental healthcare, mental health status and clinical outcomes became secondary concerns to the primary goal of cost containment. Early managed care contracts were awarded over relatively short terms (e.g., one year) and have traditionally been won through the promise of often dramatic cost savings. In general, neither preventative intervention nor service system reforms are cost-effective in the short run. Consequently, more immediate strategies such as treatment restrictions and benefit and access barriers have been implemented to manage resources. However, as the rapid implementation of managed care initiatives have driven down costs and contained increases in utilization, there is less opportunity to negotiate contracts based on real costs savings. Therefore, interest is developing in establishing the value of service provided. This requires the use of clinical measures to related to the costs of services.

The following chapter will emphasize the importance of managing the cost, quality, and outcome of mental healthcare through the use of decision support technology.   Appropriate measurement strategies for integrating clinical information into the administration of mental health services will be addressed.

In the managed mental health care system, patients are often treated as the Greek mythical figure Procrustes treated the hapless travelers who crossed his path. Procrustes tied travelers to his bed and stretched them or lopped off their legs to ensure that they would fit perfectly into his bedframe (Docherty, 1993). Similarly, rigid and sometimes seemingly arbitrary guidelines developed for the purposes of cost containment and standardization force healthcare providers to fit patients into diagnostic categories and implement treatment plans that may not be clinically optimal. These circumstances promote treatment interventions that are disproportionately influenced by ancillary considerations rather than by sound clinical judgement and reliable outcome data.

As managed mental healthcare becomes the predominant model for the organization and financing of mental health service delivery, managed care firms must avoid assuming the role of Procrustes. Rather than rigidly adhering to issues of cost containment, managed care organizations must also attend to the quality of services provided under their auspices. If managed care organizations are to successfully balance the cost and quality of services, rather than merely managing the utilization of services, then technology must be developed that provides reliable, relevant, readily available, and generalizable information on clinical dimensions that inform administrative decision-making. One of the challenges facing mental health service delivery planning is that decision models that work for general health services may not be applicable to mental health services. Psychiatric decision making is influenced by a wide range of variables and is rarely based upon a standard set of criteria; therefore, decision theory in psychiatry is more complicated than in other medical specialties. The number of varying circumstances that influence decisions are infinite and unique to each patient; thus, protocols for specific conditions are logistically and clinically difficult to develop.

A substantial body of research has documented an absence of a consistent relationship between psychiatric diagnosis and service utilization.   This is particularly true for the relationship between diagnosis and length of stay on inpatient psychiatric units (Freiman & Hendricks, 1990; Goldman et al., 1984; Michalon & Richman, 1990; Mitchell et al., 1987; Taube, Lee, & Forthofer, 1984).   The only exception appears to be that individuals with co-occurring substance abuse disorders remain in treatment or hospitalized for shorter periods of time (Faden & Taube, 1977; Lyons & McGovern, 1989). A number of nondiagnostic and service delivery variables are also associated with inpatient bed utilization.   For instance, older patients appear to stay longer than younger patients (Conwell, Nelson, Kim, & Mazure, 1983; Lyons, Pressman, Pavkov, Salk, Larson, & Finkel, 1992). Involuntary admissions have longer lengths of stay than voluntary admissions (McFarland, Faulkner, & Bloom, 1990). Provider variables, such as hospital and attending psychiatrist, also predict length of stay

(Lyons, O'Mahoney, & Larson, 1991; Scherl, English, & Sharfstein, 1988).

From a clinical perspective, the absence of a relationship between diagnosis and length of inpatient stay is not surprising. In a survey of clinicians, Mezzich and Coffman (1985) found that those involved in inpatient care saw symptomatology and social supports as more important determinants of length of stay than diagnosis. Patients are not admitted to the hospital for a psychiatric diagnosis per se but, rather, because of some specific symptoms or circumstances secondary to that disorder. In a study of emergency room decision-making, Marson (1990) found that danger to self, danger to others, and inadequate self-care were the best clinical predictors of the decision to admit. Danger to oneself can be secondary to major depression, bipolar disorder, or schizophrenia. Danger to others can be secondary to psychotic disorders or even some Axis II disorders. Problems with self-care can be secondary to most serious mental illnesses.

Emergency psychiatric patients often present with complex and troubling problems, yet decision-making in an emergency psychiatric service does not allow the luxury of observing a patient over time. Clinicians must often make their decisions in a relatively brief period of time. The cross-section of behavior sampled is the point of reference used in assessing the presence and degree of psychiatric symptoms. Special attention is given to the impact of these psychiatric symptoms on immediate safety of the patients and others. However, the assessment of dangerousness or the ability to care for oneself can vary considerably from clinician to clinician (Apsler & Bassuk, 1983). Moreover, the treatment of psychiatric disorders in an inpatient setting is rationally influenced by factors other than those necessary to justify admission. For example, medical co-morbidities can make differential diagnosis more difficult and complicate the medical management of patients on the unit (Boelhouwer & Rosenberg, 1983; Hall, Gardner, Stickney, LeCann, & Popkin, 1980). Co-existing substance abuse has also been shown to influence the course of psychiatric inpatient stays (Lyons & McGovern, 1989). A variety of social factors from housing status to family support can complicate discharge planning for patients (Drake, Wallach, & Hoffman, 1989; Miller & Willer, 1979; Rock, Goldstein, Hopkins, & Quitkin, 1990; Zaleski, Gale, & Winset, 1979). Finally, as with all interventions, individuals differ in their willingness and ability to adhere to the treatment protocol.

The psychiatric emergency service has become the central point of entry to inpatient psychiatric services as well as the primary triage site for level-of-care decisions (Feigelson et al., 1978; Gerson & Bassuk, 1980; Medel & Rapport, 1969; Tischler, 1966; Steadman, Braff, & Morrisey, 1988). In the managed care environment, crisis decision-making becomes a crucial point at which significant clinical and resource decisions are made.

The advent and rapid expansion of managed care into the mental health service system has increasingly influenced decision making in emergency psychiatric care. The role of managed care organizations in the decision-making process often means that dispositional decisions are regulated by persons who are not only removed from the actual evaluation sites but whose decisions necessarily include attention to resource utilization concerns. Thus, emergency psychiatric services must consider medical necessity criteria as the primary determinants shaping level-of-care decisions. This is particularly true for decisions that result in expensive inpatient treatment.

A variety of strategies have been proposed to balance economic and quality of care concerns. Some of these strategies include outcomes management, decision support, utilization review, quality indicators, and continuous quality improvement.

Outcomes management refers to the use of clinical outcome data to inform management decisions. Outcomes management generally requires that reliable assessments of clinical status be made by clinicians and patients at the beginning and termination of treatment. More frequent assessments allow for the monitoring of the trajectory of outcomes over the course of treatment. There are two basic assumptions of outcomes management. First, it is assumed that high-quality services result in good outcomes. Thus, adverse outcomes are used to identify problematic structures and processes in service delivery. Second, it is assumed that monitoring outcomes increases provider motivation to offer quality services.

Decision support refers to strategies through which clinically relevant information is exchanged between clinicians and/or case managers. These strategies are intended to facilitate consistent, high quality decision making on matters such as level-of-care, duration of treatment, and discharge placement. Decision support technologies are designed to monitor clinicians' decision-making rather than to distance them from the treatment process. The most common decision support tools involve hospital admission criteria. If a patient does not meet the specified criteria, the case manager (or clinician) may need to justify why this particular case warrants an exemption.

Utilization review is conceptually similar to decision support but is accomplished through concurrent or retroactive review between a provider and a third party. In utilization review strategies, utilization decisions are monitored for clinical appropriateness and medical necessity. These reviews are returned to providers and/or case managers so that adjustments in practice can be made based on experience informed by data. Frequently, rather than reviewing all cases, some selection process is used to identify specific cases for review. The most common strategy is a random selection process to ensure a representative sample of cases. However, a combined decision-support-utilization review strategy that triggers review when a "deviant" decision is made can also be used as a targeted sampling procedure.

Quality indicators refer to the characteristics, such as process and outcome information, considered when evaluating the quality of care provided. Rather than directly measuring quality, these indicators provide information that may lead administrators to engage in a more detailed study of a specific aspect of service delivery. For example, the distribution of days between initial contact and first appointment at an outpatient clinic might be an indicator. Longer waits might point to insufficient staff, more referrals, or a particularly difficult client mix.

Finally, **continuous quality improvement (CQI)** refers to both an organizational philosophy and a technology of identifying, studying, and refining service delivery processes. This is accomplished through focused, short-term studies of specific, limited aspects of the service delivery system. The results of these time-limited studies inform administrators of the need for new programming or for changes in existing program policies. The literature on CQI identifies numerous strategies to enhance quality through targeted investigations of structures, processes, and outcomes. Frequently these strategies combine components of the techniques described above so that CQI becomes an overarching philosophy of service management and development.

MEASUREMENT IN MANAGED MENTAL HEALTH CARE

The common denominator in each of these five strategies of integrating clinical information into the administration of service delivery is the need for appropriate measurement. The utility of measures for these purposes should be evaluated on the following dimensions: clinical relevance, reliability, ease-of-use, and generalizability.

In order to be **clinically relevant**, measures must assess constructs that are important to the clinical aspects of mental health service delivery. Any measure used to facilitate or evaluate level-of-care decisions must include a reliable and valid measure of this construct. For example, a measure of "ego strength" may be a valid measure of the construct of ego strength but is not relevant to level-of-care decisions or outcomes. Suicide potential, on the other hand, is important to clinical decisions regarding level of care.

Reliability refers to the ability of multiple individuals to use the same measure similarly. For example, clinicians and case managers must be able to use the measure equivalently. Likewise, patients must be able to understand and complete the measure reliably.

Ease-of-use refers to both the time it takes to complete the measure and the degree of difficulty in understanding the directions or definitions. Few resources are available to maintain the quality and integrity of data collection, thus extensive training in the use of measures is usually not pragmatic. The longer and more cumbersome the measure, the less likely people will complete it fully and reliably. Similarly, if a form is ambiguous, it may be incorrectly or partially completed.

Generalizability refers to the extent to which the information collected can be widely understood and applied to a variety of treatment settings. If a managed care program wishes to apply standard clinical criteria across providers and/or settings, it is necessary that these criteria generalize appropriately—that is, that they remain valid and applicable regardless of setting.

DECISION SUPPORT FOR ACUTE PSYCHIATRIC SERVICES

Decision support technology provides a means for systematically managing the cost, quality, and utilization of mental health services. Moreover, decision support tools facilitate communication between providers and managed care organizations. Their development and use are predicated on an understanding that the delivery of mental health care be overseen by professionals and guided by sound clinical judgement. Decision support tools measuring the severity of illness for psychiatric inpatients will be discussed below.

The Psychiatric Severity of Illness (PSI) rating, as described by Horn, Chambers, and Sharkey (1989), predicts between one-third and one-half of the variation in length of stay (LOS) within specific diagnosis-related groups (DRGs). However, one of the dimensions of the PSI assesses the "rate of response to therapy," which, by definition, is related to the need for continued resource use. "Resolution of acute symptoms" is also difficult to rate independent of the course of the hospital stay. The PSI, although developed rationally, was not based on clinical features associated with decisions to admit.

Another example of a measure of severity of illness is the Computerized Psychiatric Severity Index (CPSI), as reported by Stoskopf and Horn (1992). The CPSI, when combined with twenty-two other patient variables, predicted 27.5 percent of the variance of LOS on a sample of 243 patients with affective disorders, and 70.3 percent of the variance of LOS on a sample of sixty-one patients with schizophrenia.   The ratio of variables to patients in this study makes the variance estimates difficult to interpret. Glazer, Kramer, Montgomery, and Myers (1991) reported the development of a "medical necessity" scale, but they did not report any associations of this measure to utilization of inpatient services.

In order to predict length of psychiatric hospital stay, a twelve-item measure, the Severity of Psychiatric Illness rating scale, was developed. The scale was based on research modeling the decision to admit to a psychiatric facility, and on prior research on the course of inpatient treatment (Essock-Vitale, 1987; Friedman, 1983; Marson, 1990). The research on psychiatric decision making in the emergency room suggests that the variables influencing the decision to admit need to be considered both independently and in relation to one another (Marson et al., 1988). In an attempt to gain a more complete clinical understanding of the nature of inpatient care, the potential complications of the case and the severity and persistence of the disorder must be considered in addition to the reasons for admission. To the extent that resource use is clinically justified, then prediction of length of stay should be based on these variables. One approach to understanding the dimensions of psychiatric illness relevant to either the decision to admit or to the course of treatment is through a chart review or concurrent decision support system.

In order to address the needs of our managed care program, we have developed a measurement strategy for providing clinically relevant information regarding the use and outcomes of acute psychiatric services. It is based on several well-founded assumptions regarding the nature of mental health service delivery. The system, called PSYMON, has evolved into one that can be used for outcomes management, decision support, utilization review, quality indicators, and continuous quality improvement.

PSYMON consists of two primary components, the Severity of Psychiatric Illness (SPI) and the Acuity of Psychiatric Illness (API). There are essentially three critical dimensions relevant to the measurement of acute psychiatric services: level-of-care decision, duration-of-service decision, and outcome. The SPI is a case-mix measure that models level-of-care decisions and provides a risk-adjusted estimate for the duration of acute treatment. The API is an immediate and sensitive measure of short-term outcome of acute psychiatric services. The SPI and API are reliable and easy to use, and the resulting data can be generalized across sites.

Severity of Psychiatric Illness

There is evidence that emergency psychiatry decision-making can be predicted reliably using multivariate prediction models (e.g., Marson, 1990). Several decision support tools reliably modeling this process have been developed (Gray & Glazer, 1994). The first of these was developed by Warner (1961) and modified by Whittington (1966). These were designed to be retrospective utilization review tools. However, since psychiatric emergency decision making can be reliably modeled using empirical data, it is possible to support decision-making as it occurs (decision support) or evaluate the appropriateness of decisions retrospectively (utilization review).

The SPI is an empirical strategy designed to support utilization management. It is founded on the clinical decision logic for inpatient psychiatric treatment. This decision logic is guided by the identification of the clinical dimensions that influence the need for inpatient services. The three primary justifications for inpatient stays include danger to self, danger to others, and severe problems with self-care; however, in practice, a number of other complicating factors have been shown to affect the need for and continuation of acute psychiatric services. Factors such as participation in outpatient treatment, medical and social complications, severity of symptoms, and premorbid levels of adjustment have each demonstrated a relationship with the decision to admit. The SPI was developed from the existing mental health services research literature and from focus group discussion with acute care providers.

For each of twelve dimensions, carefully anchored scales were developed and tested. The SPI can be reliably rated prospectively by a clinician based on contact with the patient, a case manager based on discussion with the clinician, or retrospectively using chart review. The reliability of the items of the SPI range from .92 to .85 using weighted kappa. The average reliability of the SPI has been estimated to be about .88.

With a simple and reliable set of criteria that are clinically relevant to level of care decisions, it is possible to accurately predict the majority of decisions to admit. However, for the purposes of decision-support, the "misses" provide the most interesting information. One use of this technology has been to routinize the obviously defensible admission decisions and require greater surveillance when a decision is requested that is inconsistent with the prediction model. This strategy can save time and money and improve clinician and patient satisfaction.

For purposes of utilization review, the patients who are admitted despite low probabilities in the model represent potentially inappropriate admissions. On the other hand, the "deflections," patients who are not admitted despite high probabilities in the model, are of interest to programs attempting to reduce inpatient utilization while maintaining patient safety. The SPI provides the potential for empirically defining hospital deflection. It has been used successfully to model level-of-care decisions and duration of acute care services across multiple hospitals, partial hospitals, and emergency departments and within a managed care environment.

Acuity of Psychiatric Illness (API)

It is important for risk adjustment and decision support goals to measure case-mix characteristics of patients seeking acute psychiatric services; however, this information is insufficient to evaluate the outcome of these services. Thus, the SPI can reliably model level-of-care decisions and resource use in acute care settings, but it does not measure the degree of clinical change experienced by the patients during service delivery.

Acute psychiatric services are conceptually quite distinct in their emphasis from other mental health services such as outpatient psychotherapy. The goals of acute services are immediate and consistent with the reasons acute care is required. The API, therefore, is designed to allow for the measurement of these goals.

The API is divided into two domains: clinical status and nursing status. Like the SPI, it is based upon carefully anchored ratings. Changes in clinical and nursing status can be assessed by using this rating scale at several points across the patient's stay.

Two outcome indices were developed for both the clinical and the nursing dimensions. The first is referred to as **benefit**. The clinical benefit is the measure of the standardized change in the sum of the clinical status measures from admission to discharge. The standard score used is the T score, which has a defined mean of 50 with a standard deviation of 10. A clinical benefit of 10 or more represents an improvement of at least one standard deviation, which in clinical trials research has often been used as a definition of a "clinical responder." The same strategy is applied to the patients' change in nursing status. Benefit scores can be used for individual patients, aggregated by program or clinician, or averaged by case manager.

The second outcome index developed for the API is referred to as **value**. Value includes consideration of both the benefit and the cost. For psychiatric inpatient services, value is defined as the ratio of benefit to length of stay. This ratio translates into a clinical or nursing change per day. As with the benefit outcome score, the value score can be calculated across hospitals, clinicians, or case managers or used on a per-patient basis.

Theoretically, when determining value, it is important to demonstrate a dose-response relationship between a service and its outcome. Dose response is a quasi-experimental marker of efficacy. If a service is effective, then more service should be more effective than less service. Failure to find a correlation between the amount of service and amount of clinical change (i.e., dose response relationship) suggests that either the service does not work or the outcome measure is not appropriate. Outcome research has often failed to find a dose-response relationship for acute psychiatric services using standard psychiatric symptom assessments. Some have claimed that this indicates that inpatient services are not effective. Consistent dose-response relationships have been demonstrated across hospitals using the API, suggesting that prior research has been using inappropriate measures of outcome.

Examples of Uses

PSYMON has been used in a variety of different ways to address issues of decision support and outcomes management. In the Northwestern Managed Mental Health Program, the SPI serves to predict probability of admission and is used to identify potentially inappropriate admissions for utilization review. In a recent panel of 106 admissions, five cases of predicted probabilities of admission of below .50 were identified. Four of these cases proved to be inappropriate hospital admission on review; the fifth was a mistaken use of the rating system.

In an evaluation of brief (forty-eight - hour) admission cases, the SPI and API were used to study not only the admission but the outcome of the cases. Results revealed that while brief admission patients were less acutely ill at admission, they did benefit from their short stays in terms of reduced acuity. Patients high on Suicide Potential were most likely to be among the short-stay group. Interestingly, much of the symptom improvement occurred from the time of treatment in the emergency room to the first twenty-four hours of the admission. Two SPI dimensions, Residential Instability and Family Disruption, predicted significant change from the emergency room to the first day. Thus, patients hospitalized from unstable environments experienced rapid symptom remission. These findings suggest that an environmental intervention might allow the deflection from the hospital of these rapid remitters.

SUMMARY

In keeping with the original goals of managed care, finding an optimal balance between cost containment, quality of care, and utilization of services is essential. Outcomes management, decision support, utilization review, quality indicators, and continuous quality improvement reflect the hallmarks of the next generation of managed mental healthcare. Through the identification of inefficient, inappropriate, and ineffective services, these strategies provide a systematic way of managing mental healthcare. By integrating clinical information into the financing, administration, and delivery of mental health services, cost and quality of care can be effectively addressed and negotiated. What will evolve are outcomes-based practice patterns indicative of a comprehensive and accountable system of care that responds to the interests of providers, payors, and patients.

Education Issues

12

Implications of the Contradictions in Behaviorism for a Scientifically Based Public Policy

E. Rae Harcum

This chapter asserts that successful public policy must be based on a useful conception of the nature of human beings, beginning with the assumption that they are free to choose for themselves a system of governance and to select political leaders who will execute that system with justice and judgment. This thesis assumes that the experts in behavioral science will provide the coherent scientific underpinning for a technology of social change that will guide the political and educational leaders in planning and instituting the necessary prosocial practices.

Unfortunately, the experts in behavioral science have not as yet met the challenge of providing this fundamental orientation to setting public policy. When policy planners look to psychology for the crucial answers, they are frustrated by mixed signals about the most fundamental of issues, the one involving free will—if it exists, or if all behaviors are simply determined by the interaction of inherited structure and experiential factors, many of them accidental. In fact, this issue divides psychologists themselves into two—so far—irreconcilable groups. The critical detail is whether the term *voluntary* is merely a convenient way to refer to the effects of a history of reinforcements, as the behaviorists claim, or to an independent act of free will that can transcend the reinforcement history, as the humanists claim.

The behaviorists propose that some gifted leaders rise within society and simply select by scientific means the appropriate goals for everyone and shape behaviors toward those goals through contingent rewards. The opposing, humanistic view concedes the important role of contingent rewards in improving society but holds also that human beings have some freedom of a will that can, at times, overcome the exigencies of heredity and contingent rewards and respond on the basis of perceived personal agendas, including caring and cooperation. The purpose of the present chapter is to discredit the behavioristic approach by discussing some contradictions within the view itself and by pointing out certain common practices of behaviorists that conflict with their own professed orientation.

The controversy within behavioral science over this issue has undoubtedly contributed to the public's confusion over the role of free will in public policy (Harcum, 1994), as illustrated by the following letter to the editor of a newspaper concerning the violent behavior of a teenager:

I don't blame [name]; everyone of us are [sic] to blame for his actions. We didn't offer the proper training he needs. It would be to his benefit now for us to back off and let him stand on his own feet and accept responsibility for his own actions.

The name and reference have been omitted because they are not relevant. I agree that each of us must take ultimate responsibility for our choices of behaviors, even though our neighbors did not help us make the right decisions. But note that the author shifts abruptly from "It's our fault" to "You must stand on your own two feet without any help from us," from strict determinism to libertarianism with no acknowledgment of a middle ground. This is the legacy of behaviorism because it recognizes no middle ground, the middle ground represented by the humanistic view.

Because the opposing views of behaviorists and humanists are metaphysical in nature, their truth or falsity cannot be decided by direct empirical evidence. Only one of them can be the consistent basis for human guidance, however, because in the present practical context they are mutually exclusive. The choice about which one to follow must be based on their relative utility in solving given social problems (Harcum, 1990).

Baum (1994), presenting an authentic behaviorist view—by all indications—argued that the behaviorists diametrically oppose the humanists' contention that democracy and morality are dependent upon a belief in free will. In contrast, he argued that actually the behavioristic approach to social problems will foster these important social behaviors. Because this argument entails an empirical issue, not a metaphysical one, it should therefore be amenable to solution by scientific methods. This chapter exposes the inherent scientific and practical weaknesses of the behavioristic view in psychology, ones that lead to inherent contradictions, and suggests that the humanistic view offers greater practical value for the framers of public policy.

I see the following contradictions in the behavioristic position:

- Their attempts to apply the behavioristic version of scientific thinking to practical problems, as in behavior therapy, often require the assumption of human choice as an unacknowledged importation (Harcum, 1989).
- They make gratuitous claims to account for all kinds of behaviors in terms

of a very few causal mechanisms.
- They advocate the use of science but insist on their own restrictive definition of its nature and scope.
- They promulgate straw-man arguments against the humanist view, in defiance of good science.
- They fail to acknowledge their leadership roles as scientists in promulgating their personal goals for society.

The implications for public policy of these contradictions will be discussed, as well as the advantages of the humanistic view.

IMPORTATIONS

The behaviorists emphasize the role of learning theory in behavior therapy without considering the client's necessary prior commitment and assumption of responsibility to the therapeutic process (Harcum, 1989). This point is critical if the solution to our social problems is psychotherapeutic, rather than simple behavior modification (Harcum, 1994).

PRESCRIPTIVE SCIENCE

Behaviorists advocate the use of science in establishing public policy but promulgate an unacceptable, traditional definition of science. LeShan (1990) maintained, therefore, that because of the behavioristic influence, psychology has divorced itself from the truly human aspects of persons, concentrating instead on their ratlike and machinelike features. Consequently, psychologists can solve only the problems of laboratory behavior in rats and pigeons: "If, however, the problems were of the nature of how to stop killing each other, how to stop poisoning our planet, or how to stop our steadily increasing population growth, one had better turn elsewhere" (p. 150).

LeShan (1990) summarized the effect of this conception of science on the practical application of psychology: "Psychology has so thoroughly sold its birthright, has so completely abandoned any real contact with human existence, that it is widely believed in our society that it would be useless to look to it for help in a time of overwhelming peril" (p. 157). Harman (1988) argued similarly that the successful methods of the physical sciences are limited for seeking answers to important psychological questions: "But to learn more about human consciousness, it is necessary to look not in the physics laboratory, but in the deeper recesses of the human mind" (p. 18).

Behaviorists assert that human values have no place in science. But as Prilleltensky (1989) argued, scientific decisions do involve values—for example, in the choice of the problems to be studied. The effect of these unrecognized value judgments may be the prevention of valuable social changes. According to Harman (1988), the behavioristic approach does not deal adequately with such problems as purpose, meaning in social groupings, creativity, and the concept of self because of its insistence on objectivism, determinism, and reductionism. The behaviorists think that some theoretical gremlin, composed of mysterious mechanisms, can account for the creative choices better than the postulation of a theoretical ghost, a nonmaterial spirit (Harcum, 1991, 1994).

Science itself advises us that the relative validity of these conceptions of creativity must be empirically tested in terms of their scientific and practical utility. We should not be intimidated by the behaviorists' claim to scientific rigor, on the assumption that formal rigor is always better than personal intuition and judgment. Harman (1988) pointed out that we have been "culturally hypnotized" (p. 14) to view the world as described by the traditional physical sciences, to reject the spiritual level of interpretation. We must reprogram (reeducate) ourselves to understand that science itself is a human enterprise and thus is subject to human interpretation and error.

STRAW-MAN TACTICS

Any definition of science requires the scientist to stay rigorously and scrupulously within the available facts. Nevertheless, behaviorists have consistently promulgated false conceptions about humanists despite clear statements of the humanistic view. For example, Baum (1994) began his book with the false statement—actually the cornerstone of his book—that the only real controversy over behaviorism stems from its basic argument that there can be a science of behavior. He maintained that a behavioral science is possible only if it excludes a belief in some unnatural hidden agent—a free will—as a possible cause of behavior:

The term *free will* names the supposed ability of a person to choose behavior freely, without regard to inheritance or environment. Determinism asserts that free will is an illusion based on ignorance of the factors determining behavior. Since soft determinism and compatibilist theories of free will affirm the idea that free will is only an illusion, they present no challenge to a science of behavior. Only *libertarian free will*, the idea that people really have the ability to behave as they choose (espoused by Judaism and Christianity), conflicts with determinism. (p. 15)

First, the soft deterministic view does not reduce to determinism. To support his false argument, Baum actually used the nonscientific ploy of asserting that a self-professed determinist like Donald Hebb was a soft determinist. Then, concluding that Hebb's view is actually deterministic, he asserted that the soft deterministic view is actually deterministic. Such a tactic is not science by anyone's definition.

Second, Baum's assertion that free will assumes that behavior can be chosen "without regard to inheritance or environment" is, at least, misleading because the humanistic psychologists do not deny influences of heredity and environment. In a formal statement of the humanist view, C.R. Rogers (in Rogers & Skinner, 1956) agreed with Skinner about the value of science in predicting and controlling behavior, but Rogers proposed a broader view of behavioral science: "Behavior, when it is examined scientifically, is surely best understood as determined by prior causation. This is one great fact of science. But responsible personal choice, which is the most essential element in being a person, which is the core experience in psychotherapy, which exists prior to any scientific endeavor, is an equally prominent fact of our lives. To deny the experience of responsible choice is, to me, as restricted a view as to deny the possibility of a behavioral science" (p. 1064). Rogers' view is consistent with other statements of the humanistic view by Shoben (1965), Pollio (1981), and others. Baum (1994) extended his straw-man argument into the arena of social applications:

Apart from philosophical and aesthetic considerations, the results of public policies based on an assumption of free will usually range from poor to disastrous. The assumption is often used as a justification for doing nothing. If cocaine addicts are free to choose not to take the drug, then it seems that addiction is the addicts' fault, that they should just "pull themselves together," and that no help need be given.

It seems that we are slowly learning that wise policies cannot assume free will. It is useless and self-serving to say that people growing up in urban slums choose to be ignorant and unemployed. (p. 152)

Several authors to be quoted later in this chapter would strongly disagree with his low evaluation of public policies based on the assumption of free will. To criticize the assumption of free will as an excuse for inaction is as fair as criticizing behaviorists because some people make bribes, thus using reward contingencies to foster harmful behaviors. To argue that the natural implication of the humanistic view is that drug addicts do not need help is clearly not accurate scientific reporting. This is equivalent to saying that humanists do not advocate psychotherapy—a ridiculous notion. It is equally irresponsible to imply that humanists assume that all slum dwellers choose to be uneducated and unemployed.

In summary, no psychologist, by the very definition of the field, would deny that heredity and environment have an influence on behavior. If all human behavior were produced by an act of a literally free will—unrestrained and uninfluenced by any observable environmental factors—there would indeed be no basis for understanding, predicting, or controlling human behavior, as must be obvious to everyone. There would be no principles of behavior for guidance because the action of a literally free will would be, by nature, incomprehensible and uncontrollable. Therefore, contrary to Baum's (1994) assertion, humanistic psychology holds merely that there are limits to scientific understanding.

CLOSET LEADERS

A major criticism of behavioristic theory, going back at least as far as Boring (1957), is that no one is outside of society and therefore those who would attempt to foster change in that society must somehow draw apart from the mainstream to redirect the thinking and practices of the rest, to move society in the direction they deem best. That is what it means to be a leader, and it implies that the leaders value some things differently from their constituents. How can this be possible in a deterministic world with common species inheritances and common human experience?

The behaviorists deny that they make value judgments. They maintain that they themselves are merely guided by the empirical evidence they have produced through their rigorous research. The very technology produces the best goals for human behavior, they say, because the technology shows what works best. In Baum's (1994) words: "Behavior analysts argue that as long as we go on assuming free will, we will fail to solve our social problems. If, however, we move forward in a frankly behavioral framework and try to change problematic behavior, then our focus will shift to questions about which methods to use" (p. 152).

This argument is irrelevant to humanism, appropriate only to the straw-man libertarian view. In fact, this argument cuts both ways: The behaviorists' insistence on determinism prevents them from asking some important questions about how to change behaviors. In contrast, the humanists are free to ask all the questions about the causation of behaviors.

Because the technology of the behaviorists itself is firmly based on the assumption of determinism and a belief in rigorous empirical research, as Baum (1994) asserts, behaviorism really represents an approach rather than a theory. Clearly, the behaviorists strongly advocate that approach, even in the face of substantial social and professional opposition. Therefore, the behaviorists themselves have arbitrarily selected the first goal to be achieved in a better society: The abolition of the belief in free will by the members of society. The behaviorists have not selected this goal on the basis of empirical evidence, I submit, but on the personal conviction—literally a value judgment—that such an approach to behavioral science is a useful, even necessary, goal for our society.

The behaviorists do not view this conviction as a value judgment, or even as a metaphysical assumption, but as a fact of nature. Therefore, they do not see themselves as leaders promulgating their particular point of view. They are both closet positivists and closet leaders because they believe they are merely stating the truth about the universe, without an influence of personal disposition. For example, although Baum (1994) asserts that the issue of free will versus determinism cannot be resolved by empirical evidence, but by the relative utility of each in solving social problems, he nevertheless advances the following argument for determinism: "You never choose freely to breathe, walk, or even learn to talk. These were constrained by your genes and environment. Were it possible to be free from such constraints, then we would have free will" (p. 152). This is another instance of the behaviorists' tendency to confuse doctrine with data. We can stop breathing for a time by choice, even though breathing is normally controlled by our inherited physical structure. To claim that walking and talking are acquired exclusively by the interaction of genes and environment is entirely gratuitous, presumably based on the behaviorists' view that they have superseded metaphysics by their version of science. In any case, the relevant issue is whether or not a physically capable person can choose voluntarily to walk or to talk at a given time.

This behavioristic contradiction is further reflected in the behaviorists' choice of potential variables for research. They refuse even to study the social consequences of beliefs in freedom of will on the asserted grounds that the beliefs are false. This appears very close to the value judgments they disclaim and the positivistic view of science that they generally reject.

EXTRAVAGANT CLAIMS

Behaviorists claim that contingent rewards will explain any behavioral phenomenon, but they fail to back up their claim with viable explanations for many social problems of relevance to public policy. Claims to unmask the causation of behavior in terms of contingent rewards have been successful only for simple behaviors in which the causal factors are relatively contiguous to the behaviors (Harcum, 1990, 1994). Therefore, their claims that complex social behaviors can be explained in terms of inheritances and reward-contingencies have been based on metaphysical supposition rather than on appropriate scientific evidence. Skinner himself was pessimistic about his ability to use behavioristic analyses as a basis for specific advice to the federal government on policy: "Personally, I don't try to advise anyone, in Washington or elsewhere, about specific problems. Too many variables are involved....Before I could answer any question about a practical political situation, I should have to spend a few years finding out what is going on, and probably then wouldn't know enough to apply principles of behavior directly to that situation" (Evans, 1968, 108-109).

A specific example of behavioristic failure to deal with complex human problems comes from the phenomenon of social loafing (Harcum, 1994), inferiority of performance when a task is performed in the perceived presence of one or more other individuals, compared to when it is performed alone. Because workers perform in groups, this phenomenon is an important problem for public policy.

Social loafing is controlled by many variables, such as identifiability of each worker's performance, personal characteristics of the workers, and the perceived role and function of the others who are present. No single variable seems to be crucial, and that includes reward contingencies. In fact, the most important variables concern the personal cognitive appraisal of the task by the worker. Therefore, the behavioristic approach speaks only to a small fragment of the data. The meaning of the reward with respect to appropriateness and equity with respect to the rewards given to other members of the group and the accepted social standards are far more important. Thus, a worker responds voluntarily as he or she understands the situation—an idea foreign to the behaviorists. The common sense approach of the humanists argues that the lack of identifiability of performance in a group produces an immunity from personal evaluation and responsibility. Therefore, group leadership based entirely on reward contingencies will not be effective in the long run.

DISCUSSION

If I am correct about what ails public policy today, there is no possibility for a quick fix. The immediate problem is that the standards against which the policies are established and judged have drifted downward from the high ideals on which this nation was founded. Today, the public policy decisions are not grounded on prosocial principles of morality but on selfish ones, resulting in what I call "pork policy," the policy of making decisions based on the satisfaction of personal needs rather than on the welfare of the group. Such thinking is a natural consequence of the amoral deterministic presumptions of the behaviorists.

I advocate a return to the guiding principles of a democratic government by those who are responsible for the drafting of public policy. These persons are not just the officials who are charged with voting for specific policies but also the voting public, who keep those officials in office. As the cartoon character Pogo said, "We have met the enemy, and he is us." It is up to us, the citizens, to change the bases for decisions on our own, without some benign Big Brother to change them for us. No outside agency will wave a magic wand, or a big stick, and make us into selfless persons. The behaviorists will not even try to change our dispositions, because they want to produce selfless behaviors from selfish people.

The self-remaking process must be re-educational and psychotherapeutic, and therefore it will be slow. The process will also be painful because we will be fighting ourselves, our own selfish desires. For example, we will have to vote for the legislative candidates who will assure that the pork is evenly distributed among all the peoples, not just among their personal constituents. We must change our bases for determining the reward contingencies; we must convince officeholders that selective distribution of the pork (i.e., manipulation of reward contingencies toward the goal of re-election) will not guarantee continuance in office because they will know that their constituents do not think like rats or alligators.

What about empirical evidence for the relative values of the two opposing approaches to the design of a better society? Rigorous research is essentially impossible because of problems with controlling all of the relevant variables. For example, as in psychotherapy, the major variables may reside in the personality of the guide rather than in the details of the remedial program (Ryan & Gizynski, 1971). In any case, no one doubts that reward contingencies are often important in specific and short-term contexts.

The best empirical evidence for the long-term efficacy of the voluntaristic view comes from social observers who have done behavioral analyses of a different sort, evaluating the social programs that seem to be working in the most difficult arenas and calling for the actions suggested by such programs. For example, Jackson (1990) emphasized the need for grassroots mobilization of human concerns for the common good:

Global security requires empowerment. The Earth will not be saved by powerful savants issuing edicts from afar. The environment will not be saved by corporations whose mandate is to maximize profit, nor by bureaucracies whose mandate is to manage people. The new enlightenment requires that people be empowered to change the way institutions act. Only popular mobilization can create the political force necessary for the transformation — of the laws that determine how corporations produce, the priorities that governments will pursue, the practices that people adopt. (pp. xii-xiii)

The present view is that the people must empower themselves.

In a similar vein, Raspberry (1994) argued that our problems with violence against people must be solved by fundamental and long-term methods. For example, he doubted that any likely gun control legislation would help to curb violence from guns because the basic problem is not in the availability of firearms or the efficiency of law enforcement. He said that the problem is with people:

It is simply another manifestation of a problem I have described as the "consciencelessness" of a small but significant element among us: children who have reached adolescence and beyond without having internalized any important sense of right and wrong, who have no internal brakes on their behavior, who can maim, destroy and kill without remorse.

These are the young people for whom automatic weapons fire seems a reasonable response to being cheated, cut off in traffic, or even "dissed," and who place scant value even on their own lives, let alone yours.

Worse: As the influence of these conscienceless ones increases — in schoolyards and on the streets —youngsters who were brought up as moral and responsible beings find themselves forced to choose between an utterly emasculating wimpishness and readiness to engage in retaliatory (or even preemptive) violence. (p. A12)

We must get started on making the changes now. Erickson (1990) advocated immediate action against the "fossilized institutions which suppress creativity, generosity and the human will" (p. 6): "It is easy for decision makers to pay lip service to justice and democracy while catering to an elite minority who prosper via *in*justice. For the victim, it is easy to complain about unjust conditions without changing them. It is more difficult for a determined group of people to identify and confront the root of injustice, demand an end to it, and if need be, directly intervene to prevent its continuation. But so far, that is the only approach that works" (p. 1).

The critical question is, of course, how specifically do we go about inaugurating such a drastic fundamental change in the attitudes of individual constituents. Clearly, we must start at a very basic level to make changes in the psychological science that must take the lead in the transformation. Ideally, public policy should rest on the assumptions the authors of such policy make about the nature of human beings. This would surely be the case if the framers of policy were motivated to provide the best policies for all their constituents. The main point is that the morality of policy decisions today is characterized by the reptilian mode of thinking that is displayed by the youngest and least-experienced members of our species: "I want mine and I want it now!" This attitude may have immediate survival value for an individual, but not for the society.

The survival of our society requires mutual caring and sharing that can come only from the humanistic concepts of value, voluntary choice, and personal responsibility. Raspberry (1992) quoted Robert L. Woodson, Sr., founder and president of the National Center for Neighborhood Enterprise in Washington, D.C., as saying that the successful social programs in the inner cities almost always have a spiritual element in them. By spiritual element he does not necessarily mean a religious element, but an emotional commitment and unconditional caring - something that puts meaning or significance into life. These spiritual values are the very elements the behaviorists hope and work to discard.

Beck (1994) asserted that we must strengthen and increase the funding for those service agencies that try to fill the void in the nurturance of children produced by the breakdown of our families, but the place to look for true solutions to violence among our children is in our own social attitudes:

We need to look at ourselves and what each of us can each do to help reduce the level of violence--even if it means supporting strong gun control measures and boycotting violence as entertainment in TV, the movies and rap music.

And we must try to strengthen and expand the positive influences in our society, particularly the churches, whose moral values are the necessary foundation of our society, whether or not they are so acknowledged. (p. A8)

Raspberry (1994) offers the same solution: "And we can do what is necessary to reduce at the source the supply of conscienceless youngsters - by enlisting church and community in a crusade for their academic, economic and spiritual redemption" (p. A12). He understands the implications of his proposal in terms of its timeframe and indefinite nature: "It sounds hopelessly long-term, somewhat vague and a little sappy, even to me. But I think it's the truth. Our communities won't be safe *from* our children until we first make them safe, decent and nurturing places *for* our children" (p. A12).

To be honest, given the present state of our society, any viable proposal may, in fact, seem a bit sappy because the task is indeed so formidable. But behavioral science can find the answers. It cannot be successful in solving these problems, however, if it is distracted and confused by behavioristic contradictions at the outset.

AUTHOR NOTE

The author thanks Peter L. Derks and Harvey Langholtz for helpful comments on this chapter, but remains fully responsible for the content.

———————— ♦ ————————

13

Morality, Values, and Education: Psychology's Role

Daniel J. Rybicki

*The fear of the Lord is the beginning of knowledge, but
fools despise wisdom and discipline.*
Proverbs 1:7

The battle lines have been drawn, and the conflict has begun. Only a small warning shot was fired in spring 1992 when Dan Quayle challenged television's *Murphy Brown* and raised the vanguard of Family Values. After years of steady decline and challenge to the moral underpinnings of this great nation, a mounting groundswell of indignation has begun to reclaim our government, our schools, and our communities. For the past two years the issue of family values has remained a steady topic of conversation and has begun to attract increasing attention, from friend and foe alike, with the issue winning even bipartisan support in recent months in the centers of government. But the issue is not merely one of legislation, although this is certainly a key element in the problem and in efforts at solution. The crisis lies in our very communities and homes, with public and private education playing a central role in both the problem and the prospect for recovery and solutions.

This chapter is intended to address briefly the role of psychology in dealing with issues of morals and values in education. This is a very broad topic and can span over several disciplines and over many issues of importance. This topic cannot readily be raised without bringing some potential offense to some readers. Due to the space restrictions on this chapter, it may not be possible here to fully develop all the issues or defend them in advance. While concepts outlined here may easily be misconstrued in this fashion and seen as prejudicial or discriminatory, this is not the author's intent.

In this era of "thought police" and "political correctness," compounded by intensely solicitous attitudes toward "diversity," it is only natural that any discussion of values and morals will raise the rancor of some. The cherished position of many radicals and intellectuals will be challenged as we examine the role that psychology has played in contributing to the moral crisis in America through its role in education. The timing is critical for this review to open the floor to a lively and candid debate over the future course of education in America. While space limitations restrict the depth of analysis presented here, the central themes will be outlined along with suggestions for policy and programmatic actions to implement a new and more favorable role for psychology in the arena of morals and values development. The reader is directed to many excellent works cited in the reference section for more lengthy studies in the area.

THE CRISIS IN EDUCATION AND PSYCHOLOGY'S ROLE

It has been said that those who do not know history are destined to repeat it, an axiom true today for the crisis in education. Through the cultural revolution of the 1960s to the present psychology has offered theories and concepts that have made their way into the very heart of education. Some of these concepts have been helpful in raising awareness of many social ills, but they have done so in a manner that has contributed to moral anarchy and a social nilism unrivaled throughout the world. An examination of this crisis requires a brief review of the current status of the problem in education, along with analysis of the role that psychology has played in the genesis of these concerns.

In 1983 the National Commission on Excellence in Education reported that poor performance in school was a significant problem putting our nation at risk. A steady decline on achievement test scores and a decline in student knowledge of such core subjects as English and history and geography were indications of the depths to which the performance had dropped. "The educational foundations of our society are presently being eroded by a rising tide of mediocrity that threatens our very future as a nation and a people....We have in effect been committing an act of unthinkable, unilateral educational disarmament" (*A Nation at Risk*, 1983).

A comparison of math and science skills revealed that Americans scored at the bottom while South Korean students scored at the top, performing four times the rate of U.S. students. At the same time some 68 percent of the American students stated a belief that they were good at math compared with only 23 percent of the South Korean students making this same claim. Bennett (1994) states that this demonstrates that "this country is a lot better at teaching self-esteem than it is at teaching math" (p. 29). While the educational system has tried to move away from giving test scores and "judgmental feedback" that might injure the fragile youth's self-esteem, the real tragedy has been the abandonment of standards and criterion-based education. In effect, the educational system has sold out these youth, who will one day face the rude awakening in the marketplace that they are without education - and their illusion of self-worth will be shattered.

Schools that fail to teach reading, writing, and arithmetic corrupt the proper understanding of self esteem. Educators who say "don't grade them, don't label them. You have to make them feel good about themselves" cause the problems. It makes no sense for students to be full of self-esteem if they are empty of knowledge. Reality will soon puncture their illusions, and they will have to face two disturbing facts: (1) that they are ignorant, and (2) that the adults responsible for teaching them have failed them and lied to them. In the real world, praise has to be the reward for something worthwhile; praise must be connected to reality. (Vitz, 1994, 18)

In March 1994, a new program for education was put into law in the bill known as Goals 2000. Many sources have begun to react to this latest federal boondoggle with dismay. Former congressman Bob McEwen (R-Ohio) called this legislation "the most blatant grab for power in the history of Congress" (cf. Dobson, 1994). Journalist Cal Thomas referred to Goals 2000 as the "dumbing down of a generation" (cf. Dobson, 1994). Gary Bauer of the Family Research Council notes, "Once again the bureaucrats in Washington have chosen the road to bigger government, more spending, and less learning for our children" (cf. Dobson, 1994). In keeping with these critics, psychologist James Dobson has outlined several concerns that follow from the adoption of Goals 2000 legislation, including the shifting of controls away from parents and local communities to the federal government, the creation of a costly new bureaucracy, a loss of privacy, an expansion of questionable programs for behavioral education, and the adoption of a radical philosophy known as outcome-based education. Under this system "appreciating others," "communication," and "problem-solving" will apart from content mastery, be the targets of education.

These voices of concern are contrasted with the position adopted by the American Psychological Association (APA), a champion of liberal political causes in recent years. "Psychologists are key to school reforms. New laws rely on psychologists' expertise to revamp schools and provide opportunity for the profession." Excitement over the potential role of psychology in directing the course of education is central to the APA position. "Education is based on psychological principles. We have more information that teachers, policy makers, and the public need to know to improve education" (APA, 1994 39). Clearly psychology has a great deal to offer in the area of school reform, but the direction this takes may readily be swayed by a misguided liberal agenda. This has been the case in the past when psychology took to the schools to form values education and related programs to deal with sex education, drug abuse, and cultural diversity. Indeed, the political advocacy role taken by the APA in such endeavors has led to significant challenges to its role by various members, some of who have threatened to resign as a result (e.g., *APA Monitor* letters to the editor, July 1994).

The failure of our schools is partly due to an abandonment of the central purpose of education. History tells us that the Founding Fathers sought to have an educational system that stressed the importance of basic skills in writing and calculation, along with reading, history, and geography. Bennett (1994) outlines how we have moved from Thomas Jefferson's position that stressed how "education should aim at the improvement of one's morals and one's faculties" to a system of education that is morally bankrupt and lacking in substance, owing largely to an overimportance of values clarification, pseudo-therapy, and the bolstering of children's failing self-esteem. Unfortunately, instead of teaching substance and skills that can form the foundation of legitimate self-esteem and a sense of competency, this "enlightened" form of education has created an illusion of self-worth without substance, a sham. Moreover, the version of values clarification training instituted was one deficient in a system of core values, offering only moral relativism that essentially classified all values as inert, without a basis of right or wrong to draw upon. The result has been a generation raised with relativism that lacks a fundamental set of beliefs to guide and govern their lives.

Our government with its system of checks and balances and a representative democracy was founded on an electorate that was intended to manage freedoms with responsibility. An educated electorate was seen as the surest deterrent to tyranny. This combination of fundamental knowledge and fundamental values was readily acknowledged by Thomas Jefferson, Benjamin Franklin, and others. George Washington warned in his Farewell Address, "Of all the dispositions and habits which lead to political prosperity, religion and morality are indispensable supports." John Adams stated this idea more clearly: "Our Constitution was made only for a moral and religious people. It is wholly inadequate to the government of any other." Religion and moral values, part of the core of educational instruction, were the bedrock for freedoms in our community. Thus, the abandonment of core curriculum, standards of performance, and common moral values in favor of vague expectations, programs of sensitivity and awareness, and values clarification have done what no outside political force could do: They have undermined the very foundation of our social structure.

Something's happening in America. The way people think about their country is changing. And, it's not by accident, but by design. There is an agenda behind this culture war.. . .In the early part of the 20th Century, Italian Communist Antonio Gramsci theorized . . . that it would take a long march through the institutions - meaning the media, the universities, public interest groups, etc.—before socialism and relativism would be victorious. By capturing those institutions and using their power, cultural values would be changed, morals broken down, and the stage set for the political and economic power of the West to literally fall into the hands of the radical left. (Lindsey, 1994, 15)

Few can deny that this process has taken hold of our schools, our media, and our political institutions. The causal factors are very broad and go beyond the scope of this chapter, but among the problems has been the enforcement of restrictions on religious freedoms through the 1962 Supreme Court interpretation of the Constitution position on separation of church and state. In the wake of prohibitions on Judeo-Christian values and the substitution of the moral anarchy of values clarification, our children have been left without a system of judgment or morality, without a rudder in a sea of confusion. Psychology has contributed to this decay by its role in the values clarification curriculum and similar "sensitivity" or "diversity" programs.

By way of offering some proof of this indictment, it is helpful to trace the development of the two dominant methods of values training: values clarification and moral reasoning. Values clarification got its start in 1966 with the publication of *Values and Teaching* by educational psychologists, L. Raths, M. Harmin, and S. Simon. It reflected an outgrowth of the human potential movement, taking much of its methodology from Rogerian client-centered therapy. By 1972 this was a mainstream model of educating in many American schools (Simon, Howe, & Kirschenbaum, 1972). Kilpatrick (1992) notes that this approach teaches children that values are all relative, with no moral absolutes. A heavy emphasis on feelings is central to this approach, and "...the authors of *Values and Teaching* were so committed to therapeutic nonjudgmentalism that they felt obliged to note that 'some children will choose not to develop values. It is the teacher's responsibility to support this choice also' (p.81)."

Just as Roger's model served as the basis for Values Clarification, the work on moral reasoning by Kohlberg was the foundation of another strand of the decision-making approach to morals and values education. Like Simon, Kohlberg also rejected direct character education. He wanted to turn children into moral thinkers by posing various dilemmas. Unfortunately, this approach relied heavily on Socratic teaching methods which were beyond many who tried to employ this approach. "The danger in focusing on problematic dilemmas...is that a student may begin to think of all morality as similarly problematic...students will conclude that right and wrong are anybody's guess" (Vitz, 1994, 85). The Socratic model was never intended for youngsters lacking in formal operations. Plato maintained that it was to be reserved for men over the age of thirty, "One great precaution is to not let [students] taste of arguments while they are young," lest they develop a taste for arguments rather than for the truth. Even when Kohlberg tried to implement this strategy himself in a specially designed school, he had to recognize that it was an utter disaster.

Some years of active involvement with the practice of moral education at Cluster School has led me to realize that my notion...was mistaken...[and that] the educator must be a socializer teaching value content and behavior, and not only a Socratic or Rogerian process-facilitator of development.... I no longer hold these negative views of indoctrinative moral education and I believe that the concepts guiding moral education must be partly "indoctrinative." This is true, by necessity, in a world in which children engage in stealing, cheating, and aggression. (Kohlberg, 1978 in *The Humanist*, Kilpatrick, p. 92)

Ignoring such belated warnings, educators proceeded from their untested psychological theories and failures with reasoning and values clarification to institute programs for other social ills. School programs for sex education and drug prevention were implemented, seeking with good intentions to reduce such problems as AIDS, unplanned teenage pregnancies, and the rampant spread of drug use and sales in the schools. The data on these failures speak for themselves. As early as 1976 research results from a four-year study by Blum and his colleagues at Stanford demonstrated that the "affective" approach to drug education corresponded to use of alcohol, tobacco, and marijuana at an earlier age than controls. In 1978 and 1980; comparisons with other drug programs yielded the same results: Drug education programs in fact increased drug use. By 1988 the U.S. Department of Education recommended that drug education programs based on open-ended decision-making and values clarification or "therapeutic educational strategies" should be avoided in favor of curriculums that maintain adult authority in the classroom. This model has been more in keeping with the "D.A.R.E. (Drug Abuse Resistance Education) to keep kids off drugs" approach which has gained some more favorable overall results to date.

With regard to teenage pregnancy, the results are equally appalling. "Dr. Kasun of Humboldt State University found that...with several model programs and higher than average funding of family planning, teenage pregnancies had increased at a rate ten times the national average...the increase in teenage abortions was fifteen times the national average" (Kilpatrick, 1992, 55). Kilpatrick (1994) goes on to note how a breakdown of sexual restraints hurts education, associating this with increased school failures and dropouts. Some have gone so far as to suggest an end to coeducation as one means of stemming the tide of promiscuity (Riesman, 1991).

PSYCHOLOGICAL CONTRIBUTIONS TO FUTURE SOLUTIONS

Since the Goals 2000 educational reform is now a matter of law, and since psychology has been granted a chance to play a significant role as a result, it is possible to turn the tide of mediocrity and relativism with a return to sound teaching methods and use of cognitive and social developmental models that have an empirical base. This calls for a renewed commitment to basic intellectual values as a first requirement for all education. Commenting on this problem, Kilpatrick (1992) claims that we need to put character education at the top of the list of educational objectives, along with core curriculum in content areas. Teaching students self-discipline and respect for others is central to stemming the tide of youth crime and moral decay. Taking on difficult assignments, facing failures, and learning to preserve is central to helping equip our youth for the challenges that face them in modern society. Objectivity, respect for the truth, and humility in the face of facts are central to teaching the requisite critical-thinking strategies that must be given to a new generation of citizens.

In addition to placing a stronger emphasis on the basic values required for education and learning, the solution can call for instituting new programs of values education that move from the nondirect "clarification" mode to the more instructive mode that addresses shared common mores, as some of these values surely exist.

There are still those today who claim we are now too diverse a nation, that we consist of too many competing convictions and interests to instill common values. They are wrong. ...We have always been a diverse people. Madison wrote in *Federalist No. 10* the competing, balancing interests of a diverse people can help ensure the survival of liberty. But there are virtues that all American citizens share and that we should want American students to know and to make their own: honesty, fairness, self-discipline, fidelity to task, friends, family, personal responsibility, love of country, and belief in the principles of liberty, equality, and the freedom to practice one's faith. The explicit teaching of these values is the legacy of the common school, and it is legacy to which we must return. (Bennett, 1994, 46)

Methods to implement this suggestion include using the "teachable moment," where naturally occurring incidents are used to illustrate proper behavior and social relations. In some districts, specific values training curriculums have been instituted. For example, the North Clackamas School District in Oregon has developed a four-year cycle of training for patriotism, integrity, honesty, courtesy, respect for others, respect for property, and respect for authority. Compassion, self-esteem (based on achievement rather than mere repetition of *Barney*-style mantras), self-discipline, work ethic, and patience are among the other values taught in this program. The model begins with work on comprehension of the concepts over the first four years, followed by putting these concepts into greater practice over the next four years. Definitions of terms, discussion of concepts, and generation of examples are part of the training.

At the college level others have taken to teaching specific courses in the philosophy of virtue. Kilpatrick (1992) cites Professor Christina Sommers as an example, she notes: "'Students find a great deal of plausibility in Aristotle's theory of moral education, as well as personal relevance in what he says about courage, generosity, temperance, and other virtues...Once the student becomes engaged with the problem of what kind of person to be and how to become that person, the problems of ethics become concrete and practical'" (Kilpatrick, 1992, p. 242).

Others have suggested an emphasis on reading with exposure to the classics in literature. Storytelling and use of classic examples from literature can be effective tools in the integration of moral values education and a return to an emphasis on primary literacy. Bennett and Kilpatrick are among those who advocate such an approach. The recent publication and popularity of Bennett's

Book of Virtues (1994) illustrates that we are an audience eager to put these values and methods into practice. Kilpatrick (1992) contends that ethics and moral character can be part of the ethos of a school system that uses positive moral teaching to instill in the student a passion for seeking truth and knowledge. Wynne and Ryan (1993) make similar suggestions in their book *Reclaiming Our Schools: A Handbook on Teaching Character, Academics, and Discipline*. Part of the task is to make rules, enforce them, give challenging assignments, enforce them, give challenging assignments, correct them diligently, and demand excellence while nurturing progress toward these goals. "Profound learning" is suggested by Wynne and Ryan that calls for a "serious and non-sentimental" concept of education. They provide planned activities to develop character while also instituting schoolwide expectations for behavior of faculty, staff, and students alike. Research by Edmonds in the 1970s called for such elements that are characteristics of effective schools: a safe and orderly environment, a clear and focused academic mission, instructional leadership, high expectations, student time-on-task, and frequent monitoring of student progress.

Exposing children to good character and inviting imitation of this is part of what Bennett (1994) sees as the basis for transmitting a positive moral foundation. when teachers and school administration embody sound convictions in their actions and their words, children gain the sense of right and wrong that must be part of their socialization. Several examples of significant but isolated experiments in such effective educating can be found. Joe Clark, formerly of Eastside High in Paterson, New Jersey, was an illustration, portrayed in the movie *Lean on Me*. Jaime Escalante working at East Los Angeles Garfield High was another role model of effective teaching, portrayed in yet another movie, *Stand and Deliver*. Countless other illustrations are noted by Bennett (1994), who argues that they "give the lie to the proposition that the combination of poverty, disadvantaged background, and color is destiny; that the usual rules of good habits, good behavior, and hard work don't apply in the inner city" (p. 78).

At the level of legislation and programmatic change, we can endorse and support freedom of choice in school attendance. Where this has been tried, it has met with promising results. In this model, parents have been empowered as consumers to invest their income and efforts in schools that deliver on the promise to teach. Vouchers and support for parental choice moves along the lines suggested by many in the health care debate, where the forces of the marketplace can help shape more desirable outcomes as the consumer votes with their dollars for the programs that work.

Other programmatic change can be supported by psychology, including extending the school year for a full twelve months. This would better utilize the physical plant of the school setting, decrease the opportunities for summer mischief by bored students, and increase the chances of more specific content education and achievement in the schools. Milton Goldberg, who led the research in the landmark 1983 education report *A Nation at Risk*, has endorsed this plan.

He goes on to state that we must "reclaim the academic day [because] it is filled with non-academic requirements such as personal safety, consumer affairs, AIDS awareness, family life, drivers training" (1994). It is his view that such programs should be offered after the academic day, since students currently spend less than three hours per day on core subjects. A federal commission has endorsed this view, calling for a doubling of core content curriculum to begin to match that taught by our international peers.

Research may be useful to assess experiments in education that others have suggested. Psychology could assist with such pilot projects and offer guidance in program development and program evaluation. Among the suggestions worthy of further study are recommendations for single-sex schools and for all-black schools. "In the last few years a number of black educators have been calling for all-male, all-black schools run by black, male teachers. The argument is that the boys need appropriate discipline as well as role models" (Kilpatrick, 1992, p.233). In a similar view, suggestions have been made that adolescent girls do better in all-girl schools, particularly where some uniform is the standard of dress (Riesman, 1991). The model helps to decrease some of the distractions that emerging sexual identity and peer relations issues bring with them. Further development and study of such options seems worthy of efforts by psychologists in education.

Home schooling has become a positive and viable educational option in the face of the failure of public education. However, this is not without its costs, particularly in terms of investment of parental resources and in reduction of exposure of children to other socializing agents. The argument goes that if the schools socialize poorly, it is better to have limited peer socialization on the whole. Psychology can work to remedy this problem by developing better methods for networking children and parents who are currently involved in home schooling. Parents' magazines include advertisements for curriculums for purchase and can readily help with networking of home-schooling families in a given community.

Parents can be given support by psychology to develop more meaningful and effective methods of childrearing. Too many parents have abandoned the task of parenting to the schools and to the "experts," leaving the children undisciplined and unruly. Kilpatrick (1992) notes that parents can help their children acquire character by setting limits and, in effect, produce clearer boundaries and happier, more secure children. Encouraging parental involvement in school activities and school governance is also central to the course of recovering the moral climate of education. Psychology can help with improvements in training programs for parents, encouraging parents to recover their authority in the process of setting limits and balancing nurturance with direction. In *The New Dare to Discipline* Dobson makes clear the rationale and wisdom behind a parenting model that uses both instruction and discipline. "According to a recent study, young men with high self-esteem shared some common childhood influences....The high self-esteem group came from homes where parents had been significantly more strict in their approach to discipline. By contrast, the parents in the low self-esteem group had created insecurity and dependence through their permissiveness" (Dobson, 1994). Bringing forth the research on such parenting that demonstrates the utility of more directive roles for younger children, graduated to more democratic methods for older children as they demonstrate greater self-control, will be of value in easing the fears that so many parents have of harming their child's creativity by imposing discipline.

It was Rousseau who developed the doctrine of natural goodness in its most attractive form. The theory proposed that in a natural state children could be counted on to develop natural virtues.... "To thine own self be true" would have seemed utterly foolish advice not only to Augustine but to Cicero and his contemporaries. Even in Shakespeare's play these words are put into the mouth of an old fool. But to Rousseau it was the sum and substance of wisdom. (Kilpatrick, 1992, 104-105)

Such misguided notions, as to humankind's basic nature need to give way to a more reasonable position that reflects both the good and evil inherent within us all.

Social psychological models and issues can begin to take the prominent place they deserve in developing curriculums to train morals and values. Research on altruism, helping behavior, cooperation, and team-building can be central components in such programming. Exercises and activities based on this research can be developed for use in the schools.

Social interest and a sense of interpersonal connectedness represent elements that have had prominence in family therapy and individual psychology in the past (e.g. Erich Fromm, Karen Horney, Tom Nagy). These are not dead subjects and can be readily revived in specific curriculum planning for values. Cognitive psychology and the area of self-regulation of behavior has long taught clients to plan ahead and consider the outcomes of their behavior. Kanfer (1977) has suggested that clients be taught to reflect upon their behavior in advance and to weigh their choices with consideration of the social matrix, understanding that their behavior has potential consequences for self and for others. This approach can facilitate greater consideration for others, mixing responsibility with personal freedom. Efforts have been made to apply such principles to empathy training for juvenile delinquents (e.g., Sarason, 1976), and while this approach has not produced unequivocal results, some promise yet remains. Instituting these methods into mainstream education and at early ages has greater hope of positive results, while the research appears to have offered too little, too late.

Some of this change calls for psychology to re-examine its basic assumptions, as Vitz (1994) notes in *Psychology as Religion*. For psychology has become the secularized version of a final authority for humankind, forsaking the bedrock of Judeo-Christian ethics for the emptiness of an overemphasis on the self. The emphasis on the psychology of the individual has added to the problems, helping with the social forces at work to change the family from a community of interdependent, loving persons to a collection of individuals pursuing their own path to fulfillment. "Certainly modern psychology is one of the culprits. Its emphasis has never been on family or marriage but rather on separation and individuation" (Kilpatrick, 1992, 264). Perhaps as young psychologists are trained in a more comprehensive ecological model of humankind, as they learn an eclectic model of treatment that incorporates both individual and family therapy, as they consider a bio-psycho-social matrix for behavior, they will begin to reclaim the proper perspective on the individual and the group. Part of what has been lost is a sense of shared value or purpose in humankind and, indeed, in life. The rise of humanism with the relativism it espoused, the rise of behaviorism with the natural science model it cherished, and the rise of existentialist models of therapy all undercut the more basic notions of human worth of man and the need for a spiritual foundation. Psychology has fallen prey to the misguided notion of appreciation of cultural diversity at the expense of building community first. Professor Hirsch of the University of Virginia notes that cultures and communities depend for their very existence on shared knowledge and customs. Without such specific shared information and practice, communication deteriorates and distrust and difference take hold. "Contrary to the claims of advocates of cultural diversity, the actual history of culturally diverse societies is one of discord and bloodshed. Unless there exists a common language, common religion, or common traditions to bind them, people in such societies tend to be at each other's throats" (Kilpatrick, 1992, 117).

We are rapidly reaching a point where cultural meltdown may occur unless efforts are taken to reclaim the helm of this nation. Psychology can begin to use its newfound role in the development of core curriculum in the Goals 2000 endeavor to redirect the mistakes of the past.

Even social scientists now recognize the importance of sound values and moral norms in the upbringing of children. Empirical studies confirm what most people already know. What determines a young person's behavior in academic, sexual, and social life are his deeply held convictions and beliefs. They determine behavior far more than race, class, economic background, or ethnicity. Nature abhors a vacuum; so does a child's soul. If that soul is not filled with noble sentiments, with virtue...it will be filled with something else" (Bennett, 1994, 21).

As the Roman scholar Pliny the Elder put it, "What we do to our children, they will do to society."

The issues surrounding the culture and our values are the most important ones. The convictions and principles that guide us are the most important factors in the improvement of our life together....In a country "dedicated to the proposition," dedicated to self-evident truths and self-government, the ideas of the mind and the "habits of the heart" determine almost all the important issues" (Bennett, 1994, p. 22).

Schools as Agents of Change: School-Based Barter for School and Community Development

Nelson W. Keith
Novella Zett Keith

Our chapter addresses the issue of excellence and equity for urban schools and communities by proposing a new, practical, research-supported model for creating linkages between urban schools, their students and neighborhoods, and outside agencies and communities. The model—a school-based barter network—is designed to effect change in four areas. The first two involve the school and its neighborhood: (a) identifying and documenting the sociocultural and economic capacities of local residents and by building on these (b) augmenting the resources—psychic as well as material—of school, students, and residents. The third and fourth areas involve linkages of local residents and students, via the school, with "outside" entities (c) forging or strengthening social bonds and networks among residents, educators, and civic, business, and service organizations and (d) expanding educational and training opportunities for students and community members beyond the school. The social and economic networks that result from these activities enhance mutual trust, respect, and cooperation among participants and foster community participants' sense of adequacy and bargaining power. In so doing, they provide support for inner-directed school and community development. Meaningful urban educational reform requires change in all these areas.

The chapter is divided into five sections. The first section, which briefly introduces the problem, is followed by a discussion of research findings that support our school-based barter project. In the third, interpretive section, we condense these findings into a set of research-based criteria for urban school reform initiatives and describe the barter network as a model that meets these criteria. We conclude the chapter with policy recommendations and suggest a broader policy framework for urban school reform.

DEFINITION OF THE PROBLEM

A spate of reports and pronouncements by policy-makers over the last decade has proposed a crucial link between successful educational reform and the country's ability to retain its prominence in the postindustrial, global, information age. According to their scenarios, a successful economic transition depends on schools' producing a future workforce capable of high levels of cognitive performance: We have to become "a nation of people who think for a living" (Tucker, in Edgerton, 1987).

This change, the argument continues, must not be confined to elite and middle-class institutions. One-quarter of all American children now live in poverty (the vast majority in urban centers), a condition that disproportionately afflicts minority children and their families. Projections that by the early years of the next century 40 percent of school children will be "minorities," combined with present trends of one-third to one-half of minority children in poverty, stand as stark reminders of the urgent call for policies that address the needs and potential contributions of these children, their families, and communities. Accordingly, the prominence given to the quest for excellence should not obscure the continued requirements of equity.

Comprehensive urban high schools (e.g., nonmagnet schools), however, routinely experience dropout rates as high as 40 to 50 percent. In some inner-city areas, as few as 20 percent of students entering high school graduate four years later. The "success stories," those who do graduate, often in the face of tremendous odds, are then rebuffed in their attempts to move into mainstream life and institutions; gaining meaningful employment and staying in college are difficult (American Council on Education, 1989): Their skills and knowledge, their study and work habits, are deemed insufficient and inadequate.

Explanations for the poor school performance and high dropout rate in urban schools have emphasized a number of key variables, including funding inequities (Kozol, 1991), the individual and environmental factors associated with low socioeconomic status (Coleman, 1966; Jenks et al., 1972), and school functioning (Joyce, Hersh, & McKibbin, 1983). Yet only a few of the reform initiatives (i.e., the compensatory program encapsuled by Head Start) have been demonstrably successful. Part of the difficulty is caused by the narrow focus of much research and derivative programs: the prevailing emphasis on the attributes of students and their immediate environment—self-esteem, motivation, family functioning—or on teachers and their environment, with less emphasis on structural or systemic factors. Another part is due to the way research is done: It is largely correlational and thus tells us which factors are associated with school failure rather than what causes it (Rumberger, 1994). Searching for "strong" and enduring findings through meta-analyses of large numbers of such studies may have its uses (Wang et al., 1994); however, such research cannot but replicate original study biases.

More promising explanations and attendant solutions have emerged from the work of anthropologists, cultural psychologists, and political economists (see, for instance, Jacob & Jordan, 1993; Logan & Molotch, 1987; Stigler, Shweder, & Herdt, 1990). Focusing on the role of culture on identity formation, many researchers point to the conflicting cultures that students of minority and lower socioeconomic background must negotiate. Others note the altered political and economic landscape of cities and the emergence of the urban underclass. The reconceptualization of the problem supported by such analyses suggests alternative solutions that emphasize the importance of two kinds of supportive structures: two-way "bridges" between the now largely separate worlds of family, peer group, school, work, and so on; and social and economic community development that builds on local strengths and is informed by an understanding of the broad context (historical, global) in which such development will take place. The call, then, is for comprehensive approaches to school-community change that address the interrelated nexus of cultural and social forces around a new conceptual entity: the situated person-in-relation.

School-linked barter finds support on several grounds. First, it conforms with recent findings on learning, motivation, and group process, as well as with the literature on experiential education and service learning. Second, it fits well within present reform strategies in urban education; these stress system decentralization, local community participation, school restructuring (e.g., school-based management, schools-within-schools) and partnerships with businesses, service providers, universities, professionals, and others (Asher, 1994; Fine, 1994; Dryfoos, 1994; Hess, 1993). Third, it is responsive to current fiscal stringencies and the "less government" climate propelling much of the reform effort: Models most likely to receive policy consideration are those that promote self- and mutual help and do not require large outlays of additional resources from government. Fourth, the model is responsive to the new socioeconomic and political environment created by global change patterns. Here, we refer to economic trends and related population movements that are transforming our urban centers through two major processes: the extension of microbusinesses, street vending, home-based work, and termed in general what is the informal economy; and the advance of cultural forms that are chipping away at the hegemony of Western models—what is termed cultural diversity.

Barter, or moneyless exchange, enables people and organizations to obtain needed goods and services without any cash outlay. Through barter, such economic "negatives" as unproductive use of time (as in un- and underemployment), downtime, excess industrial capacity, and excess inventory become tradable commodities. Persons in need of services but without the wherewithal to pay for them in cash can now exchange them (i.e., one person shops and run errands for a homebound person, in exchange for the latter's cooking, sewing, or other in-home activities). For participating businesses, the combined effects of constant overheads and underutilized machinery drastically reduce the cost of goods produced for barter (i.e., printed advertising), while these same goods generate revenue ("trade dollars") that would otherwise not be generated.

Our model draws from two common types of barter exchanges: (1) community-based, nonprofit barter clubs and (2) corporate, for profit barter exchanges. The "neighborhood economy" in many communities features formal and informal barter clubs through which members exchange all sorts of services, such as babysitting, repairs, and tutoring. A model for increasing services to the elderly through "service credits" (vouchers) has received considerable support in the United States (Cahn, 1987). For-profit barter transactions (countertrade), which are common features of government and corporate exchanges, account for one-fourth of world trade (Gershman, 1986). This is a well-established long-term trend that is little affected by cyclical economic downturns, although these downturns do stimulate increased barter (Stapleton & Richman, 1978). Exchanges specializing in barter brokering exist in the United States, Germany, and other countries (Offe & Heinze, 1992). The Business Information System lists eleven corporate barter organizations with operating revenues ranging from $26 million to $1 million.

CURRENT FINDINGS

The literature suggests that fostering greater student success in urban schools requires comprehensive policies that address three kinds of obstacles. The first is the prevailing orientation to inner-city students and residents as deficient (at risk) and thus requiring education and retraining in mainstream behaviors and values. A solution is provided by the "difference versus deficit" approach, which espouses epistemological diversity and, seeing inner-city residents as bearers of culture and knowledge, seeks to identify and build on their strengths and capacities. The second obstacle is the failure of solutions to be informed by a broad, historical understanding of the process and present context of change. Comprehensive change is a lengthy and painstaking process that involves changing attitudes as well as changing structures (S. Sarason, 1990; M.R. Williams, 1989); solutions need to emerge from current realities rather than nostalgia for a mythical golden past. The third obstacle is the dearth of approaches allowing for the demonstration effect of alternative views of students and the local community: We need evidence of successful programs built on the foundation of students' and community capacities.

Strengths and Capacities of Urban Communities

It may require a conscious effort to envision poor urban people, and especially inner-city people, as possessing strengths and capacities. Whether from earlier "culture of poverty" or more recent "underclass" perspectives (Wilson, 1987), the prevailing picture of the inner city is one of devastation: Bereft of connections to the formal economy (due to lack of education, skills, employment, or business ownership) and to mainstream society (due to lack of social contacts with those of higher status and class), inner-city residents are caught in "mutually reinforcing patterns of behavior and poverty" (Betancur & Gills, 1993, 193).

We cannot deny the misery we attempt to hide away in our inner cities, but focusing only on the above processes prevents us from seeing two facets of the issue: First, there are sources of hope and possibilities for change emerging from within; and second, by linking with these possibilities, institutions that are supposed to serve urban residents but often merely perpetuate the cycle of misery (including schools) can begin to enact new tales of hope. The new models stress the strengths inherent in human diversity and the resilience many inner-city youths and adults develop in the face of difficult circumstances (Linquanti, 1992; Phelan & Davidson, 1993; Werner & Smith, 1992; Williams & Newcombe, 1994). They recognize that the immediate environment presents residents with its own peculiar problems and look for accommodations made and solutions forged in this context. The attempt here is not to impose models derived from other settings (i.e., middle class, mainstream), which quickly lead to perceptions of deficiency; judgments are still made, of course, since diversity does not mean that "anything goes"; but they are made from the context of the local culture and environment—from the inside out.

Current research on intelligence supports this approach. The conclusive findings are that intelligence is multifaceted and malleable, and that it develops in the context of one's culture, through attempts to solve problems and, generally, negotiate one's environment (H. Gardner, 1991). As H. Gardner (1991) asserts, "Nearly all learning will take place in one or another cultural context. ...Far from being restricted to the individual's skull, cognition and intelligence become distributed across the landscape" (p. 109). Different environments, then, promote and make use of different intelligences.

If intelligence and cognitive abilities are not unequally distributed across classes and groups, neither are creativity, problem-solving, or exemplary behaviors. There is evidence that all adolescents "have a strong drive to *serve others*" (Fine & Mechling, 1993) and that participation in service and volunteer activities is not unusual when the circumstances are favorable. A survey conducted in 1990 found that the rate of engagement in service among African-American tenth-graders (11 percent) was higher than that of all urban students (9 percent) as well as that of all tenth-graders (7 percent) (ERIC Clearinghouse of Urban Education, 1992). It may be even higher if we assume that many service activities in the inner city go unrecorded (McClure, 1971, in Davis, 1980). Studies usually consider only visible involvement in organizations: advisory boards, voluntary organizations, pressure or social action groups, school activities, and so on; the community participation that occurs through informal helping networks and relationships in the personal sphere is usually invisible.

Also uncounted as potential assets are the contributions from nonmainstream organizations and cultural responses. Assertive cultural, art and music forms such as rap, breakdancing, graffiti "murals," and the like speak of a creativity that persists in the midst of want (Lusane, 1993;I. Miller, 1993; Ransby & Matthews, 1993). These activities are not just individual but are supported by peer groups that call forth extraordinary commitment. This is not to romanticize gang involvement and the like; it is merely to call attention to one of its less-noticed sides. Recent "peace" initiatives by gangs also demonstrate that these groups have organizational talents that may at times be put to the use of community development, and community leadership by former gang members provides a wealth of local knowledge useful in creating organizations responsive to the environment (Vigil, 1993): Indeed, some researchers suggest that inner-city youth organizations should learn from the successes of gangs in both the social and economic sphere (Fine & Mechling, 1993). It is by building on such strengths, for instance, that Nation of Islam security patrols in low-income projects are able to succeed where mainstream approaches have failed miserably.

Additional evidence of strengths comes from McLaughlin, Irby, and Langman's (1994) extensive study of "urban sanctuaries" - successful inner-city organizations for youth. Their research demonstrates that youth behaviors such as community service, volunteering, and assuming responsibility became quite common when organizations simply offered "support and optimism, fun and friendship," rather than being premised on *preventing* at-risk behaviors (1994, p. 8). They assert: "The public's discouraging conclusions and myths about the interests, motivation, and capacities of inner-city youth are in urgent need of revision. Many adolescents *do* want to belong to organizations that help them escape inner-city despair, imagine and move toward positive, hope-filled futures" (McLaughlin, Irby, & Langman, 1994, 5-6).

This study and others counter the usual conclusion that since participation is strongly correlated with socioeconomic status, few residents of the inner city would be available to participate in change-oriented activities. Research conducted in the mid-1970s in 100 American cities (Lamb, 1975, in M.R. Williams, 1989, 107) revealed that one in twelve respondents were community leaders and that two-thirds of these (one in eighteen) were actively involved in civic and social change issues. Although social and economic problems have deepened since then, the synthesizing work of Krentzmann and McKnight (1990) uncovered in many cities across the nation, large numbers of local initiatives built around the activities of community organizations and drawing strength from community "assets," including local organizations and individuals. It led them to develop "community assets maps" as alternatives to the more common "community deficits maps." This research is supported by the continued relevance of organizations such as the Alinsky-style Industrial Areas Foundation and the Poverty and Race Research Action Council. The literature on parent involvement in urban schools also includes a number of cases that can be characterized as "parent empowerment" (Delgado-Gaitan, 1993).

From these perspectives new patterns emerge: The difficulties experienced by mainstream organizations, including schools, in promoting the involvement of parents and local residents are less a matter of the low socioeconomic status and attributes of nonparticipants than of the "borders" (Phelan, Davidson, & Yu, 1993, 52) created by the very organizations that claim to seek involvement. K.E. Davis (1980) argues that organizational variables such as power distribution and group homogeneity or heterogeneity mediate participation by minority group members. Inner-city residents often see mainstream organizations as maintaining "the established distribution of power, resources and decision-making that characterize the community....[Thus] many instrumental organizations that operate in local communities are incongruous with the needs of the majority of the Black population" (p. 140).

Cynicism and apathy among inner-city residents are real enough; but rather than being fundamental attributes of personality, they are more easily changed reactions to organizations and programs perceived as noninviting, irrelevant, and condescending. Encouraging involvement by inner-city residents, then, requires less thought about motivating "unmotivated" individuals and more about offering appropriate projects and activities and fostering an inviting climate. The parents in studies by McCaleb (1994), the students in the schools featured by Wehlage, Rutter, Smit, Lesko, and Fernandez (1989), and the youths in the successful inner-city organizations found by McLaughlin, Irby, and Langman (1994), for instance, want to collaborate and succeed and when they are welcomed, willingly participate in organizations that respond to their interests and needs. Such organizational successes are due, in no small part, to the leaders' "local knowledge."

Alternative Learning Environment

As our review suggests, promoting school success among urban students requires change within the schools and beyond. Differences can become strengths if learning environments become shorn of their own *organizational* deficits. Banks (1994), Boykin (1994), and Vasquez (1994) have reviewed the research on learning environments in which minorities are more likely to succeed. These authors conclude that schools should be responsive to diverse styles of learning, cognition, and motivation. The minority students studied tended to learn more when knowledge was presented in context (field sensitive), when the learning process was collaborative, when they could see the relationship between their efforts and accomplishments, and when they engaged in activities that allowed repeated experiences with success and therefore promoted patterns of internal attribution. Finally, as learning involves more than learning tasks, relationships were also important: More learning occurred when teachers were perceived as caring.

These findings have implications for the ways learning is structured. They put a premium on integrated learning experiences that draw from the community and other involvements outside the classroom. With the current momentum of school reform pushing toward system decentralization, they raise the possibility of a variety of local public schools, attuned to the cultural preferences and socioeconomic needs of particular segments of the urban student population. The growing demand for Afrocentric curriculums and the emergence of Afrocentric schools is a case in point.

Integrating schools within the community and community knowledge and culture into schools can be achieved partly through service learning; this is a demonstrably effective approach to experiential education that fosters academic and affective growth and, moreover, is quite applicable to urban schools (Conrad & Hedin, 1989; Keith, 1994) As one source comments: "Service learning involves and immerses students in relational learning environments and engages multiple senses and intelligences. Learning becomes more accessible by expanding the definition of competence and redefining the relationship of teacher to student and student to learning. The teacher, rather than simply being the provider of information and the evaluator of competence, is the creator of environments where students learn by doing, working with others, and reflecting on their experiences" (McPherson & Nebgen, 1991, 1).

Service learning, then, may contribute to school improvements not only by providing developmentally sound learning tasks but also by changing the quality of relationships between students and teachers (Shumer, 1994): Leveling power differences, it helps promote the reciprocity and cooperation that facilitate learning. When the focus of service or other student-teacher experiential learning is on community knowledge and community development, the potential for improving relationships broadens further, reaching from the school to the local community (see Harkavy & Puckett, 1991, on the WEPIC project).

Other approaches that hold promise for fostering learning while improving relationships include learning communities or schools-within-schools and schools as communities of support. The first usually include 250 to 300 students and fifteen to twenty teachers organized around interdisciplinary themes, team teaching and curriculum planning, and career options (Fine, 1994). The second describes a number of different programs of proactive interventions in areas where different students need special supports, for instance, nurseries and related experiential learning curriculums for teen parents, and in-school teams (mentors, parents, community members) ready to help students with problems and provide assistance that may be beyond the scope of teachers or professional service providers (Rumberger & Larson, 1994; Wehlage et al., 1989).

Such approaches are part of the necessary task of reconstruction, but more is needed: Ultimately, improving learning and relationships in urban schools cannot be done in isolation from the local community. This is so for two main reasons. First, local community needs to make visible and address the disabling educational practices that characterize most urban schools and are embedded both in the school and the school system (Cummins, 1986; Weiner, 1993; M.R Williams, 1989). Schools' expectations (embedded in teachers as well as in the system) are not only academic but cultural. There is growing evidence that the mainstream cultural premises and expectations embedded in the schooling process are detrimental to learning for inner-city students; they impose added burdens on students who are culturally different and must bear the entire responsibility of adjusting to the teachers' and school's culture and expectations. Second, at a fundamental level, school improvements must be linked to community development: A difficult life may promote resilience as opposed to powerlessness and a sense of lack of control, but the presence of resilience does not obviate the need to ameliorate the conditions that necessitate it in the first place.

Community development—which has social as well as economic aspects— can begin by creating two-way bridges between the school, people and institutions in the local community, and the wider community. There is a growing literature promoting the development of partnerships in urban school reform efforts. We agree. But what kind of partnerships are needed? The next two sections help clarify this issue.

Contexts of Reform

As we saw above, there is growing recognition that members of poor communities should not be seen as deprived recipients of assistance but as capable of the creativity and innovation necessary to devise alternative development strategies. The requirement for such self-sustaining projects will increase in the 1990s and beyond, when a growing gap is predicted between needs and available investment capital and aid. A report by the Organization for Economic Cooperation and Development notes: "The internal catalytic effect of loosening the constraints placed by the regulatory framework on small scale producers finds its macro-economic rationale [in this lack of resources]. The assumption is that the indigenous entrepreneurial energies released by the removal of unnecessary and inhibitory regulations will compensate in part for lack of foreign investment and will in any case make more efficient use of available resources than is now the case" (Lubell, 1991, 14). The removal of regulations is not sufficient, however, to uplift the poorest groups. In the absence of appropriate policies, it may even increase the degradation of labor and the environment.

The report relates to the developmental needs of countries of the so-called Third World. But more and more, similar processes are affecting cities in the Western countries. There is no denying the bleakness bestowed on inner cities by the structural changes in the economy and, especially, in the economic role of cities as the country shifted from a manufacturing to a service base. While a few cities have succeeded in attracting and retaining lucrative services such as legal, financial, commercial, and insurance transactions, others must apparently settle for services at the lower end, including "specializing" as waste disposal sites (Logan & Motloch, 1987). This process of deindustrialization, as Wilson (1987) and others have well argued, is responsible in large measure for the advent of a large, semipermanent urban underclass that is marginal to the formal labor force. For its part, the growing "dual" nature of the labor market consigns the vast majority of those poor minorities who are employed to menial, temporary, and underpaid service jobs without benefits, security, and a future. Budget deficits and taxpayers' revolts have contributed to a deterioration of government-funded services and declining support for equity-promoting programs: Federal aid to cities, which stood at $47.2 billion in 1980, dwindled to $21.7 billion in 1992 (*USA Today*, May 5, 1992).

The tale is not entirely negative, however. The levels of need and deprivation found in the inner-cities do trigger many coping mechanisms (see, for instance, Warren, 1981); and while the formal economy has been in flux, a process of informalization that used to be a trademark of "Third World" countries has been flourishing in major North American and European cities (Wiegand, 1993). The informal sector includes unrecorded, nonpermanent, or marginal activities such as street vending, piecework, and the provision of various services. Sassen-Koob's (1989) study of New York City revealed informalization in key economic sectors such as apparel, construction, furniture, and electronics. Other studies conducted in Los Angeles, Miami, and Detroit, as well as in European cities, share her findings.

Informalization is reinforced and given new life by one development—immigration from underdeveloped or Third World countries. The most successful forms of entrepreneurship in inner-city areas of New York, Los Angeles, and most large cities are found among immigrant populations (Offe & Heinze, 1992). With current immigration policies ensuring the continuing flow of these populations into the United States, inner-city areas may become a more stable environment in which informalization will thrive. As the host community progressively loses faith in old formulas (including the ability of education to "pay off") and witnesses the success of these practices, there may be a tendency to follow suit.

Supportive practices have also made their appearance along with informal exchange relations. Among these is informal banking, known to flourish in immigrant communities (Jamaicans in Hartford, Connecticut, and New

Brunswick, New Jersey; and Koreans in Detroit; see Goozner, 1987). Informal exchanges (living accommodation for a variety of chores) and related informal social practices such as barter exchange and mutual assistance—child care, apprenticeships, lending societies, and burial societies—seem also to be spreading, especially in college environments.

The picture of the informal economy is not entirely positive, however: As Portes, Castells, and Benton assert, it "simultaneously encompasses flexibility and exploitation, productivity and abuse, aggressive entrepreneurs and defenseless workers" (1989, 11; see also Tiano, 1987). Thus the issue is how to use this "panacea for the growing unemployment problem" (Todaro, 1989, 268) in ways that maximize opportunities.

Previous experience demonstrates that projects that target whole communities and stress participation and self-help are much more likely to succeed (Poulton & Harris, 1988) and contribute to the "quality of life," human dimensions of development (Lineberry, 1989). Recent research on economic development efforts undertaken in East Central Los Angeles after the "Rodney King riots" lends further support: Community-based efforts are significantly more successful than outsider-initiated attempts to bring investment and jobs into the community (Johnson, Farrell & Jackson, 1994).

School-Community Linkages

The research discussed so far supports the notion that approaches that focus on at-risk behaviors and, generally, "deficits" are problem ridden. From the youths' perspective, the process of dropping out can now be seen as one of gradual disengagement and can be conceptualized in terms of the cultural dissonance of the "different worlds" to which they belong, and of identity politics: Schools and other mainstream institutions often fail to provide support for the development of talents and positive identity for lower-class, minority youth; disengaging from such "negative" environments, many of these youth then resort to peer groups and nonmainstream inner-city institutions (e.g., gangs) for support, developing oppositional identities in the process. The causes of failure thus reside both in social structures (including schools) that send subtle and not-so-subtle messages of inadequacy and "difference-as-deficit" and in the response to such messages by inner-city youths and adults (Boykin, 1994; Gordon & Yowell, 1994; Ogbu, 1990; Phelan, Davidson, & Yu, 1993; Willis, 1977).

In the last few years urban school reform efforts have increasingly focused on building partnerships between schools and "stakeholders" such as businesses, service agencies, higher education institutions, and the like. Partnerships are bridge-building activities: many are concerned with helping motivate youth to work toward future possibilities, including career and further education. Initiatives include career-oriented academic programs, mentoring, and school-to-college transition programs. The Clinton administration has proposed creating

German-style work apprenticeships for 300,000 youth (for a review, see Kantor, 1994).

Such efforts are not useless - mentors, resources, internships, and information about careers and further educational opportunities can help expand social networks and provide bridges to the mainstream that counter the isolation of most inner-city youths. This isolation serves as a barrier on many levels, including, for instance, misunderstandings and misinformation about the attributes of "good" schools and "successful" students. Maeroff (1994) describes students whose "objective" performance was quite low (e.g., third-grade reading level in ninth grade), who nonetheless considered they were doing "pretty well" in school. Goodman (1994) reports on students and parents who only fully realized the inferiority of their children's schooling when a video project compared their school with another one in a more mainstream neighborhood; school authorities, used to glossing over such differences, were upset.

Bridge building to match students with worthwhile jobs, however, is more likely to be successful for the few than for the many. Past trends suggest that most employers, especially so in the current economic climate, are not interested in hiring young high school graduates for the better jobs in the primary labor market (Kantor, 1994). And as Wilenski and Kline (1988) note, students know this even though many adults do not acknowledge it. In the context of structural unemployment, the dual labor market, and the growth of "informal" economic activities, meaningful planning for linking school and work for the majority of minority urban students requires serious rethinking. There are presently too few consistent experiences of success to dispel the pervasive sense of irrelevance of school, not only for everyday life but also as preparation for future work (Payne, 1984; Wilenski & Kline, 1988; M.R. Williams, 1989). In the face of structural unemployment, informal economy activities can be seen as having positive potential.

Schools should acknowledge these trends and build bridges that go the other way, into the community, by forging links with microbusinesses, for instance, and not only with jobs, careers, and mentors in the formal economy. In so doing, they would be following in the steps of the World Bank, the United Nations, and the International Labor Organization (ILO), who often tie their assistance packages to less-developed countries to self-help schemes and microbusinesses linked to the informal sector (Drakakis-Smith, 1987; House, 1984; Lubell, 1991).

The experience of these projects suggests that community development cannot be achieved by relying only on incentives to stimulate market mechanisms. Supporting microdevelopment projects has been found to lead to organizational strengthening and encourage efficiency, self-reliance, and the spread of projects (see de Soto, 1990, 73-74; Sethuraman, 1985, 727-729). We must thus envision new and reformulated social and economic networks in which urban (and especially inner-city) youth and other residents can participate.

Activities should be geared to elevating coping mechanisms into viable exchanges integrated into formal and informal economic and social networks operating both at the local level and in the wider social structure. In this, educators can be assisted by what Drucker (1989) calls the "third sector" of volunteers, a group large enough to constitute, he claims, a counterculture. These volunteers can certainly be tapped to help create bridges to the mainstream for poor minority youth. We have to be careful, though, about one-way partnerships that may mirror the disabling effects of schools.

INTERPRETATION OF FINDINGS

Criteria For Reform Projects

Our review of the pertinent literature leads to the formulation of several research-based criteria for projects focusing on school-community development in the inner city. These criteria, which are summarized in Table 14.1, comprise a comprehensive, systemic approach to change and cannot be seen in isolation: Addressing the problem of school success for inner-city youth requires much more than isolated attempts to improve teachers, students, and the school.

Table 14.1
Criteria for Urban School Reform Projects

I.   **Community Environment**

Focus on Development

- promotes awareness and documentation of community strengths;

- recognizes and fosters quality in community and school activities;

- engages multiple and intersecting networks and organizations providing social, cultural, and emotional supports;

- expands community economy: community-based production and circulation of goods and services (within and outside local community); emphasis on development of microbusinesses, cooperatives, and mutual aid societies.

Table 14.1
Criteria for Urban School Reform Projects *(continued)*

II.   **Learning Environment**

Local Knowledge and Talent Development

- focuses on talent development and providing many experiences with success;

- employs diversity of pedagogical approaches, including experiential learning, community service (service learning), and cooperative learning;

- involves curriculum and pedagogy built on local knowledge and culture and informed by community capacities perspective;

- uses real-life standards used to measure quality;

- fosters positive, humane relationships among teachers, students, and parents;

- uses peer support and peer group to foster engagement, commitment, and positive identity.

III.   **School-Community Links**

Two-Way Bridges

- provide school and outsiders with information on and experience with local community capacities;

- build relationships and activities on the basis of equalization of power and reciprocal exchange of resources;

- promote local and outside community presence (actual and symbolic) in school and school presence in community (via mentors, field experience and/or apprenticeships, community service, and service learning projects);

- make school a center for learning for community members *and* educators.

Criterion One: Community Environment—Focus On Development

In the course of navigating a difficult environment, local residents have developed storehouses of knowledge and skills that are infrequently tapped.

These need to be made visible, appropriated, and applied to project development. Building on local knowledge and capacities is important for at least two reasons: to improve the chances of success of a given project and to foster a sense of efficacy and empowerment among residents. Of course, there should be a good fit between local development activities and supportive systemic trends (in our case, decentralization, globalism, informalization, diversity, and so on).

Criterion Two: Learning Environment—Local Knowledge and Talent Development

The research clearly demonstrates that social groups and networks in the inner city need not be built on oppositional cultures and behaviors. Given appropriate approaches (e.g., see criterion two), the majority of youths and adults want to participate in peer and support groups and social networks that foster values, attitudes, and behaviors conducive to community development. Leaders, mentors, and teachers should have local knowledge, be committed and caring, and have the ability to bridge borders between worlds.

The mainstream and its institutions should not be assumed to be the norm. Mainstream knowledge must be taught in the context of local knowledge and capacities. Learning experiences should emphasize a diversity of approaches that build on field sensitivity, enable learners to experience a series of successful outcomes, and support the development of internal locus of control. Standards of quality should be informed by real-life measures.

Criterion Three: School-Community Links—Two-Way Bridges

Our review suggests that bridges need to be created between urban neighborhoods, schools, and the mainstream (including agencies, businesses, and the like). These bridges must function as multidirectional, equalizing structures, that is, they must serve to validate the worth and contributions (social, cultural, economic, and so on) of local residents in the eyes of both those residents and representatives of mainstream society and they must bring new resources into the local community. Bridge-building efforts should take into account the layers of distrust and skepticism that have accumulated as a result of the history of mainstream-subordinate group relations.

Building On Community Strengths: The Barter Network

The barter network we have designed meets all the criteria for successful urban school reform, as outlined in Table 14.1. A crucial point is that the network becomes much more than a means for exchanging goods and services; it builds on the strengths of students and their peer groups as learners by providing opportunities for experience-based service learning, cooperative learning, curriculum infusion with local knowledge, and experience with real-life exchange relationships and quality standards; it reduces barriers and improves relationships between school and community by involving community members as skilled participants in educational activities (in the school and outside it) and teachers as learners and participants in the community; it increases community resources by building on community knowledge and skills and by connecting school and community to outside resources; and it improves motivation for learning by making the school and other organizations more "inviting" and expanding the scope of future options. We address these in more detail as we describe the model and its phases of development; however, for the sake of clarity, we have also summarized them in Table 14.2.

Table 14.2
Barter Network Activities Meeting Successful Reform Criteria

I. **Community Environment**

Focus on Development

- quality control of barter network services;

- "certification" of members' skills;

- barter inside local community; "for cash" services outside;

- skills, capacities, and infrastructure developed to support microbusinesses.

II. **Learning Environment**

Local Knowledge and Talent Development

- student-teacher-run barter network integrated into curriculum;

- community members (barter network participants) integrated into school functioning;

- collaborative groups encouraged to participate in the barter network together.

III. **School-Community Links**

Two-Way Bridges

- through community service curriculum, students and teacher survey of community capacities (individual, group, and organizational);

- service to the school provided by barter network members as part of their network commitment;

- local community services by teachers advertised in their home communities (e.g. through church);

Table 14.2
Barter Network Activities Meeting Successful Reform Criteria *(continued)*

- internships in exchange for barter network goods and services by outside members provided;

- skills of would-be barter members without credentials "certified" by skilled workers, others.

Phase 1: Planning and Organizational Development

1. A team of students, teachers, and community members (the "Leadership Team") provides leadership for conducting a survey of the community, "mapping" community strengths (individual, organizational, and physical assets) and identifying community needs. Assets identified include informal and non-formal educational opportunities available locally. This activity yields more than a survey: it becomes a developmental cooperative learning exercise undertaken in the spirit of participatory research; as experiential or service learning, it can become part of the curriculum in the areas of social studies, English, math, science, and so on. It identifies, in addition, community members interested in working to improve the schools and contributing to school activities through their knowledge and assets.
2. Information from the "mapping" research becomes part of a computerized database for planning and outreach: In order to enable their members to meet their needs through barter, the network must include a variety of goods and services for exchange. Thus outreach becomes an ongoing activity designed to meet members' needs in areas where there are gaps. Outreach at this stage may include local businesses and professionals whose services are needed, such as printers, computer programmers, and so on. The computerized database is eventually developed into a sophisticated information management system with many of the features of a banking operation. It allows multiparty exchange facilitated through currency substitutes (i.e., barter-checks) issued by the barter sponsoring organization. The computerized system maintains a databank of goods and services for barter, matches offerers and users of goods and services, tracks transactions, maintains quality control information, and generates monthly statements of member transactions in "barter dollars."
3. Since the success of the barter network depends on the quality of work produced by members, planning must include the development of quality control mechanisms. Three such mechanisms are required: "certification" of skills (for instance, those acquired in the informal economy); character references; and evaluation of services rendered. For certification and character references, the leadership team can call upon skilled personnel and trusted leaders in local organizations and institutions. Evaluation requires a system of feedback from users of services, more intensive during a "trial" period before members become fully certified. This process introduces high standards of quality that are based on real-life requirements.
4. Planning for organizational development includes developing the skills of the leadership team, acquiring initial resources, and securing an ongoing resource base for the organization. Developing the first (which in itself adds to the students' learning and

development of community capacities) and second are the only aspects of the project that may require outside resources, to be obtained either through professional volunteers or through small grants for organizational development and training. The third requirement can be met through the contributions of members, much as it happens in cooperative ventures, these contributions include a small annual fee ("investment capital") and a small number of hours of free service to be donated annually by each member to the barter network. The leadership team needs to decide where such service will be put to best use so as to contribute to school and community development, as well as support the network; service to the school may include assistance to classroom teachers, and guidance and other counselors, participation in school committees, and tutoring service for community development may include workshops and training for community residents, including in areas relevant for small business development and the support of informal sector activities and exchanges.

Phase 2: Community Barter

1. With the publishing of a directory of available goods and services, and a telephone service for users, the project is ready to officially begin. The tasks of outreach, quality control, and updating of available goods and services are ongoing. At this point, the barter network is itself a community microbusiness, serving as an incubator for additional microbusinesses and the strengthening of informal sector activities.
2. As appropriate, the network supplements its activities with workshops, training, and internships for students and community learners offered by network members.
3. Membership in the leadership team becomes rotating, thus providing opportunities for other students, teachers, and community members to participate in the learning processes involved.
4. At the conclusion of a pilot period, the network conducts an evaluation to determine the appropriate "mix" of members (i.e., skilled, unskilled; types of professions, businesses, technical and personal services, etc.) to ensure the viability of the network. The results of this evaluation inform outreach and quality control activities, including extending membership to qualified community residents, seeking new corporate members, and extending the list of services offered through barter in the areas of training and experiential education. Based on its quality control operations, the barter network issues qualifying community participants certificates and references attesting to their ability to deliver goods and services. This features serves to facilitate entry into the formal economy for those members wishing to do so.

Phase 3: Reaching Outside the Local Community

Outreach initiated in the first two phases is here extended in two ways.

1. Since augmenting community resources requires increasing the money in circulation in the community, the network facilitates the provision of for-cash services by members to residents of surrounding wealthier areas. Teachers and other community leaders with outside connections can become useful "bridges" for such activities by speaking on behalf of network members to other colleagues, members of organizations to which they belong, and so on.

2. Outside professionals, businesses, and providers of goods and services are encouraged to provide internships, work experiences, and services for students and barter members. Where desirable and possible, they may do so on a barter basis. Thus professionals and local organizations that might otherwise be approached with requests for volunteering and "giveaways" will have new incentives to become involved with the school and community, through linkages based not on charity but on mutually beneficial exchange.

FUTURE DIRECTIONS AND IMPLICATIONS

We began this chapter by noting the need for both equity and excellence for poor urban schools and asserting that likely approaches would focus on building capacities and linkages that support both school and community development. The barter network described in this chapter is not a panacea; it is, however, a promising model. As an element of a comprehensive strategy designed to rebuild inner-city neighborhoods "from the inside out," it can become part of the foundation for community organization that captures the assets of local residents, maximizes their use, and redistributes resources from outside the neighborhood.

As we apply it, the barter network goes well beyond its usual functions in the area of exchange, addressing other tasks of school and community development; ultimately, however, the full scope of such tasks is beyond its reach. Thus policy makers and implementers will reap more benefits if they insert the network into a more comprehensive strategy. We conclude by briefly identifying four tasks required for such a strategy.

Economic tasks are defined as the production and exchange of services and goods in ways that benefit the local community. They include not only jobs but education and training for productive economic roles and the availability of other resources - most importantly capital. Strengthening local assets requires social, symbolic, and economic supports for local initiatives, including identity affirming and socially bonding experiences of success; task-oriented projects such as cooperatives, incubators, internships, new approaches to certification, revolving credit schemes, and special insurance arrangements, and the like, must be conducted in ways that support the building of relationships and "inviting" organizational arrangements.

Cultural tasks involve establishing connections to the community's strengths and contributions and the enrichment of community life. Given a focus on diversity, they include the validation of the experiences, history, culture, and knowledge of the neighborhood's diverse groups. Although schools have a special role to play here in introducing a curriculum in which learning is contextually located, communities also need to recognize and facilitate education as a lifelong process.

Social tasks are defined as the strengthening of community institutions and networks in ways that provide supports for youth, families, and other residents. They include such areas of life as safety, stability, housing, recreation, and the social bonds of mutual help and friendship (Lyon, 1987, 152-159). Included here is the task of reintegrating community institutions such as schools, youth-centered organizations, and service providers into the fabric of the community. Given the context of community diversity, such efforts must also span ethnic, race, and class divisions and improve relations with groups in the wider community (including, for instance, relations between residents on the one hand and police, service providers, and business owners on the other).

Political tasks involve the development of the community's voice, the creation of channels for meaningful participation in social and public life and institutions, and the wherewithal to press for equity in the creation and distribution of material and nonmaterial resources. It is important here to recognize that the needed shifts in the relations of power that govern the value of one's "resources" (economic, symbolic, etc.) may come about through the play of relationships and influence as well as advocacy and social action.

15

Positive Agents of Change in the Transformation of Social Systems: A Role for Education

Kathi L. Wilhite

This chapter considers the role of change agents in the transformation of service systems for children and youth with multiple needs and their families. The potential for schools to fill this role is also examined. The chapter is divided into four sections. Section one introduces the concept of service system change and defines terminology used throughout the chapter. Section two explores factors indicative of service system needs for this population and considers influencing social issues such as poverty, divorce, changing family structures, and crime rates. (Influencing system issues such as limited coordination, limiting financial structures, and territorial boundaries are discussed briefly as well.) This section also looks at the decline of the American education system in recent decades. Section three gives two examples of service system change initiatives started by social entities outside of education and reviews two service system change efforts spearheaded by education. Section four suggests proposed changes in the current service system structure. This last section concludes by delineating the implications of proposed service system change for policy development.

INTRODUCTION AND DEFINITIONS

Established systems tend to resist change until it is demanded out of necessity. The rising cost of traditional treatment modes for children and youth with emotional and behavioral disorders, coupled with indications of increasing ineffectiveness, is creating a demand for change in systems serving this population. Successful change occurs when efforts are consumer driven, streamlined to eliminate the duplication of service, provide ease in accessibility, acknowledge the role of the family and the community in the provision of appropriate services to children and youth, and encourage the responsible use of available resources. A key factor underlining these assumptions is the belief that a multidisciplinary approach is essential in the provision of appropriate services to children and youth with multiple needs. The commitment and participation of institutions such as education, mental health, public welfare, juvenile justice, corrections, families, family service providers, and local communities is required for positive service system change.

This chapter focuses on school-aged children and youth, hereafter referred to as students, exhibiting a complexity of emotional, behavioral, social, and familial disorders. Students exhibiting these disorders are given a variety of labels dependant upon the identifying entity. Typical labels include emotionally disturbed, behavior disordered, juvenile delinquent, child in need of services (CHINS), conduct disordered, and socially maladjusted. This is certainly not an exhaustive list; however, it does give a frame of reference as to the students being addressed. The wide variety of services needed to address this complexity of disorders is the basis for identification of these students as having multiple needs, or *multi-needs*, the term that will be used in this chapter. Systems referred to in this document include education, mental health, public welfare, social service agencies, juvenile justice, corrections, families, family service providers, local communities, and other local, state, or federal agencies or groups with an obligation for service provision to students and families.

CURRENT FINDINGS IN SYSTEMS SERVING MULTI-NEEDS STUDENTS

Social Issues

Multiple factors have been cited as contributing to the increase in number and severity of multi-needs students. One major factor is the economic status of the United States. The proportion of American children living in poverty grew by 23 percent in the nine years from 1979 to 1988. At the current rate, one in four American children could soon be living in poverty (Children's Defense Fund, 1990). Students living in poverty are likely to experience many related problems such as hunger, poor health, and homelessness, all of which will result in both educational and social challenges (Children's Defense Fund, 1991).

Divorce has become an accepted fact in American culture and an additional factor in the increasing number of students with multiple needs. Estimates indicate that as many as 40 percent of American students will experience parental divorce before reaching age eighteen (Hodgkinson & Mirga, 1986). Two additional factors, possibly related to the increasing divorce rates and identified as "at risk indicators" by the U.S. Department of Education are single mothers and working mothers (Carson, Huelskamp, & Woodall, 1991). In 1988, 51 percent of all children younger than six had mothers in the workforce (Children's Defense Fund, 1991).

The past three decades have been years of major change in the structure of the American family and the view of society toward the family. Coleman (1972) wrote that in the society of the 1970s, there was no longer a place for the child in most homes. The productive family activities that were once required in American families were not needed in modern homes. Coleman (1972) further commented that "all of this leads to an inescapable conclusion. The school of the future must focus on those activities that in the past have largely been accomplished outside school."

Baker (1991) gave a startling glimpse into the trends and statistics of juvenile crime in the Untied States today: (1) the number of senseless, random acts of violence is on the rise; (2) juveniles are involving themselves in criminal activity at an earlier age; (3) for commission of FBI Index property crimes among both adults and juveniles, the peak age is sixteen; (4) for crimes of violence among both adults and juveniles, the peak ages are seventeen and eighteen; and (5) between 1984 and 1989 the rate for arrests of juveniles ages ten through seventeen for murder doubled. "Even nondelinquents are becoming immune to the violence around them" (Baker, 1991).

Situations resulting in socioeconomic and family stress have been considered accurate predictors of risk for the development of emotional and behavioral disorders. As a result, an increase in the number of students requiring multiple services is anticipated (Emery, 1982). Given the social, economic, and political environment of the 1970s through the early years of the 1990s, multiple factors must be considered when charting a course for change. As phrased by Kahn (1991): "The social and economic problems confronting people today are debilitating. They sap energy and destroy morale."

System Issues

Knitzer (1982) found that typically, multi-needs students are passed from agency to agency, never receiving effective treatment. The situation is "dismal" in all social systems with responsibilities to multi-needs students including education, welfare, mental health, and juvenile justice (Knitzer, 1982).

There is no doubt that as society increases in complexity, no single service system can adequately address all of the needs. Knitzer, Steinberg, and Fleisch (1990) spoke of the American tradition that recognizes the benefit of education and mental health collaboration. This should lead to an increase in collaboration among the professions. It is unfortunate that the opposite appears to be true.

Since the late 1970s there has been decreasing support, both fiscally and philosophically, for the development of collaboration between agencies (Knitzer et al., 1990). "The professions have become increasingly convergent and specialized. This has worked against the type of thinking and interdisciplinary effort that is necessary" (Skrtic, 1991). Skrtic (1991) further discussed the convergent, specialized approach of service systems resulting in the expenditure of much time and "energy on the politics of winning converts and defending" (p.4) the specialized area from outside attacks.

Many social systems today are mandated to provide services to students with multiple needs and their families. Mandates often apply to the same or similar service and the same or similar client. The result of service system mandates operating simultaneously without coordination is either a duplication of service or a lack of service. By operating in isolation, social service systems are guilty of building one of the most significant barriers to an effective service system for students with multiple needs.

The lack of coordination, coupled with the consistent lack of adequate dollars, has lead to a guarding by agencies of the limited resources they possess. Territorial attitudes contribute to the failure of service systems. No agency can continue to "administer separate systems of service....Separate systems are not economical, effective, or ethically justified" (O'Connell & Sontag, 1992, 110). By coordination of resources and collaboration of service provisions, a comprehensive service system for multi-needs students is possible. Without coordination and collaboration, service systems are destined to continue in failure.

Education System Failure

Factors cited in this chapter leave no doubt that there will be increasing numbers of multi-needs students in the future. Research indicates, however, that multi-needs students are currently being underserved by existing educational systems. The number of students identified, on the federal level, as eligible for services through special education as seriously emotionally disturbed stands at approximately 2 percent of the population. The estimated prevalence of students that should meet the eligibility criteria for special education services as seriously emotionally handicapped is between 6 percent and 10 percent of the population (Glidwell & Swallow, 1968; Graham, 1979; Reinert, 1976).

Throughout the past two decades, the American educational system has been greatly criticized (Goodlad, 1983; Kozol, 1980). American education is not meeting the needs of all American students, as documented in the report of the National Commission on Excellence in Education (1983). This report, and the nation's response to it, has elevated education and student service systems to the front of many agendas, resulting in the sweeping educational reform movements of the past ten years (O'Connell & Sontag, 1992). As McNulty (1992) stated, while educators look at the reasons for the failure of the education system, it is impossible not to ponder the need for a student service system "that reflects the dynamic and interactive nature of today's complex milieu" (p. 25). Lipp (1992) stated, "In examination of collective conscience, educators have determined that they do not bear the sole responsibility for the failure of the system." Nor can education change the student service system alone. Changes in service systems for multi-needs students must be grounded in a holistic approach that includes interagency cooperation and service delivery collaboration (McNulty, 1992). Stroul & Friedman (1986) also expressed that the only way the complex needs of this group could possibly be met is by a system that is collaborative and integrates all helping systems working together for the benefit of the student and their family.

SERVICE SYSTEM CHANGE INITIATIVES

Service System Initiatives Outside of Education

Numerous models of service system change have emerged from a variety of service agencies. The two initiatives to be discussed in this section are the Child and Adolescent Service System Program (CASSP) and the Alaska Youth Initiative (AYI). These initiatives, while originating from different sources, have both provided significant information regarding service system change at both the implementation and policy levels.

The first initiatives, CASSP, began in 1984, funded as part of the public health budget. The funds are used to provide small grants to states and local entities to assist in the development of comprehensive, integrated mental health services for multi-needs students. The initial goals of this small federal program were (1) to encourage leadership at the state level in the area of children's mental health, (2) to establish the concept of interagency responsibilities, and (3) to develop demonstration systems at the local community level (Knitzer et al., 1990). While targeting mental health services, CASSP requires close collaboration with other service providers. Although CASSP itself is not a service delivery model, one of the major products that has emerged from the CASSP initiative is the document "A System of Care for Severely Emotionally Disturbed Children and Youth" (Stroul & Friedman, 1986). "This document describes a model of service delivery [frequently referred to as the CASSP Model] that is both comprehensive and based on interagency collaboration" (Duchnowski, 1991, 15). The CASSP Model has been used in many states as the beginning point for service system change efforts. The CASSP Model details components of a service system including: mental health services, social services, educational services, health services, vocational services, recreational services, and operational services. The CASSP Model proposes supplying the needed services to the student and his or her family through a continuum of care based in the local community. The CASSP Model also recommends the consideration of cultural issues in treatment decisions. One key element in the CASSP Model is the use of case management, "described as the glue that holds this system together" (Duchnowski, 1991).

The Alaska Youth Initiative (AYI) began as a state initiative to establish community-based services for a small group of students being served in residential treatment centers out of state. The impetus for the initiative was twofold: First, the cost of out-of-state residential treatment was creating a financial burden; and second, for students placed out of state, even high-cost treatment was not working. Agency representatives reported a lack of positive outcomes. The AYI is a major departure from previous service system models because it does not use a categorical structure in defining students or services. The key components in the AYI are (1) an individualized (often termed "wrap-around") needs-based services (2) determined by an interdisciplinary services team (including the parent or guardian, the teacher, the therapist, the psychiatrist, a services coordinator, and any other persons with influence in the student's life) that is, (3) based on major life domains (a place to live, a family, a social group, educational needs, medical needs, psychological and/or emotional needs, legal needs, safety needs, and student-specific needs). The AYI is extremely successful in Alaska and is now being used as the basis for initiatives in several other states Duchnowski, 1991; Knitzer et al., 1990; VanDenBerg, 1992).

Service System Initiatives Lead by Education

School districts across the nation have implemented collaborative arrangements with other service systems. The most common of these is the school and mental health partnerships that thrive in many communities. However, in very few instances have schools lead the way in the creation of a comprehensive student service system that encompasses the multiple factors crucial to success with multi-needs students (Knitzer et al., 1990; Fiske, 1991). This section will look at two initiatives, lead by education agencies, that are addressing the need for service system change in working with multi-needs students and their families.

Since the late 1980s, many communities in New Jersey have been part of the New Jersey School-Based Youth Services Program. The concept of one-stop-shopping has lead to the creation of numerous "full-service" model schools. At the local community full-service school, services in health, mental health, including substance abuse and family counseling, employment, and recreation are available. Such schools are viewed as a way to coordinate efforts of various service systems and make services readily available in a safe environment. New Jersey's success with the one-stop-shopping concept has lead to the development of similar programs in Kentucky and Iowa. Two federal departments - Education, and Health and Human Services - are jointly considering the benefits of the full-service school model (Fiske, 1991; Knitzer et al., 1990).

In 1987 the state of Indiana began the first steps toward a comprehensive, statewide change effort in the provision of services to multi-needs students and their families. Various segments of the service systems change are referred to as the Challenge of Change initiatives. All of the initiatives are based on the beliefs that: (1) the students being served by these initiatives exhibit multiple needs and, therefore, are the responsibility of multiple state and local entities; (2) services must be cross-disciplinary, because multi-needs students can no longer afford the inefficiencies and ineffectiveness of multiple service systems working in isolation; (3) services must be child and family centered; (4) services must be easily accessible; and (5) service gaps and service duplication must be eliminated. In addition to these basic beliefs, all initiatives are considered in relation to four specific factors: legal issues, fiscal issues, programmatic issues, and interdisciplinary issues. The Indiana approach appears, at first glance, to be fragmented and without a cohesive structure. In reality, the undertaking of an entire state service system is of such magnitude that multiple initiatives, occurring simultaneously, are required to achieve the overall change effect. An overview of some of the key initiatives is given below, followed by a brief report on the status of the Challenge of Change in Indiana.

Bringing Hoosier Children Home. The early Indiana effort began in a manner similar to the previously described Alaska Youth Initiative. The Indiana Department of Education had a number of students placed out of state in high-cost residential facilities. In addition to the financial implications of these placements, was the concern that students placed out-of-state were not making substantial progress. In the few cases where a student did progress at an out- of-state facility, upon the student's return to the local community environment the gains were often lost. This group of students was the initial target group for the Challenge of Change: Bringing Hoosier Children Home initiative. The return of these students has been a springboard to effect multiple service system change efforts.

Child Service Coordinators. In 1992 Indiana initiated several three-year grant projects introducing the concept of the Child Service Coordinator (CSC). CSCs fulfill two main roles in the systems change initiatives. First, the CSCs gather information regarding barriers to local collaboration. This information is essential to other components of the systems change project, providing information for future strategies. The CSC model also provides technical assistance to local communities utilizing a cadre of trained professionals from a variety of service backgrounds. That include special education, education administration, mental health, social work, public welfare, probation, corrections, and parents. CSCs provide assistance and information regarding the wrap-around service concept, collaboration, team building, and problem solving.

Training and Retraining. When a major shift in the service system occurs, a corresponding shift in the training of new service system workers is essential. A preservice cross-disciplinary training program has been started at one state university. The initial training targets teachers and will branch out into other service system areas (nursing, social work, political science, criminology, etc.) and to other universities via a distance education format.

Existing service system workers must also be given information as to new service system structure. Several initiatives are addressing this retraining need. (1) A series of informative video broadcasts began in January 1991 with additions to the series continuing. (2) A training is being developed for local community based teams. The training will provide additional information on wrap around services, collaboration, team building, and problem solving. (3) A mentoring component is being developed to provide a multi-disciplinary mentor team to newly formed community teams. (4) Challenge education sites have been built around the state for use with students, families, community teams, and agency personnel. The purpose of the Challenge Education sites is to provide another means for training in the concepts of collaboration, team building, and problem solving.

Information Services. Information is a key element in system change progress. A statewide electronic mail network now links educators to other service providers around the state as well as to pertinent bulletin board information on student and family issues. Work is also underway on a cross-referenced database that will facilitate planning at the local community level as well as at the state level.

Project CONNECT. Project CONNECT is a federally funded grant project that is doing in-depth work with two school districts, one rural and one urban. Project CONNECT will provide recommendations for interagency agreements, multi-agency forms, and other documents that will be of assistance to local community teams. Project CONNECT will also provide data collection and additional inservice training material in the form of self-study modules.

Legislative Change. Service system change is not an easy undertaking. Many barriers are identified as change progresses. Some barriers are removed by training, some by the provision of information. A few barriers, however, require legislative changes. The Indiana service system change initiatives have sought legislative removal of barriers when necessary.

The Indiana Challenge of Change Initiatives have resulted in two recent documents, the Indiana Consolidated Plan and the Indiana Collaboration Project. The Indiana Consolidated Plan is the result of the work of a multidisciplinary group at the state agency level. This group identified two key pieces of information: the number and amount of federal funding streams coming into the state of Indiana and the number of state-level resources going out into local communities. Based on the gathered information, the Indiana Consolidated Plan outlines recommendations for the responsible use of existing resources. The Indiana Collaboration Project, also resulting from the work of a multidisciplinary, state-level group, details a plan for local communities to follow when they, as a local community planning team, come across barriers they cannot remove alone. As in other Indiana service system change initiatives, these barriers may be legal or legislative in nature, they may be programmatic barriers, interdisciplinary issues, or fiscal barriers. The Collaboration Project has appointed problem-solving teams, in a tiered format, to address barriers as they are identified. The first tier is local community-level problem-solving team built on existing Step Ahead Councils. The next tier is a county-level multi-agency problem-solving team. From the county-level team, an issue would move to a state-level working group. If the barrier cannot be removed at the state-level working group tier, several tiers remain to be accessed, including the Indiana Policy Council, the Region V Team, and at the federal level, the White House Empowerment Board Working Group. This tiered barrier removal and/or problem-solving approach forms the basis for continued refinement of the service system in Indiana. The Consolidated Plan and Collaboration Project have received praise and support from President Bill Clinton. In a letter addressed to Evan Bayh, governor of Indiana, President Clinton spoke of the usefulness of Indiana's plan as an information source to the Domestic Policy Council, the National Economic Council, the Departments of Agriculture, Education, Health and Human Services, Housing and Urban Development, Justice, and Labor. (W. Clinton, President of the United States of America, personal communication to E. Bayh, Governor of Indiana, January 5, 1994).

IMPLICATIONS FOR SYSTEMS SERVING MULTINEEDS STUDENTS FUTURE DIRECTIONS AND IMPLICATIONS FOR POLICY DEVELOPMENT

Proposed Components of Service Systems

Kahn (1991) believed that despite the multitude of issues, "problems can be solved if people learn to work collectively." The multiple needs of this population demand responses that are cross-disciplinary, requiring the commitment and participation of education, mental health, public welfare, and social service agencies; of healthcare and family service providers; and of juvenile justice and corrections facilities; of families, and of local communities, and local business, as well as of other local, state, or federal agencies with responsibility to or concern for the coordinated provision of appropriate services to students with multiple needs. No single entity can change student service systems. To succeed in their own primary objectives, each entity must forge alliances and working relationships with others. Together, the fabric of a successful service system can be woven (Fiske, 1991).

Creating a climate for change may be the most important goal in the process of systems change (Polsgrove, Skiba, Wilhite, Marra, Jackson, Quick, & Dare, 1993). The involvement of multiple entities in service provision to students with multiple needs is essential; however, there are critical considerations in these collaborations. Interaction among agencies must respect the values and assumptions of each individual collaborator. Decision making must be open and take into account the view of all entities involved. Roles must be renegotiated and redefined. Current knowledge concerning effective interventions for multi-needs students must be utilized. Sufficient training, cross-disciplinary in nature, must be available. Service acquisition and provision must be streamlined. In addition, families must be active participants in the collaboration (Bower, 1989; Duchnowski, 1991; Lipp, 1992).

"People are changed, not by coercion or intimidation, but by example" (Bird, 1992, 12). Sharing effective models of system change assists in letting others know what is being done to improve services for multi-needs students. Sharing successful efforts also documents for policy makers the characteristics of endeavors that have resulted in positive system change. The information discussed in this chapter shows that service system change can have many beginnings. Advocates in multiple systems are calling for change in existing service systems. The change being called for places decision making at the local level based on comprehensive, coordinated service assisting the family and the community along with the student (O'Connell & Sontag, 1992). Although there is no single entity that must lead the way, many look to education to provide leadership in efforts for children and youth. "Schools have been viewed by Congress primarily as instruments of social change" (Maeroff, 1982). The Children's Defense Fund, (1991, cited in O'Connell & Sontag, 1992), envisioned the school's becoming the "hub for collaborative service delivery systems" (p. 109). As Edward J. Tetleman of the New Jersey State Department of Human Services observed, in many communities the school represents the one place "where families and children and youth gather, and it's the correct place for us [service providers] to be in order to give them access to needed services" (as cited in Fiske, 1991).

Implications for Policy Development

Regardless of the origins of service system change, new policies must be visionary. "The call is for a new kind of policy development that hinges on an understanding of the new world view and that reflects the dynamic and interactive nature of today's complex milieu" (Lipp, 1992, 25). In the development of policies that affect multi-needs students, several guiding principles are recommended: Policies should be client focused, field driven, and integrated with service delivery. Policies should foster communication between stakeholders. They should streamline processes and encourage innovation; they should also encourage citizen involvement. As well, policies should structure a framework that allows for future evolutionary changes that will further strengthen services (based on principles of reorganization outlined in the Indiana

Government Operations Committee Report, November 1989). Change is truly a "process that takes time to evolve—it is not a discrete event...[but] requires a high degree of commitment and continuous attention" (Berreth, 1992). Service system change involves a series of formidable tasks, but change can be successfully undertaken and ultimately accomplished.

AUTHOR NOTE

Much of the information in this chapter is a result of my years of work with the Indiana Department of Education, Division of Special Education. The information contained in this document does not necessarily reflect the views of the Indiana Department of Education, however.

My thanks to Robert Marra, assistant director of the Division of Special Education, for his vision, leadership, example, and belief in the importance of service system change.

16

New Directions: Innovative Programs to Reach At-Risk Students

Robert G. Monahan
Sheila B. Marino
Rosemary Miller

At the Education Summit in Charlottesville, Virginia, in 1989, the president of the United States and its governors set forth six education goals for the nation: (1) by the year 2000, all children in American will start school ready to learn, (2) the high school graduation rate will increase to at least 90 percent, (3) students will participate and demonstrate competency in rigorous school curricula, (4) students will become life-long learners to assure success in the workplace and to exercise the rights and responsibilities of responsible citizens, (5) all schools will be drug- and violence-free, and (6) American students will be first in the world in science and mathematics achievement.

The focus of these goals is on students who are at risk, students who according to a Phi Delta Kappa study are likely to fail either in school or in life. Examples of failure may include a grade in school or physical, sexual, or drug abuse in life. According to Frymier and Gainsneder (1989) failure in school or in life provides evidence that a youngster is at risk.

A variety of initiatives have been shown to be effective strategies for addressing the needs of at-risk students. This chapter will discuss the following initiatives: early intervention; behavior management and social skills training; instructional strategies, including text adaptations, reading, recovery, cooperative learning and whole language reading instruction; and finally community involvement through the Foster Grandparents Program and multicultural education.

EARLY INTERVENTION

Amendments to the Education of the Handicapped Act of 1975 (PL 94-142) address services for children ages birth to six (PL 99-457) and the development of national educational goals, the first of which states that all children will enter school ready to learn, to assure early intervention for the at-risk and developmentally-delayed preschool population.   Inherent in the legislative language as well as the objectives cited for Goal 1 by the National Educational Goals Panel is an emphasis on interagency collaboration, the assurance that parents participate as full partners in the educational planning and implementation process, and that comprehensive service delivery systems are available to all eligible children.

Communities throughout the United States have multiple agencies that provide various services to young children with special needs. However, there are often gaps or duplications in the provision of these services. Parents may be subjected to repeated requests for the same information by different agencies only to learn that they are not eligible for services. Agency caseload maximums may result in placement on a waiting list, causing the loss of critical intervention time. In an effort to coordinate service delivery efforts Congress mandated that under Part H of PL 99-457 an Interagency Coordinating Council (ICC) be established in every state. Many states have furthered the concept of interagency collaboration by requiring that local councils be established to assure dialogue between service providers at the grassroots level.

"Best practice" guidelines for exemplary early childhood services are characterized as being (1) integrated, (2) comprehensive in assessment, planning, programming, service coordination, and evaluation, (3) adaptable to support different family needs, (4) peer and family referenced to assure communication between families and service providers, and (5) outcome based to assure appropriate programming and transition planning (McDonnell & Hardman 1988). With multiple local agencies that may include health, education, social services, counseling, mental retardation, Head Start, daycare, and private preschool, the task of assuring best practice is staggering. The local ICC provides a vehicle for communication among service providers that may result in exemplary programs. Broadening the scope of the local ICC to include all young children ages birth to six assures that services can be provided across agencies and settings. Specific activities local ICC's may promote include agency information sharing, collaborative "child-find" activities, cross-agency assessments and educational placements, public relations, and political action.

Agency information sharing can be a program feature of ICC meetings. Using a preestablished format, each agency is given time to present an overview of the purpose, guidelines, and services provided. Handouts that can be placed in a notebook provide a written resource for the participants to refer to at a later date. The outcome of this knowledge is increased trust among agency personnel.

With increased trust comes a willingness to communicate and when people begin to talk with each other, interagency collaboration begins to occur. Simply stated, *knowledge* brings *trust*, which fosters *communication*, which results in *collaboration*.

"Child Find" is an activity mandated in PL 94-142 and PL 99-457. It requires public education agencies as well as the lead agency in a state responsible for services for the birth-to-three population to assure a comprehensive system of identification and screening of all children who may have a disability. The ICC provides a vehicle for planning comprehensive interagency child-find activities. Resources can be pooled and multiple sites such as child-care centers, Head Start programs, or preschools other than those in public schools can be used as screening sites. Because parents are equal members of the ICC, they can participate in the child-find process and provide support to families who may have a child who demonstrates some significant developmental delays.

Cross-agency assessments and service delivery options can be structured by the local ICC to meet the needs of the community. An assessment center could be set up with all the equipment and materials needed housed in one location. With agency collaboration, costs can be shared through in-kind contributions as well as financial contributions. Because agencies are participating in the assessment at the same time, parents are spared the inconvenience and cost of multiple visits to multiple sites and are present to actively participate in the evaluation process.

Services for children who are at risk for or are developmentally delayed are best provided in integrated settings, settings that group disabled children and nondisabled children together for instructional and/or social activities (Peck, Odom, & Bricker, 1993; Salisbury & Smith, 1991). Through collaboration within the context of the ICC, these integrated settings can be established with positive outcomes for disabled and nondisabled children (Bailey & Bricker, 1985; Hoyson, Jamieson, & Strain, 1984). Children with language delays taught in clinical settings make disappointing transfers of language training (Cooke, Raver, Cooke, & Apolloni, 1965), whereas those instructed in an interactive communicative approach using classroom activities as instructional time make significantly more generalizations of new language skills (Raver, 1987). Nondisabled and at-risk children also benefit from the incidental language instruction that occurs during classroom routines.

Preschool children with identified delays may receive services from multiple agencies. Extended-day programs might be provided by one agency, educational services provided by a second agency, and intervention services by a third agency. All these services could be provided in one setting through a collaborative service delivery approach developed by the ICC.

Public relations and political action are two additional activities the ICC can engage in to the benefit of all children. Through newspaper articles and radio and television spots, the public becomes better informed about the needs of this population as well as those services that exist. With an informed public, identified needs become the focus of political action. If funding for programs for preschool disabled and at-risk children is to continue, political action is critical.

Local and state agencies that provide services to young children at risk for school success are challenged to develop innovative ways to assure that the needs of this population are met. Interagency coordinating councils provide a means of pooling resources and ideas to better meet best practice guidelines for exemplary services.

BEHAVIORAL MANAGEMENT

Behavioral management can be directed in many ways. Perhaps one of the most important aspects of any behavior change program is its relationship to the maintenance of acquired skills over time and ultimately to their generalization to other settings and other behaviors. One area that has been widely addressed in the United States today is the area of self-management. It consists of four components: self-assessment, self-instruction, self-determination of reinforcement, and self-admiration. Today the field is burgeoning with research on cognitive behavior modification (CBM). This research has provided many techniques to promote behavior change through self-regulation. Self-monitoring, particularly of on-task behavior, has been a topic of much research. Based on the array of literature supporting self-monitoring, it would certainly be worthy of consideration. Behavior change strategies affords persons working in the field with a wide variety of options for motivating and managing children who require behavior management. Systematic use of positive reinforcement can increase appropriate behavior. Using the Premack principle, behaviors can be shaped in a positive manner. Behavior management is a power tool that must be used systematically and carefully with constant evaluation so that behaviors will be modified in the students' best interest. At-risk students can benefit from positive behavior management programs through the use of contingency contracting and token economics, as backed up by years of research in the field.

Another consideration is the home-school coordination. Two common methods that have produced positive results are the *daily report card*, which is sent home daily for communication, and the *passport*, which takes the form of a notebook that travels with the student back and forth from the school to home. Teachers, parents, and others such as the bus driver, can make regular notations. The major thought to keep in mind is that behavior is learned, and therefore it can be shaped and changed.

The area of social skills has been heavily explored by researchers over the past twenty-five years. In the United States, several commercially produced social skills curricula are available to teachers. Teachers, of course, are encouraged to develop their own social skills programs to match the needs of their students. Using both behavioral and the social strategies the teacher may need to employ a variety of approaches to increase appropriate social and behavioral skills and decrease inappropriate ones. Teachers in the United States have their behavioral expectations rooted in the Anglo-American culture. Learning to socialize begins at birth and develops throughout life. Persons with inappropriate social skills need to have an opportunity to modify their learned skills or learn appropriate new ones. Today in the United States with the diverse cultures assimilating together social skills need to be developed on an individualized basis. A variety of strategies can be used to develop the area of social skills. These strategies can be designed to enhance the self-concept and increase the ability to engage in positive social skills in the community and in society. Teachers can combine the social skill training with their behavior management training to work toward the positive goal of having the students accepted by their peers and by their own community.

INSTRUCTIONAL STRATEGIES

At-risk students often have difficulty succeeding in general education classrooms because the instructional material is beyond their skill level. Many instructional strategies have been shown to be effective interventions for fostering classroom success for these students. The instructional strategies to be reviewed include text and instructional modifications and student-directed strategies to foster content mastery, the Reading Recovery Program and whole language reading instruction to improve reading skills; and cooperative learning to enhance self-esteem and engagement in the learning process.

Textbook modifications may be necessary especially if the discrepancy between the reader and the text is so great that the decoding of words, not the comprehension of the concepts, becomes the focus of the task. Textbooks are often the primary vehicle for disseminating information in the content area classroom. If the student's reading skills are well below the readability of the textbook, the student is at risk for failure in that class. Tape recording the material, highlighting key concepts, and simplifying the content by addressing the text organization are examples of modifications that may be used by the classroom teacher to foster comprehension.

Tape recording a textbook is a simple but time-consuming process. Students or adult volunteers can be used, but care must be taken to assure that they read clearly and at a reasonable rate. The students with reading problems can listen to those tapes to reinforce the concepts (Wood & Wooley, 1986). To further enhance the comprehension of the material, inserting summaries, emphasizing key vocabulary words, explaining graphic information, or instructing students to listen for answers to specific questions can be included in the recording of the text.

The simplification of vocabulary and sentence structure is another textbook modification strategy. However, shorter sentences and simpler vocabulary do not necessarily mean that the text will be easier to read. It is important that cohesive ties such as coordinate and subordinate conjunctions, pronoun referents, and signal words such as first and next are not eliminated (Armbruster & Anderson, 1988). Topic sentences for each paragraph and transition sentences to the next paragraph improve comprehension, so care must be taken to ensure that these are not eliminated or shortened so that their effect is minimized. Graphic information needs to be evaluated for its importance to the comprehension of the text and questions embedded in the text so that visual presentations of information are used as learning tools (Reynolds & Salend, 1990). When simplifying vocabulary, the repetition of key words rather than the use of synonyms and the inclusion of examples after the definition have been shown to improve comprehension.

Alternative materials may be used to modify or supplement the text. Many excellent computer programs are available that provide a well-organized and logical presentation of the material and allow students to interact with the computer program to receive immediate feedback and remediation (Reynolds & Salend, 1990). Films and videotapes can also be used as alternative materials. High-interest, low-vocabulary materials may need to be used with students whose reading skills are significantly low. Care must be taken, however, to assure that the required concepts are addressed and that through the simplification process important background information has not been omitted.

Highlighting key concepts can be an effective textbook modification strategy. Color coding words or sentences using highlighter pens to identify important information can aid comprehension, assuming that marking in the textbook is acceptable. Wood and Wooley (1986) suggest using three colors, one for important terms, one for definitions, and a third for important facts.

Content simplification can be achieved through effective organization of the information presented in the text. All textbooks do not lend themselves to writing a basic outline of the concepts presented. Research has found that many content area texts are not well structured (Armbruster & Anderson, 1988). Transitions from topic to topic are often abrupt and confusing, chronological sequences are confusing, and graphics may be used more for decoration than comprehension (Armbruster & Anderson, 1988). Beech (1983) suggests the following guidelines be used when simplifying content to assure effective organization of the material: present ideas logically, sequence events in chronological order, cluster related information, and eliminate extraneous information. Vocabulary can be simplified by the repetition of key words rather than using synonyms and the inclusion of examples after a definition is given.

INSTRUCTIONAL MODIFICATIONS

Instructional modifications that are based on what is known about teaching reading comprehension are effective tools for helping students with poor reading skills become efficient users of content area textbooks. Providing advance organizers and study guides, previewing the text using text organizational strategies, preteaching critical vocabulary, shortening the length of assignments, and modeling effective reading strategies are examples of methods that have proven effective.

Providing students with advance organizers prior to independent reading has been shown to improve comprehension. Advance organizers help the students tap their prior knowledge of a topic so that they can integrate it with new information obtained from the reading. Research in schema theory demonstrates the importance of prior knowledge in the comprehension of the information to be presented (Bos & Vaughn, 1991). Semantic mapping is one strategy that can be used to activate background knowledge (Pearson & Johnson, 1978). Through free association, the students and teacher develop a list of words that pertain to the topic and then arrange them in a network that shows their relationship to each other. Advance organizers that are presented orally and followed by discussion have been shown to be more effective than those read silently by the students and then discussed (Rinehart & Welker, 1992).

Study guides are an effective means of enhancing comprehension by emphasizing major headings and cueing students as to the location of answers to questions (Reynolds & Salend, 1990). These guides also set the purpose for reading the passage and focus the students' attention on the important concepts.

Previewing the assignment by focusing on the organization of the textbook is another effective method for improving comprehension. Making students aware of the headings, subheadings, introduction, and summary enables them to more easily read the material on their own. Archer and Gleason (1989) have suggested a teacher-directed chapter warm-up procedures:

- Read the chapter title and introduction.
- Read the headings and subheadings.
- Read the chapter summary.
- Read the questions at the end of the chapter.
- Tell what the chapter will talk about.

The pre-teaching of critical vocabulary has been shown to enhance comprehension. The specialized terms and new words should be presented in context. This not only provides the definition of the term but establishes how the term is used in the particular content (Bos & Vaughn, 1991). The use of specific examples when defining terms is also important to the retention of the meanings as well as their use in new settings.

Adapting a textbook or altering instructional procedures does not have to be a complicated and time-consuming process. These strategies can be integrated into the instructional routine, thus enhancing the learning of all participants. Also, the use of the adaptation process by the teacher can serve as a model for the students to develop their own strategies for content mastery.

STUDENT DIRECTED STRATEGIES

Student-directed strategies do not require the teacher to spend as much time modifying materials, but they do require considerable direct instruction time to teach the student how to apply them systematically and effectively. Students must also believe that the strategy will benefit them (Reynolds & Salend, 1990). The University of Kansas Institute for Research in Learning Disabilities (UK-IRLD) has developed a teaching sequence for instruction in the use of learning strategies that includes obtaining a commitment to learn the strategy, describing and modeling the strategy for the students, having the students verbally rehearse the strategy steps and practice using the steps in controlled materials, and finally using the strategy to master content in regular classroom materials (Ellis, Deshler, Lenz, Schumaker, & Clark, 1991). Many other learning strategies have been devised and studied for their effectiveness, including Multipass, self-questioning, study cards, and SOS. One of the earliest content learning strategies is known as SQ3R (Robinson, 1946). This acronym represents the steps of the strategy which are Survey, Question, Read, Recite, Review. Multipass is a similar strategy developed at UK-IRLD (Schumaker, Deshler, Alley, Warner, & Denton, 1982). This strategy includes three passes through the passage, reading only that which is necessary for each pass. The Survey Pass requires the students to read the title, headings, illustrations, chapter introduction, and chapter summary. The second or Size-Up Pass requires the students to read the chapter questions and identify the ones they cannot answer. These questions are answered by skimming the chapter to find the answers. The Sort-Out Pass requires the student to test his knowledge of the content by reviewing the chapter questions again, checking off the ones known, and returning to the chapter to locate forgotten information. Although this strategy is complex and requires some prerequisite skills, it has been demonstrated to be effective.

Self-questioning strategies have been developed based on the research that demonstrates that questioning plays an important role in the comprehension process. Wong and Jones (1982) developed a strategy for upper elementary-age children that focuses on the main ideas in a passage. After instructing the students in finding main ideas, teach them to ask themselves the following questions:

Step 1:   Determine why you are studying this passage.
Step 2:   Find the main ideas and underline them.
Step 3:   Think of a question about the main idea.

Step 4:   Write the question in the margin.
Step 5:   Learn the answer to the question.
Step 6:   Always look back at the previous questions and answers to see how they relate to each other.

Active Reading (Archer & Gleason, 1989) is a similar strategy designed to involve the students in verbally hearing and monitoring their comprehension of textbook passages through self-questioning. The student proceeds paragraph by paragraph thinking about the topic sentence and important details, reciting what each paragraph is about, and checking to see that the recitation is correct. These self-questioning strategies can also be used by students as they listen to a taped text. Instead of the teacher inserting the questions, the student develops his or her own questions based on the main ideas and details.

Study cards are often used to review material prior to taking a test. Rooney (1988) detailed a system for producing study cards that combines self-questioning and comprehension strategies. Students read the subtitle and paragraphs under the subtitle. On separate index cards, they write important vocabulary, dates, names, and so on. Next, the students go back to turn the subtitles into questions and write these questions on the index card that has the correct answer on it. This procedure is repeated until a set of study cards has been produced that covers all of the material. These cards can now be used to self-question using both the main ideas and the answers as questions.

A vocabulary learning strategy, SOS, was developed by R. Miller (1985). The acronym stands for Search, Operate, and Study, and the purpose of the strategy is to facilitate the mastery of content material that has a focus on specific vocabulary such as that in science and computer courses. The process is similar to other reading comprehension strategies. It differs in that it requires the student to record the material in a specific format that results in an outline that places the content-specific vocabulary in context. The student searches through the chapter for vocabulary by reading the title, introduction, summary, headings, subheadings, charts and graphs, and questions. As vocabulary words are encountered, they are recorded with the page number beside them. The second pass through the material is the Operate step, in which the student records the definition of the words and gives examples. When these two steps are completed, the student has a chapter outline that focuses on the vocabulary. The final step is to study the vocabulary word and their meanings using the Study process.

The process of determining the most effective adaptation approach must be based on the specific strengths and weaknesses of the students as well as on the teacher's personality. Martens, Peterson, Witt, and Cirone (1986) identified treatment acceptability as a critical factor in the strategy choice. Treatment acceptability refers to the ease of implementation. According to Reynolds and Salend (1990) educators should consider student strengths and weaknesses, the time involved in implementing the strategy, the course content-strategy match, and the impact of the strategy on all students in the class.

Text modifications, instructional modifications, and student-generated learning strategies are effective methods of accommodating at-risk students in the classroom. The first two are teacher implemented, whereas the learning strategies foster independent learning. Effective teachers may well determine that a combination of teacher and student modifications provides the optimum learning environment for students at risk for school failure.

READING RECOVERY PROGRAM

The Reading Recovery Program provides intensive one-to-one intervention for at-risk young children. Designed to be a preventative program for young children who are having difficulty learning to read during their first year of reading instruction, the program was developed in 1982 in New Zealand by Marie Clay, a leading educator and psychologist. The program is short-term, usually lasting from twelve to fifteen weeks, and it uses one-to-one instruction for thirty minutes each day to provide strategies for reading. The materials used in the program include hundreds of simple books from picture books and wordless books to books adept first-grade readers can read by the end of the year.

The thirty-minute lesson has five components: reading familiar books, rereading the previous lesson's new book and assessing reading ability, working with letters, writing a story, and reading a new book (Bos, 1991). In the first part of the lesson the teacher and child reread books that are familiar to the child. This rereading allows the child to participate in fluent reading in much the same way that using language experience stories written by the child allows for ownership of the printed page. After this initial rereading the child is requested to reread the previous lesson's new book and the teacher takes on the role of observer and recorder to determine how the child is using word identification, comprehension, and monitoring strategies. Working with letters will follow so the child will begin to recognize and write the upper and lowercase letters. The child will then compose a brief story or message usually one to two sentences in length. In this situation, the child discovers sound-symbol relationships and participates in structural and phonic analyses. At the end of each lesson the teacher introduces the child to a new book.

This innovative program attempts to reduce failure through early intervention and to help young at-risk children to become independent readers and develop essential literacy skills with a positive self-concept. Children are taught how to use a variety of word identification and comprehension strategies and how to utilize the strategies while attending to the text. Children are taught not only the "skills" of reading but through this program, the "love" of reading.

WHOLE LANGUAGE PROGRAMS

Literacy begins within the family when members respond to signs, logos, and labels, share books, and scribbling notes. Whole language programs have emerged as an effective means of teaching integrated communication skills. In whole language programs children are able to learn from materials written for a variety of purposes. Writing becomes an integral part of reading in whole language programs, and skills are taught in context as children need them (Harp & Brewer, 1991). Basic tenets of whole language programs involve a totally integrated approach to language instruction focusing on students' experience and interests, with students engaged in oral language and writing activities and teachers serving as language models and researchers who observe students learning for classroom application (Stoodt, 1988).

Whole language programs provide the flexibility to accommodate for the needs of young at-risk children. The programs use a variety of materials, build on the experimental background of the children, and involve the students in active learning.

COOPERATIVE LEARNING PROGRAMS

Programs that incorporate cooperative learning strategies enhance the self-esteem of the at-risk young child (Dick, 1991). Young children learn to cooperate with others and help others solve problems. Johnson and Johnson (1987) have found that children tend to like each other more when they work cooperatively in the classroom. Thus, when students of different ethnicity and academic ability learn cooperatively, prejudice diminishes and ridicule subsides. Through cooperative learning settings young children are able to develop acceptance for others (Slavin, 1983). Children learn to prize the uniqueness and special abilities of each member of the group (Barbour, 1990).

Kagan (1989) notes there is a large repertoire of cooperative learning strategies or procedures. Each of these is based on several common ideas that include dividing the class into small groups who work together cooperatively to complete an academic task, giving tasks at different levels of difficulty, and providing guidelines to inspire cooperation and interdependence within each group.

Cooperative learning programs incorporate an alternative method of learning that is successfully combatting the low self-esteem of at-risk students, enhancing their social skills, and assisting them in their mastery of the basic skills (Slavin, 1989).

COMMUNITY INVOLVEMENT: THE FOSTER GRANDPARENT PROGRAM

One of the programs that has been successful in focusing on the at-risk school-age child is the Foster Grandparent Program. The program sponsored by A.C.T.I.O.N. provides low-income sixty-year-olds and over, an opportunity to share themselves with at-risk children in public schools and private settings. Foster grandparents receive a modest tax-free stipend, a hot meal, transportation allowance, accident insurance, and an annual physical examination. They attend forty hours of preservice orientation and have monthly inservice programs.

The program in Laurens County, South Carolina, was first funded in 1988. Volunteers work at a variety of workstations throughout the community such as the public schools, Head Start, and institutional settings. The National Foster Grandparent Program started in 1965 now funds 245 different programs in the United States. These programs serve more than 19,000 grandparents and serve over 67,000 children with special needs.

MULTICULTURAL EDUCATION

In the absence of appropriate programs in regular and special education, students are at a higher risk of being misidentified and their educational experiences may not take into account the reality that linguistic and cultural characteristics coexist and interact with disability-related factors (Garcia & Malkin, 1993). Culture provides a worldwide view that influences our ways of perceiving the world around us. As a result, the culture and subcultures of the school are likely to impact what and how children should be taught, as well as when and how successfully it is taught (Lynch, 1992).

Intercultural competence is an essential ingredient in teachers' ability to implement multicultural education. As diversity in U.S. society continues to increase, students must be prepared to become members of a workforce that is much more heterogeneous. Multicultural education assists all students to increase their appreciation of diversity, to develop a positive self-concept, to respect individuals' civil and human rights, to understand the historical context in which prejudice, oppression, and stereotyping occur, and ultimately to fulfill their own potential while resisting and challenging stereotyping and barriers to success that exist in the society (Sleeter, 1992).

CONCLUSIONS

The program initiatives discussed here are only a few of many that have been demonstrated to be effective in working with at-risk students. Early intervention through effective collaboration, innovative instructional strategies that involve the student to foster independence, and community programs that cause all citizens both young and old to invest themselves in the educational process are viable strategies that will move us closer to meeting our national goals. However, it is the position of these authors that if we are to see the fruits of our labors, two key issues must be addressed. First is the need for schools to become family-focused rather than child-focused. Students live in community with other family members, and the needs of the family directly affects their success or failure in school. Second is the need to implement in a coordinated and consistent system across all communities the initiatives that have been demonstrated as effective.

Our public schools have been challenged to meet the needs of all students by the year 2000. If we as professionals are to meet this challenge, we must affirm our attitudes on individual differences, interests, and abilities, begin to rejoice in our likenesses and differences, and view at-risk students as capable learners and valuable citizens.

References

Aaron, H. J. (1973). *Why is welfare so hard to reform?* Washington, DC: Brookings Institution.

Acs, G. (1993). The impact of AFDC on young women's childbearing decisions (Discussion Paper No. 101193). Madison, WI: Institute for Research on Poverty.

Adams, C. F., Jr., Landsbergen, D., & Cobler, L. (1992). Welfare reform and paternity establishment: A social experiment. *Journal of Policy Analysis and Management, 11*, 665-687.

Adams, P. F., & Hardy, A. M. (1989). *Current estimates from the National Health Interview Survey: United States, 1988 national health statistics,10*(173). Washington, DC: National Center for Health Statistics.

AFLCIO Proceedings of the 5th Constitutional Convention of the AFLCIO. Washington D.C.: Government Printing Office.

Alford, R. R. (1975). *Health care politics: Ideological and interest group barriers to reform.* Chicago: University of Chicago Press.

Allport, G, & Postman, L. (1947). *The psychology of rumor.* New York: Henry Holt.

AMBHA/Foster Higgins (1994). *Managed behavioral healthcare quality and access survey.* New York: AMBHA.

American Council on Education (1989). *Minorities in higher education.* Eighth Annual Status Report. Washington, DC: Council on Education, Office of Minority Concerns.

American Psychiatric Association (APA)(1994). *Diagnostic and statistical manual for mental disordersIV.* Washington, DC: American Psychiatric Association Press.

Anderson, E. (1991). Neighborhood effects on teenage pregnancy. In C. Jencks & P. E. Peterson (Eds.), *The urban underclass* (pp. 375-398). Washington, DC: Brookings Institution.

Andreck, William S. (1994, September/October). Balancing the budget at the bedside. *The Healthcare Forum Journal.*

Angle, H. L., & Van de Ven, A. H. (1989). Suggestions for managing the innovation journey. In A. H. Van de Ven, H. L. Angle & M. S. Poole (Eds.), *Research on the management of innovation,* New York: Harper & Row.

Appelbaum, P. S. (1994). *Almost a revolution: Mental health law and the limits of change.* New York: Oxford University Press.

Apsler, R., & Bassuk, E. (1983). Differences among clinicians in the decision to admit. *Archives of General Psychiatry, 40*, 1133-1137.

Archer, A., & Gleason, M. (1989). *Skills for school success.* Boston: Curriculum Associates.

Armbruster, B., & Anderson, T. (1988). On selecting "considerate" content area textbooks, *RASE*, *9*(1), 47-52.

Arnold, C. A. (1989). Beyond self interest: Policy entrepreneurs and aid to the homeless. *Policy Studies Journal*, *18*(Fall), 47-66.

Arnold, R. D. (1990). *The logic of congressional action*, New Haven, CT: Yale University Press.

Aronowitz, S. (1994). A different perspective on educational inequality. In F. Pignatelli & S. W. Pflaum (Eds.), *Experiencing diversity* (pp. 25-46). Thousand Oaks, CA: Corwin.

Asher, C. (1994). Improving the school-home connection for poor and minority students. In J. Kretovics & E. J. Nussel (Eds.), *Transforming urban education* (pp. 360-374). Boston: Allyn & Bacon.

Associated Press. (1994, October 23). School trustee calls homework "unfair," seeks ban. *Chicago Tribune*, p. 14.

Avery, G. (1985). Effects of social, cultural, and economic factors on brain development. In J. Freeman (Ed.), *Prenatal and perinatal factors associated with brain disorders*. Washington, DC: Department of Health and Human Services.

Ayers, William. (1991, May). Perestroika in Chicago's schools. *Educational Leadership*, pp. 41-43.

Bagley, R., Allard, H., McCormier, N., Proudfoot, P., Fortin, D., Oglivie, D., RaeGrant, Q., Gelinas, P., Pepin, L., & Sutherland, S. (1984). Sexual offenses against children. In *Committee on sexual offenses against children and youth*. Ottawa: Canadian Government Publishing Centre.

Bailey, E. & Bricker, D. (1985). Evaluation of a three-year early intervention demonstration project. *Topics in Early Childhood Special Education*, *5*, 52-65.

Baker, F. (1991). *Saving our kids from delinquency, drugs, and despair*. New York: Harper Collins.

Bandura, A. (1983). Psychological mechanisms of aggression. In R. G. Green & E. I. Donnerstein (Eds.), *Aggression: Theoretical and empirical reviews*. New York: Academic Press.

Banks, J. (1994). Ethnicity, class, cognitive, and motivation styles: Research and teaching implications. In J. Kretovics & E. J. Nussel (Eds.), *Transforming urban education* (pp. 274-290). New York: Teachers College Press.

Barbour, N. (1990). Flexible grouping: It works. *Childhood Education*, *67*, 66-67.

Bardach, E. (1972). *The skill factor in politics*, Berkeley, CA: University of California Press.

Bardach, E. (1977). *The implementation game: What happens after a bill becomes a law*, Cambridge, MA: MIT Press.

Barker, Arthur, J. (1993). *Paradigms, the business of discovering the future*. New York: Harper Business.

Bartfeld, J., & Meyer, D. R. (1994). Are there really deadbeat dads? The relationship between ability to pay, enforcement, and compliance in nonmarital child support cases. *Social Service Review*, *68*, 219-235.

Bartunek, Frank. (1994). Intergovernmental relations in education. *Education Canada*, pp. 4-7.

Bassi, L. J., & Barnow, B. S. (1993). Expenditures on children and child support guidelines. *Journal of Policy Analysis and Management*, *12*, 478-497.

Baum, W. M. (1994). *Understanding behaviorism*. New York: Harper Collins.

Baumeister, A. A., Dokecki, P. R., & Kupstas, F. D. (1991). The new morbidity. In R. Batey & A. Garcia (Eds.), *Current perspectives in psychological, legal, and ethical issues: Vol. 1., Children and families.* Greenwich, CT: JAI Press.

Baumeister, A. A., & Kupstas, F. D. (1990). The new morbidity: Implications for prevention and amelioration. In A. Clark & P. Evans (Eds.), *Combating mental handicap: A multidisciplinary approach.* London: A. B. Academic Publishers.

Baumeister, A. A., Kupstas, F., & Klindworth, L. M. (1991). The new morbidity: A national plan of action. *American Behavioral Scientist, 34*(4), 468-500.

Baumeister, A. A., Kupstas, F. D., & Zanthos, P. W. (1993). *Guide to state planning for the prevention of mental retardation and related disabilities associated with socioeconomic conditions.* Washington, DC: President's Committee on Mental Retardation.

Baumgartner, F. R., & Jones, B. D. (1991). Agenda dynamics and policy subsystems. *Journal of Politics, 53*(4), 1044-1074.

Beck, J. (1994,). The frustrating job of ending a culture of violence. *Daily Press* September 10, p. A8.

Becker, G. S. (1964). *Human capital.* New York: Columbia University Press.

Becker, S., & McPherson, S. (1986). *Poor clients.* Benefits Research Unit, University of Nottingham: Department of Social Administration and Social Work.

Beech, M. C. (1983). Simplifying text for mainstreamed students. *Journal of Learning Disabilities, 16*(7), 400-402.

Bennett, W.J. (1994). *The devaluing of America.* Colorado Springs, CO: Focus on the Family Publishing.

Bergman, A. B. (1986). *The discovery of sudden infant death syndrome: Lessons in the practice of political medicine,* New York: Praeger.

Berreth, D. G. (1992). Restructuring: Where we've been and where we're going. *The Special Education Leadership Review, 1*(1), 510.

Besharov, D. J. (1989). Targeting longterm welfare recipients. In P. H. Cottingham & D. T. Ellwood (Eds.), *Welfare policy for the 1990s* (pp. 146-164). Cambridge, MA: Harvard University Press.

Betancur, J. J., & Gills, D. C. (1993). Race and class in local economic development. In R. D. Bingham & R. Mier (Eds.), *Theories of local economic development: Perspectives from across the disciplines* (pp. 191-209). Newbury Park, CA: Sage.

Betson, D., Evenhouse, E., Reilly, S., & Smolensky, E. (1992). Tradeoffs implicit in childsupport guidelines. *Journal of Policy Analysis and Management, 11,* 120.

Bigelow, R. (1972). The evolution of coopeation, aggression, and selfcontrol. In J. Cole & D. Jenson (Eds.), *Nebraska symposium on motivation.* Lincoln: University of Nebraska Press.

Bird, K. M. (1992). Restructuring & special education: A local administrator's perspective. *The Special Education Leadership Review, 1* (1), 11-12.

Bishop, S. J., Murphy, J. M., Jellinek, M. S., Quinn, S. D., & Poitrast, F. G. (1992). Protecting seriously mistreated children: Time delays in a court sample. *Child Abuse and Neglect, 16,* 465-474.

Blank, R. M. (1994). The employment strategy: Public policies to increase work and earnings. In S. H. Danziger, G. D. Sandefur & D. H. Weinberg (Eds.), *Confronting poverty: Prescriptions for change* (pp. 168-204). Cambridge, MA: Harvard University Press.

Bloom, D., Fellerath, V., Long, D., & Wood, R. G. (1993). *LEAP: Interim findings on a welfare initiative to improve school attendance among teenage parents*. New York: Manpower Demonstration Research Corporation.

Bloom, D., & Sherwood, K. (1994). *Matching opportunities to obligations: Lessons for child support reform from the Parents' Fair Share pilot phase*. New York: Manpower Demonstration Research Corporation.

Blum, R. H., Blum, E., & Garfield, E. (1976). *Drugfree education: Results and recommendations*. Lexington, MA: Lexington Books.

Bockoven, J. S. (1963). *Moral treatment in American psychiatry.* New York: Springer.

Bodwin, Marc A. (1993). *Medicine, money, and morals*. New York: Oxford University Press.

Boelhouwer, C., & Rosenberg, M. (1983). Length of stay: A retrospective computer analysis. *Psychiatric Annals, 13*, 605-611.

Boring, E. G. (1957). When is human behavior predetermined? *Scientific Monthly, 84*, 189-196.

Borus, J., Howes, M., & Devins, N. (1988). Primary healthcare providers recognition and diagnosis of mental disorders in the patients. *General Hospital Psychiatry, 10*, 317-321.

Bos, C. S., & Vaughn, S. (1991). *Strategies for teaching students with learning and behavior problems*. Boston: Allyn & Bacon.

Bower, E. M. (1989). A brief history of how we have helped emotionally disturbed children and other fairy tales. In S. Braaten, F. H. Wood & G. Wrobel (Eds.), *Celebrating the past, preparing for the future: 40 years of serving students with emotional and behavioral disorders* (pp. 11-21). Minneapolis: Minnesota Council for Children with Behavioral Disorders and Minnesota Educators of Emotionally/Behaviorally Disordered.

Boykin, A. W. (1994). Harvesting talent and culture: African American children and educational reform. In R. J. Rossi (Ed.), *Schools and students at risk: Context and framework for positive change* (pp. 116-138). New York: Teachers College Press.

Brennen, M. H. (1973). *Mental illness and the economy*. Cambridge, MA: Harvard University Press.

Brock, T., Butler, D., & Long, D. (1993). *Unpaid work experience for welfare recipients: Findings and lessons from MDRC research*. New York: Manpower Demonstration Research Corporation.

Broman, S., Nichols, P., Shaughnessy, P., & Kennedy, W. (1987). *Retardation in young children*. Hillsdale, NJ: Erlbaum.

Brown, L. D. (1983). *Politics and health care organization: HMOs as federal policy*. Washington, DC: Brookings Institution.

Brown, L. D. (1991). Knowledge and power: Health services research as a political resource. In E. Ginzberg (Ed.), *Health services research: Key to health policy*. Cambridge, MA: Harvard University Press.

Burgess, R. L. & Garbarino, J. (1983). Doing what comes naturally? An evolutionary perspective on child abuse. In D. Finkelhor (Ed.), *The dark side of families: Current family violence research*. New York: Harper Business.

Burkett, L. (1993). What ever happened to the American dream? *Chicago*: Moody.

Burns, J. M. (1978). *Leadership.* New York: Harper & Row.

Burtless, G. (1989). The effect of reform on employment, earnings, and income. In P.

H. Cottingham & D. T. Ellwood (Eds.), *Welfare policy for the 1990s* (pp. 103-140). Cambridge, MA: Harvard University Press.

Burtless, G. (1994). Public spending on the poor: Historical trends and economic limits. In S. H. Danziger, G. D. Sandefur & D. H. Weinberg (Eds.), *Confronting poverty: Prescriptions for change* (pp. 51-84). Cambridge, MA: Harvard University Press.

Butler, A. D. (1992). The changing economic consequences of teenage childbearing. *Social Service Review, 66,* 131.

Cahn, E. S. (1987). The Florida Service Credit Project: Implementation of the service credit concept. Unpublished manuscript. Cited in Offe and Heinze, 1992.

Campbell, J. P., & Pritchard, R. D. (1976). Motivation theory in industrial and organizational psychology. In M. D. Dunnette (Ed.), *Handbook of industrial and organizational psychology* (pp. 63-130). Chicago: RandMcNally.

Carlson, M., & Castro, J. (1993). What price mental health? *Time, 141*(22), 59, 60.

Carnegie Corporation of New York (1994). *Starting points: Meeting the needs of our youngest children.* New York: Author.

Carson, C. C., Huelskamp, R. M., & Woodall, T. D. (1991). *Perspectives on education in America.* Albuquerque: Sandia National Laboratories, Systems Analysis Department.

Caton, C., & Gralnick, A. (1987). A review of issues surrounding length of psychiatric hospitalization. *Hospital & Community Psychiatry, 38,* 858-863.

Chandler, B., Stiles, L., & Kitsuse, J. (Eds.) (1962). *Education in urban society.* New York: Dodd, Mead & Co.

Chase, L., & Sweitzer, D. (1978) in American Association of Colleges for Teacher Education. In Commission on Multicultural Education (Ed.), *State legislation, provisions, and practices related to multicultural education.* Washington, DC: Department of Education, Congressional Research Service. (1965).

Children's Defense Fund. (1990). *The state of America's children.* Washington, DC: Author.

Children's Defense Fund. (1991). *The state of America's children.* Washington, DC: Author.

Children's Defense Fund (1994). *The State of America's Children, 1994.* Washington, DC: Author.

Chilman, C. S. (1992). Welfare reform or revision? The Family Support Act of 1988. *Social Service Review, 66,* 349-377.

Clark, M. E. (1989). *Ariadne's thread: The search for new modes of thinking.* New York: St. Martin's Press.

Cobb, R. W., & Elder, C. D. (1972). *Participation in American politics: The dynamics of agenda building.* Boston: Allyn & Bacon.

Cohen, M., March, J., & Olsen, J. (1972). A garbage can model of organizational choice. *Administrative Science Quarterly, 17*(March), 125.

Coleman, J. S. (1966). *Equality of educational opportunity.* Washington, DC: Government Printing Office.

Coleman, J. S. (1972). Of education and human community. In J. Bowman, L. Freeman, P. A. Olson & J. Pieper (Eds.), *A symposium of leaders in experimental education* (pp. 69-75). Lincoln: University of Nebraska Curriculum Center.

Committee on Energy and Commerce, U.S. Congress (1988). *Medicaid and the mentally retarded.* Washington, DC: Government Printing Office.

Committee on Ways and Means, U.S. House of Representatives (1993). *1993 green book: Background material and data on programs within the jurisdiction of the Committee on Ways and Means.* Washington, DC: Government Printing Office.

Conrad, D., & Hedin, D. (1989). *High school community service: A review of research and programs.* Madison, WI: National Center on Effective Secondary Schools, University of Wisconsin, Madison.

Conwell, Y., Nelson, J., Kim, K., & Mazure, C. (1983). Elderly patients admitted to the psychiatric unit of a general hospital. *Journal of the American Geriatrics Society, 31*, 792-796.

Cooke (Raver), S., Cooke, T., & Apolloni, A. (1965). Generalization of language training with the mentally retarded. *Journal of Special Education, 10*, 299-304.

Cooper, C. S., Peterson, N. L. & Meier, J. H. (1987). Variables associated with disrupted placement in a select sample of abused and neglected children. *Child Abuse and Neglect, 11*, 75-86.

Corbett, T. (1993). Child poverty and welfare reform: Progress or paralysis? *Focus, 15*(1), 117.

Cottingham, P. H., & Ellwood, D. T. (Eds.). (1989). *Welfare policy for the 1990s.* Cambridge, MA: Harvard University Press.

Creighton, S. J. (1988). The incidence of child abuse and neglect. In K. Browne, C. Davies & P. Stratton (Eds.), *Early prediction and prevention of child abuse.* Chichester: Wiley.

Cummings, N., & Follette, W. (1968). Psychiatric services and medical utilization in a prepaid health plan setting: Part II. *Medical Care, 6*, 31-41.

Cummins, J. (1986). Empowering minority students: A framework for intervention. *Harvard Educational Review, 56*(1), 18-36.

Cyert, R. M., & March, J. G. (1963). *A behavioral theory of the firm.* Englewood Cliffs, NJ: Prentice Hall.

Dahl, R. A. (1961). *Who governs? Democracy and power in an American city.* New Haven, CT: Yale University Press.

Dahl, R. A. (1984). *Modern political analysis* (2nd ed.). Englewood Cliffs, NJ: Prentice Hall.

Danziger, S. K., & Nichols-Casebolt. (1988). Teen parents and child support: Eligibility, participation and payment. *Journal of Social Service Research, 11*, 120.

Davis, K. E. (1980). An alternative theoretical perspective on race and voluntary participation. *Journal of Voluntary Action Research, 36*, 126-142.

Davis, Stanley M. (1987). *Future perfect.* Menlo Park, CA: AddisonWesley.

Delgado Gaitan, C. (1993). Research and policy in reconceptualizing family school relationships. In P. Phelan & A.L. Davidson (Eds.), *Renegotiating cultural diversity in American schools* (pp. 139-158). New York: Teachers College Press.

de Soto, H. (1990). *The other path: The invisible revolution in the Third World.* New York: Harper & Row.

Deutsch, A. (1948). *The shame of the states.* New York: Harcourt, Brace. Deutsch, K. W. (1985). On theory and research in innovation. In R. L. Merritt & A. J. Merritt (Eds.), *Innovation in the public sector*, (pp. 17-35). Beverly Hills, CA: Sage Publications.

Dick, K. (1991). Cooperative learning: Mastering the bundle of sticks. *Childhood Education, 67*, 179.

Dill, A., & Rochefort, D. (1989). Coordination, continuity and centralized control: A policy perspective on service strategies for the chronic mentally ill. Journal of Social Issues, *45*,(3), 145-159.

Dingwall, J., Miller, N. E., Doob, L. W., Mowrer, O. H., & Sears, R. (1989). *Frustration and aggression*. New Haven, CT: Yale University Press.

Dobson, J. (1992). *The new dare to discipline*. Wheaton, IL: Tyndale.

Dobson, J. (1994, July). *Focus on the Family Bulletin*.

Docherty, D. (1993). One size doesn't fit all: Mental health care requires providers to find a good fit. *Business Insurance*.

Doig, J. W., & Hargrove, E. C. (1990). Leadership and political analysis. In J. W. Doig, & E. C. Hargrove (Eds.), *Leadership and innovation* (pp. 1-22). Baltimore: Johns Hopkins University Press.

Downs, A. (1967). *Inside bureaucracy*. Boston: Little, Brown.

DrakakisSmith, D. (1987). *The Third World city*. New York: Methuen.

Drake, R., Wallach, M., & Hoffman, J. (1989). Housing instability and homelessness among aftercare patients in an urban state hospital. *Hospital & Community Psychiatry, 40*, 46-51.

Drucker, P. (1989). *The new realities*. New York: Harper & Row.

Drucker, P.F. (1985). *Innovation and entrepreneurship: Practice and principles*. New York: Harper & Row.

Dryfoos, J. G. (1994). *Fullservice schools: A revolution in health and Social services for children, youth, and families*. San Francisco: Jossey Bass.

Duchnowski, A. J. (1991). Helping children who have severe behavior disorders: The need for collaboration. In S. Braaten & G. Wrobel (Eds.), *Perspectives on the diagnosis and treatment of students with emotional/behavioral disorders* (pp. 51-60). Minneapolis: Minnesota Educators of the Emotionally Disturbed, Minnesota Council for Children with Behavioral Disorders.

Duhl, L. J. (1990). *The social entrepreneurship of change*, New York: Pace University Press.

Duncan, G. J., BrooksGunn, J., & Klebanov, P. K. (1994). Economic deprivation and early childhood development. *Child Development, 65*, 296-318.

Dutton, D. G. (1991). An ecological nested theory of male violence toward intimates. Paper presented to the Canadian Psychological Association annual convention, Toronto, Canada.

Eaton, W. W. (1980). *The sociology of mental disorders*. New York: Praeger.

Edelman, M. (1964). *The symbolic uses of politics*, Urbana: University of Illinois Press.

Edgerton, R. (1987). The Spring Hill statement. *AAHE Bulletin, 40*(3), 34.

Ellis, A., Canfield, R., & Bierbower, J. (1989). *Elementary language arts instruction*. Englewood Cliffs, NJ: Prentice Hall.

Ellis, E. S., Deshler, D. D., Lenz, B. K. Schumaker, J. B., & Clark, F. (1991). An instructional model for teaching learning strategies. *Focus on Exceptional Children, 23*(6), 123.

Ellwood, D. T. (1988). *Poor support: Poverty in the American family*. New York: Basic Books.

Ellwood, D. T. (1989). Conclusion. In P. H. Cottingham & D. T. Ellwood (Eds.), *Welfare policy for the 1990s* (pp. 269-289). Cambridge, MA: Harvard University Press.

Emery, R. E. (1982). Interparental conflict and the children of discord and divorce.

Psychological Bulletin, 92 (2), 310-330.

Enns, C. Z. (1992). Toward integrating feminist psychotherapy and feminist philosophy. *Professional Psychology: Research and Practice, 23*, 453-466.

Erickson, B. (1990). Forward on all fronts, In B. Erickson (Ed.), *Call to action: Handbook for ecology, peace and justice.* (pp. xi-xiii). San Francisco: Sierra Club Books.

Escalona, S. K. (1982). Babies at double hazard: Early developments of infants at biologic and social risk. *Pediatrics, 70*, 670-675.

EssockVitale, S. (1987). Patient characteristics predictive of treatment costs on inpatient psychiatric wards. *Hospital & Community Psychiatry, 38*, 263-269.

Evans, R. I. (1968). *B. F. Skinner: The man and his ideas.* New York: E. P. Dutton.

Eyestone, R. (1978). *From social issues to public policy.* New York: Wiley.

Faden, V., & Taube, C. (1977). *Length of stay of discharges from nonfederal general hospital psychiatric units: United States, 1975.* Mental Health Statistical Note 133. Rockville, MD: National Institute of Mental Health.

Falkson, J. L. (1980). *HMOs and the politics of health system reform.* Chicago: American Hospital Association and Robert J. Brady Co.

Famularo, R. A., Stone, K., Barnum, R., & Wharton, R. (1986). Alcoholism and severe child maltreatment. *American Journal of Orthopsychiatry, 56*, 481-485.

Farkas, Steve, & Johnson, Jean. (1993, October). The politics of education reform. *Education Digest*, pp. 4-7.

Feldman, P. H., Putnam, S., & Gerteis, M. (1992, Winter). Impact of foundationfunded commissions on health policy. *Health Affairs, 11*, 207-225.

Fenno, R. F., Jr. (1973). *Congressmen in committees,* Boston: Little, Brown.

Ferleger, N., Glenwick, D. S., Gaines, R. R. W., & Green, A. H. (1988). Identifying correlates of reabuse in maltreating parents. *Child Abuse and Neglect, 12*, 41-49.

Ferman, B. (1990). When failure Is success: Implementation and Madisonian government. In D. J. Palumbo & D. J. Calista (Eds.), *Implementation and the policy process* (pp. 39-50). New York: Greenwood Press.

Fine, G. A., & Mechling, J. (1993). Child saving and children's cultures at century's end. In S. B. Heath & M.W. McLaughlin (Eds.), *Identity and innercity youth* (pp. 120-146). New York: Teachers College Press.

Fine, M. (Ed.). (1994). *Chartering urban school reform; Reflections on public schools in the midst of change.* New York: Teachers College Press.

Finkelhor, D. (1984). *Child sexual abuse: New theory & research.* New York: Free Press.

Fiorina, M. P., & Shepsle, K. A. (1989). Formal theories of leadership: Agents, agenda setters, and entrepreneurs. In B. D. Jones (Ed.), *Leadership and politics* (pp. 17-40). Lawrence: University Press of Kansas.

Fiske, E. B. (1991). *Smart schools, smart kids.* New York: Simon & Schuster. Fitch, F. J. & Papantonio, A. (1983). Men who batter: Some pertinent characteristics. *Journal of Nervous and Mental Disease, 171*, 190-192.

Follette, W., & Cummings, N. (1967). Psychiatric services and medical utilization in a prepaid health plan setting. *Medical Care, 5*, 25-35.

Fossett, M. A., & Kiecolt, J. K. (1993). Mate availability and family structure among AfricanAmericans in U.S. metropolitan areas. *Journal of Marriage and the Family, 55*, 288-302.

Fox, D. M., & Leichter, H. M. (1991). Rationing care in Oregon: The new accountability.

Health Affairs, 10(2), 727.

Frank, R., & Lave, J. (1985). The psychiatric DRGs: Are they different? *Medical Care, 23,* 1148-1163.

Freiman, M., & Hendricks, M. (1990). Psychiatric facilities and DRG weights. *Administration and Policy in Mental Health, 17,* 125-137.

Freud, S. (1920). *Beyond the pleasure principle.* 1955 translation. New York: Hogarth Press.

Friedman. (1994, March/April). Making choices: A sense of loss. *The Healthcare Forum Journal.*

Friedman, R. (1983). Hospital treatment of psychiatric emergencies. In S. Soreff (Ed.), *Emergency psychiatry (the psychiatric clinics of North America),* vol. 6, (pp. 293-304), Philadelphia: W. B. Saunders.

Frohlich, N., Oppenheimer, J. A., & Young, O. R. (1971). *Political leadership and collective goods.* Princeton, NJ: Princeton University Press.

Fromm, E. (1973). *The anatomy of human destructiveness.* New York: Fawcett.

Frymier, J., & Gainsneder, (1989). *A study of students at risk: Collaborating to do research.* Bloomington, IN: Phi Delta Kappa Educational Foundation.

Furstenberg, F. F., Jr., Sherwood, K. E., & Sullivan, M. L. (1992). *Caring and paying: What fathers and mothers say about child support.* New York: Manpower Demonstration Research Corporation.

Gabrielle de Groot & American Psychological Association (1994, July). Psychologists' key to school reform, *APA Monitor,* 38, 39.

Garbarino, J.,& Kostelny, K. (1992). Child maltreatment as a community problem. *Child Abuse and Neglect, 16,* 455-464.

Garcia, S., & Malkin, D. (1993). Toward defining programs and services for culturally and linguistically diverse learners in special education. *Teaching Exceptional Children, 26,* 52-58.

Gardner, H. (1991). *The unschooled mind: How children think and how schools should teach.* New York: Basic Books.

Gardner, J. W. (1986). *Leadership and power.* Paper published as part of series sponsored by Independent Sector.

Garfinkel, I. (1992). *Assuring child support: An extension of social security.* New York: Russell Sage Foundation.

Garfinkel, I., & Klawitter, M. M. (1990). The effect of routine income withholding of child support collections. *Journal of Policy Analysis and Management, 9,* 155-177.

Garfinkel, I., & McLanahan, S. (1994). Single mother families, economic insecurity, and government policy. In S. H. Danziger, G. D. Sandefur & D. H. Weinberg (Eds.), *Confronting poverty: Prescriptions for change* (pp. 205-225). Cambridge, MA: Harvard University Press.

Garfinkel, I., & Melli, M. S. (1992). The use of normative standards in family law decisions: Developing mathematical standards for child support. In I. Garfinkel, S. S. McLanahan & P. K. Robins (Eds.), *Child support assurance: Design issues, expected impacts, and political barriers as seen from Wisconsin* (pp. 203-228). Washington: Urban Institute Press.

Garfinkel, I., & Oellerich, D. T. (1992). Noncustodial fathers' ability to pay child support. In I. Garfinkel, S. S. McLanahan & P. K. Robins (Eds.), *Child support assurance: Design issues, expected impacts, and political barriers as seen from*

Wisconsin (pp. 55-78). Washington: Urban Institute Press.

Garfinkel, I., & Robins, P. K. (1993). *The relationship between child support enforcement tools and child support outcomes* (Discussion Paper No. 100493). Madison, WI: Institute for Research on Poverty.

Gaus, R. (1994, October). Improving the quality of health care through research: The challenges ahead. *Academic Medicine, 69*(10), 243-251.

Gelles, R. (1983). An exchange/social control theory. In D. Finkelhor, R. J. Gelles, G. T. Hotaling & M. A. Straus (Eds.), *The dark side of families.* Beverly Hills: Sage Publications.

Gelles, R. J. & Maynard, P. E. (1987). A structural family systems approach to intervention in cases of family violence. *Family Relations, 36*, 270-275.

Gelles, R. J., Straus, M. A. & Harrop, J. W. (1988). Has family violence decreased? A response to Timothy Stocks. *Journal of Marriage and the Family, 50*, 286.

Gershman, M. (1986). *Smarter barter: A guide for corporations, professionals, and small businesses.* New York: Viking Penguin.

Gibbs, N. (1994, June 20). The vicious cycle. *Time*, pp. 24-33.

Gilder, G. (1984). *The spirit of enterprise.* New York: Simon & Schuster. Glazer, W., & Bell, N. (1993) *Mental health benefits: A purchaser's guide.* Brookfield, WI: International Foundation of Employee Benefit Plans Press.

Glazer, W., Kramer, R., Montgomery, J., & Myers, L. (1991). Use of medical necessity scales in concurrent review of psychiatric inpatient care. *Hospital & Community Psychiatry, 42*, 1199-1200.

Glidwell, J. C., & Swallow, C. S. (1968). *The prevalence of maladjustment in elementary schools.* Chicago: Joint Commission on the Mental Health of Children, University of Chicago.

Goffman, E. (1961). *Asylums.* New York: Doubleday Anchor.

Goldberg, E. M., & Warburton, W. (1979). *Ends and means in social work.* London: Allen & Unwin.

Goldberg, M. (1994, July). In speaking to the public. *Family Voice, 16*(7), 17.

Golden, H. (1977). The children are waiting: *The failure to achieve permanent homes for foster children in New York City.* New York: New York City Comptroller's Office.

Goldman, H., Pincus, H., Taube, C., Jeffreys, M., & Stellbaum, K. (1984) Prospective payment for psychiatric hospitalization: Questions and issues. *Hospital & Community Psychiatry, 35*, 460-466.

Goldstein, Gary (1995, January). How much lower can healthcare costs go? *Northern California Medicine.*

Goode, E. A. (1994, March 14). How much coverage for mental illness? *U.S. News and World Report, 116*(10) (March 14), 56, 57.

Goodlad, J. I. (1983). *A place called school.* New York: McGrawHill.

Goodman, S. (1994). Talking back: The portrait of a student documentary on school inequity. In F. Pignatelli & S.W. Pflaum (Eds.), *Experiencing diversity: Toward educational equity* (pp. 47-69). Thousand Oaks, CA: Corwin.

Goozner, M. (1987, July 19). Age old tradition bankrolls Koreans. *Chicago Tribune,* C67.

Gordon, E. W., & Yowell, C. (1994). Cultural dissonance as a risk factor in the development of students. In R.J. Rossi (Ed.), *Schools and students at risk: Context and framework for positive change* (pp. 51-69). New York: Teachers College Press.

Gorman, M. (1948). Oklahoma attacks its snakepits. *Reader's Digest, 53*, 139-160.

Gottschalk, P., McLanahan, S., & Sandefur, G. D. (1994). The dynamics and inter generational transmission of poverty and welfare participation. In S. H. Danziger, G. D. Sandefur & D. H. Weinberg. (Eds.), *Confronting poverty: Prescriptions for change* (pp. 85-108). Cambridge, MA: Harvard University Press.

Graham, P. J. (1979). Epidemiological studies. In H. C. Quay & J. S. Werry (Eds.), *Psychopathological disorders of childhood*, (2nd ed.). New York: Wiley.

Gray, B. H. (1992). The legislative battle over health services research. *Health Affairs, 11*(4), 38-66.

Gray, G., & Glazer, W. (1994, January/February). Psychiatric decision making in the 90's: The coming era of decision support. *Behavioral Healthcare Tomorrow*, pp. 7-54.

Greenberg, D., & Wiseman, M. (1992). *What did the workwelfare demonstrations do?* (Discussion Paper No. 96992). Madison, WI: Institute for Research on Poverty.

Greenberg, P., Stiglin, L., Finklstein, S., Foundries, D., Stevenson, A. (1990). The economic burden of depression in 1990. *Journal of Clinical Psychiatry*, 73-78.

Grob, G. (1973). *Mental institutions in America, social policy to 1875*. New York: Free Press of Glencoe.

Grob, G. (1983). *Mental illness and American society, 1875-1940*. Princeton, NJ: Princeton University Press.

Gronfein, W. (1985). Incentives and intentions in mental health policy: A comparison of the Medicaid and community mental health programs. *Journal of Health and Social Behavior, 26*, 192-206.

Gueron, J. M., & Pauly, E. (1991). *From welfare to work*. New York: Russell Sage Foundation.

Gunn, J. (1991). Human violence: A biological perspective. *Criminal Behavior and Mental Health, 1*, 344-354.

Hagen, J. L., & Lurie, I. (1993). The job opportunities and basic skills training program and child care: Initial state developments. *Social Service Review, 67*, 198-216.

Hall, R., Gardner, E., Stickney, S., LeCann, A., & Popkin, M. (1980). Physical illness manifesting as psychiatric disease. Analysis of a state hospital inpatient population. *Archives of General Psychiatry, 37*, 989-995.

Hallett, C. (1988). Research in child abuse: Some observations on the knowledge base. *Journal of Reproductive and Infant Psychology, 6*, 119-124.

Halsey, C. L., Collin, M. F., & Anderson, C. L. (1993). Extremely low birthweight children and their peers: A comparison of preschool performances. *Pediatrics, 91*, 807-811.

Harcum, E. R. (1989). Commitment to collaboration as a prerequisite for existential commonality in psychotherapy. *Psychotherapy, 26*, 200-209.

Harcum, E. R. (1990). The relative utility of complementary disparate views on voluntarism and determinism. *The Journal of Psychology, 125*, 217-228.

Harcum, E. R. (1991). Parity for the theoretical ghosts and gremlins: Response to Pollio/Henley and Rychlak. *The Journal of Mind and Behavior, 12*, 151-162.

Harcum, E. R. (1994). *A psychology of freedom and dignity*. Westport, CT: Praeger.

Hargrove, E. C. (1989). Two conceptions of leadership. In B. D. Jones (Ed.), *Leadership and Politics* (pp. 57-83). Lawrence: University Press of Kansas.

Harkavy, I., & Puckett, J. (1991). *Academically based public service in a university's local community as a possible strategy for integrating teaching, research, and service.* Paper presented for the Wingspread Conference on Setting the Agenda for Effective Research in Combining Service and Learning in the 1990s. Racine, WI: Johnson Foundation, Wingspread.

Harman, W. W. (1988). The transpersonal challenge to the scientific paradigm: The need for a restructuring of science. *ReVision, 11*, 13-21.

Harp, B., & Brewer, J. (1991). *Reading and writing: Teaching for the connections.* New York: Harcourt, Brace, & Jovanovich.

Haveman, R., & Buron, L. (1993). Escaping poverty through work: The problem of low earnings capacity in the United States, 1973-88. *Review of Income and Wealth, 39,* 141-157.

Haveman, R. H., & Scholz, J. K. (1994). *The Clinton welfare reform plan: Will it end poverty as we know it?* (Discussion Paper No. 103794). Madison, WI: Institute for Research on Poverty.

Hayes, M. T. (1992). *Incrementalism and public policy.* New York: Longman.

Hershovits, Melville, J. (1948). *Man and his works.* New York: Dreyden Press.

Herrenkohl, R. C., Herrenkohl, E. C., Egolf, B., & Seech, M. (1979). The repetition of child abuse: How frequently does it occur? *Child Abuse and Neglect, 3,* 67-72.

Herrnstein, R. J. & Murray, C. (1994). *The Bell Curve: Intelligence and class structure in American life.* New York: Free Press.

Hess, G. A. (Ed.). (1993). *Empowering teachers and parents: School restructuring through the eyes of anthropologists.* Westport, CT: Bergin & Garvey.

Hirschi, T. (1969). Exploring alternatives to integrated theory. In S. F. Messner, M. D. Krohn, & A. E. Liska (Eds.), *Theoretical integration in the study of deviance and crime.* Albany: State University of New York Press.

Hodgkinson, H. L., & Mirga, T. (1986, May 14). Today's numbers, tomorrow's nation. *Education Week, 5*(34), 14, 15.

Hofman, P. B. (1993, January/February). Healthcare reform begins at home. *Healthcare Executive,* pp. 25-27.

Hollister, R. G., Jr., Kemper, P., & Maynard, R. A. (Eds.). (1984). *The national supported work demonstration.* Madison: WI University of Wisconsin Press.

Horn, S., Chambers, A., Sharkey, P., & Horn, R. (1989). Psychiatric severity of illness. A case mix study. *Medical Care, 27,* 69-87.

Houk, V. N., & Thacker, S. B. (1989). The Centers for Disease Control program to prevent primary and secondary disabilities in the United States. *Public Health Report, 104,* 226-231.

House, W. (1984). Nairobi's informal sector: Dynamic entrepreneurs or surplus labor? *Economic Development and Cultural Change, 12*(2): 277-302.

Hoyson, M., Jamieson, B., & Strain, P. (1984). Individualized group instruction of normally developing and autisticlike children: A description and evaluation of LEAP curriculum model. *Journal of the Division for Early Childhood, 8,* 157-172.

Hudson, C. G. (1983). An empirical model of state mental health spending. *Social Work Research and Abstracts, 23,* 312.

Hudson, C. G. (1990). The performance of state community mental health systems: A path model. *Social Service Review, 64*(1), 94-120.

Hudson, C. G. (1993). The United States. In D. Kemp (Ed.), *International handbook on mental health policy* (pp. 413-446). Westport, CT: Greenwood Press.

Hutchens, R. M. (1986). The effects of the Omnibus Budget Reconciliation Act of 1981 on AFDC recipients: A review of studies. In R. G. Ehrenberg (Ed.), *Research in labor economics: Vol. 8 (part B)*. Greenwich, CT: JAI Press.

Institute of Medicine (1985). *Preventing low birthweight*. Washington, DC: National Academy Press.

Irvine, R. (1988). Child abuse and poverty. In S. Becker & S. McPherson (Eds.) *Public issues private pain, insight*, p. 126. New York: Harper & Row.

Isaac, R. J. & Armat, V. C. (1990). *Madness in the streets: How psychiatry and the law abandoned the mentally ill*. New York: Free Press.

Jackson, J. L. (1990). Preface. In B. Erickson (Ed.), *Call to action: Handbook for ecology, peace and justice* (pp. xi-xiii). San Francisco: Sierra Club Books.
Jacob, E., & Jordan, C. (Eds.). (1993). *Minority education: Anthropological perspectives*. Norwood, NJ: Ablex.

Jencks, C. (1992a, Fall). Can we put a time limit on welfare? *The American Prospect*, pp. 32-40.

Jencks, C. (1992b). *Rethinking social policy: Race, poverty, and the underclass*. Cambridge, MA: Harvard University Press.

Jenks, C., Carlson, G., & Murnicka, V. (1972). *Inequality: A reassessment of the effect of family and schooling in America*. New York: Holt, Rinehart, & Winston.

Johnson, A. B. (1990). *Out of bedlam: The truth about deinstitutionalization*. New York: Basic Books.

Johnson, D. W. & Johnson, R. (Eds.). (1987). *Joining together group theory and group skill*. New Jersey: Prentice Hall.

Johnson, J. H., Farrell, W. C., & Jackson, M. R. (1994). Los Angeles one year later: A prospective assessment of responses to the 1992 civil unrest. *Economic Development Quarterly, 8*(1), 19-27.

Jones, B. D. (1989). Causation, constraint, and political leadership. In B. D. Jones (Ed.), *Leadership and politics* (pp. 314). Lawrence: University Press of Kansas.

Jones, B. D., & Bachelor, L. W. (1986). *The sustaining hand: Community leadership and corporate power*. Lawrence: University Press of Kansas.

Jones, D.P.H. (1987). The untreatable family. *Child Abuse and Neglect, 11*, 409-420.

Jordan, D. (1992). Editor's note, in Militarization and development. *Peace Psychology Bulletin and Newsletter, 1*(2), 8.

Joyce, B. R., Hersh, R., & McKibbin, M. (1983). *The structure of school improvement*. New York: Longman.

Kagan, S. (1989). *Cooperative learning resources for teachers*. San Juan Capistrano, CA: Resources for Teachers.

Kahn, S. (1991). *Organizing: A guide for grassroots leaders*. Washington DC: National Association of Social Workers Press.

Kalichman, S. C. & Brosig, C. L. (1992). The effects of statutory requirements on child maltreatment reporting: A comparison of two state laws. *American Journal of Orthopsychiatry, 62*, 284-296.

Kanfer, F.H. (1977). The many faces of selfcontrol, or behavior modification changes its focus. In P. B. Stuart, ed., *Behavioral selfmanagement*. New York: Brunner/Mazel.

Kanter, R. M. (1983). *The change masters: Innovation and entrepreneurship in the American corporation*, New York: Simon & Schuster.

Katz, M. B. (1983). *Poverty and policy in American history*. New York: Academic

Press.

Kaus, M. (1992). *The end of equality*. New York: New Republic/Basic Books.

Keith, N. Z. (1994). School-sponsored community service: Answers and more questions. *Journal of Adolescence, 17*(3) 114.

Kemp, D. R. (1994). *Mental health in the workplace: An employer's and manager's guide*. Westport, CT: Quorum.

Kennedy, M. M., Sears, N., & Fendry, B. (1986). *Poverty, achievement and the distribution of education services*. Washington, DC: United States Department of Education.

Kesler, R., et al. (1994). Lifetime and 12 month prevalence of DSM IIIR psychiatric disorders in the United States; Results from the National Comorbidity Study. *Archives of General Psychiatry, 51*, 819.

Kiesler, C. A. (1982). Mental hospitals and alternative care: Noninstitutionalization as potential public policy for mental patients. *American Psychologist, 35*, 1066-1080.

Kiesler, C. A., (1995). Mental health should be independent of health policy. In W. Barbour (Ed.), *Mental illness: Opposing viewpoints*. (pp. 245-251). San Diego, CA: Greenhaven Press.

Kiesler, C. A. & Sibulkin, A. E. (1987). *Mental hospitalization: Myths and Facts about a national crisis*. Newbury Park, CA: Sage Publications.

Kilpatrick, W. (1992). *Why Johnny can't tell right from wrong*. New York: Touchstone.

Kingdon, J. W. (1981). *Congressmen's voting decisions*. (2nd ed.) New York: Harper & Row.

Kingdon, J. W. (1984). *Agendas, alternatives, and public policies*. Boston: Little, Brown.

Kitzhaber, J., & Gibson, M. (1991). The crisis in health care - the Oregon Health Plan as a strategy for change. *Stanford Law & Policy Review, 3*(Fall), 64-72.

Klawitter, M. M., & Garfinkel, I. (1992). The effect of routine income withholding of child support on AFDC participation and cost. In I. Garfinkel, S. S. McLanahan & P. K. Robins (Eds.), *Child support assurance: Design issues, expected impacts, and political barriers as seen from Wisconsin* (pp. 255-278). Washington, DC: Urban Institute Press.

Knitzer, J. (1982). *Unclaimed children: The failure of public responsibility to children and adolescents in need of mental health services*. Washington, DC: Children's Defense Fund.

Knitzer, J., Steinberg, Z., & Fleisch, B. (1990). *At the schoolhouse door: An examination of programs and policies for children with behavioral and emotional problems*. New York: Bank Street College of Education.

Kohn, Alfie. (1991, March). Caring kids: The role of the schools. *Phi Delta Kappan*, pp. 101-110.

Kohut, H. (1973). Thoughts on narcissism and narcissistic rage. *Psychoanalytic Study of the Child, 27*, 360-400.

Korr, W. S. (1991). The current legal environment. In C. G. Hudson & A. J. Cox (Eds.), *Dimensions of state mental health policy*. (pp.58-63). New York: Praeger.

Kozol, J. (1980). *The night is dark and I am far from home*. New York: Continuum.

Kozol, J. (1991). *Savage inequalities*. New York: Crown.

Kretovics, J., & Nussel, E. J. (Eds.). (1994). *Transforming urban education*. Boston: Allyn & Bacon.

Kretzmann, J. P., & McKnight, J. L. (1993). *Building communities from the inside out*.

Kretzmann, J. P., & McKnight, J. L. (1993). *Building communities from the inside out.* Evanston, IL: Northwestern University, Center for Urban Affairs and Policy Research.

LeShan, L. (1990). *The dilemma of psychology.* New York: E. P. Dutton.

Levine, M. (1981). *The history and politics of community mental health.* New York: Oxford University Press.

Lewis, A. (1992, September). Urban youth in community service: Becoming part of the solution. *ERIC Clearinghouse on Urban Education Digest, 81*(EDO-UD-92-4), 1-2.

Lewis, E. (1980). *Public entrepreneurship: Toward a theory of bureaucratic political power.* Bloomington, IN: Indiana University Press.

Lipp, M. (1992). An emerging perspective on special education: A developmental agenda for the 1990s. *Education Leadership Review, 1*(1), 19-39.

Lindsey, H. (1994). *Planet Earth—2000 a.d..* Palos Verdes, CA: Western Front.

Lineberry, William P. (Ed.). (1989). *Assessing participatory development: Rhetoric versus reality.* Boulder, CO: Westview Press.

Linquanti, R. (1992, October). *Using community-wide collaboration to foster resiliency in kids: A conceptual framework.* Western Regional Center for Drug-Free Schools and Communities.

Logan, J. R., & Molotch H. L. (1987). *Urban fortunes: The political economy of place.* Berkeley: University of California Press.

Loomis, B. (1988). *The new American politician: Ambition, entrepreneurship, and the changing face of political life.* New York: Basic Books.

Lubell, Harold (1991). *The informal sector in the 1980s and 1990s.* Paris: Development Centre of the Organization for Economic Cooperation and Development.

Lusane, C. (1993). Rap, race, and politics. *Race & Class, 35*(1), 41-56.

Lynch, J. (1992). *Education for citizenship in a multicultural society.* New York: Cassell.

Lynn, L. E., Jr. (1993, Fall). Ending welfare reform as we know it. *The American Prospect*, pp. 83-92.

Lyon, L. (1987). *The community in urban society.* Philadelphia: Temple University.

Lyons, J., Colletta, J., Devens, M., & Finkel, S. (1994). The construct and predictive validity of the Severity of Psychiatric Illness in a sample of psychogeriatric patients. *International Psychogeriatrics* (in press).

Lyons, J., & McGovern, M. (1989). Use of mental health services by dually diagnosed patients. *Hospital & Community Psychiatry, 40*, 1067-1069.

Lyons, J., O'Mahoney, M., & Larson, D. (1991). The attending psychiatrist as a predictor of length of stay. *Hospital & Community Psychiatry, 42*, 1064-1066.

Lyons, J., Pressman, P., Pavkov, T., Salk, P., Larson, D., & Finkel, S. (1992). Psychiatric hospitalization of older adults: Comparison of a specialty geropsychiatric unit to general units. *Clinical Gerontologist, 12*, 1-18.

Maeroff, G. I. (1982). *Don't blame the kids—The trouble with America's public schools.* New York: McGraw-Hill.

Maeroff, G. I. (1994). Withered hopes, stillborn dreams: The dismal panorama of urban schools. In J. Kretovics & E.J. Nussel (Eds.), *Transforming urban education* (pp. 32-42). Boston: Allyn & Bacon.

Magnet, M. (1992, August 10). The American family, 1992. *Fortune*, pp. 42-47.

Maisel, A. Z. (1948). Bedlam 1946. *Life, 2*, 102-118.

Majone, G., & Wildavsky, A. (1984). Implementation as evolution. In J. Pressman & A. Wildavsky (Eds.), *Implementation* (3rd ed.), pp. 163-180, Berkeley: University of California Press.

Manion, C. (1992, December). A moral primer for schools. *Wall Street Journal, 8*, 14.

March, J. G., & Olsen, J. P. (1984). The New institutionalism: Organizational factors in political life. *American Political Science Review, 78*(3), 734-749.

March, J. G., & Olsen, J. P. (1989). *Rediscovering institutions: The organizational basis of politics.* New York: Free Press.

March, J. G., & Simon, H. A. (1958). *Organizations.* New York: Wiley.

Marson, D. (1990). *Two studies of decision-making in the psychiatric emergency service.* Doctoral dissertation, Northwestern University.

Martens, B. K., Peterson, R. L., Witt, J. C., & Cirone, S. (1986). Teacher perceptions of school based interventions. *Exceptional Children, 53*, 213-223.

Martin, J. (1983). Maternal and paternal abuse of children. In D. Finkelhor, R. J. Gelles, G. T. Hotaling & M. A. Straus (Eds.), *The dark side of families.* Beverly Hills: Sage.

Mayhew, D. R. (1974). *Congress: The electoral connection.* New Haven, CT: Yale University Press.

Mayor's Advisory Panel on Decentralization of the New York City Schools (1967). *Reconnection for learning: A community school system for New York City.* New York: Ford Foundation.

McCaleb, S. P. (1994). *Building communities of learners: A collaboration among teachers, students, families, and community.* New York: St. Martin's Press.

McDonnell, A., & Hardman, M. (1988). A synthesis of "best practice" guidelines for early childhood special services. *Journal of the Division for Early Childhood, 12*, 328 -341.

McFarland, B., Faulkner, L., & Bloom, J. (1990). Predicting involuntary patients' length of stay. *Administration and Policy in Mental Health, 17*, 139-149.

McGauhey, P., Starfield, B.. Alexander, C., & Ensminger, M. (1991). The social environment and vulnerability of low birthweight children: a social-epidemiological perspective. *Pediatrics, 88*, 954-953.

McGuire, A. (1989). Fires, cigarettes and advocacy. *Law, Medicine & Health Care, 17*(1), 73-77.

McKenzie-Mohr, D., & Winter, D.D.N. (1992). The case for approaching global issues systematically: Militarization and development. *Peace Psychology Bulletin, 1*(2), 9 -11.

McKibben, L., DeVos, E., & Newberger, E. (1989). Victimization of mothers of abused children: A controlled study. *Pediatrics, 81*, 531.

McLanahan, S. S., Brown, P. R., & Monson, R. A. (1992). Paternity establishment in AFDC cases: Three Wisconsin counties. In I. Garfinkel, S. S. McLanahan & P. K. Robins (Eds.), *Child support assurance: Design issues, expected impacts, and political barriers as seen from Wisconsin* (pp. 137-158). Washington, DC: Urban Institute Press.

McLaughlin, M. W., Irby, M., & Langman, J. (1994). *Urban sanctuaries: Neighborhood organization in the lives and futures of inner-city youth.* San Francisco: Jossey-Bass.

McNulty, B. A. (1992). Restructuring—A state administrator's perspective. *The Special Education Leadership Review, 1*(1), 13-17.

McPherson, K., & Nebgen, M. K. (1991). Setting the agenda: School reform and community service. *Network, 2*(3), 1, 4 (published by the Constitutional Rights Foundation, 601 South Kingsley Drive, Los Angeles, CA).

Mead, L. M. (1986). *Beyond entitlement: The social obligations of citizenship.* New

York: Free Press.

Mead, L. M. (1990). Should workfare be mandatory? What research says. *Journal of Policy Analysis and Management, 9,* 400-404.

Mead, L. M. (1992). *The new politics of poverty: The nonworking poor in America.* New York: Basic Books.

Mechanic, David. (1994). Trust and informed consent to rationing. *Millbank Quarterly, 72*(2).

Mechanic, D., & Rochefort, D. (1994). Deinstitutionalization of the mentally ill: Efforts for inclusion. In D. Mechanic (Ed.), *Inescapable decisions: The imperatives of health reform* (pp. 165-212). New Brunswick, NJ: Transaction Publishers.

Mechanic, D., & Trust, R. (1994). *Care Provision in the Twentieth Century.* New York: Free Press.

Meltsner, A. J. (1976). *Policy analysts in the bureaucracy,* Los Angeles, CA: University of California Press.

Menard, A. E., & Salius, A. J. (1990). Judicial response to family violence: The importance of message. *Mediation Quarterly, 7,* 293-302.

Merkel-Holguin, L. A., & Sobel, A. J. (1993). *The child welfare stat book, 1993.* Washington, DC: Child Welfare League of America.

Meyer, D. (1993). Child support and welfare dynamics: Evidence from Wisconsin. *Demography, 30,* 45-62.

Meyer, D. R., (1993). *Supporting children born outside of marriage: Do child support awards keep pace with changes in fathers' incomes?* (Discussion Paper No. 1026-93). Madison, WI: Institute for Research on Poverty.

Meyer, D. R., & Bartfeld, J. (1992). *How routine is "routine" withholding? Evidence from Wisconsin.* (Discussion Paper No. 987-1106) Madison, WI: Institute for Research on Poverty.

Mezzich, J., & Coffman, G. (1985). Factors influencing length of hospital stay. *Hospital & Community Psychiatry, 36,* 1262-1270.

Michalon, M., & Richman, A. (1990). Factors affecting length of stay in psychiatric intensive care unit. *General Hospital Psychiatry, 12,* 303-308.

Miller, G., & Willer, B. (1979). Length of hospitalization predicted by self-assessment of social competence. *Canadian Psychiatric Association Journal, 24,* 337-339.

Miller, I. (1993). Guerrilla artists of New York City. *Race & Class, 35*(1), 27-40.

Miller, R. (1985). *The effects of a vocabulary learning strategy on the comprehension of science concepts.* Unpublished doctoral dissertation, University of Arizona.

Milward, B. H. (1980). Policy entrepreneurship and bureaucratic demand creation. In H. M. Ingram & D. E. Mann (Eds.), *Why policies succeed or fail* (pp. 255-277). Beverly Hills, CA: Sage Publications.

Mitchell, J., Dickey, B., Liptzin, B., Marshfield, K., & Sansone, T. (1987). Bring psychiatric patients into the Medicare prospective payment system: Alternatives to DRGs. *American Journal of Psychiatry, 144,* 610-615.

Moffitt, R. (1992). Incentive effects of the U.S. welfare system: A review. *Journal of Economic Literature, 30,* 1-61.

Moffitt, R. (1993). The effect of work and training programs on entry and exit from the welfare caseload (Discussion Paper No. 1025-93). Madison, WI: Institute for Research on Poverty.

Moffitt, R., & Wolfe, B. (1992). The effect of the Medicaid program on welfare participation and labor supply. *The Review of Economics and Statistics, 74,* 615-626.

Moll, L. C., Humphrey, K. L., & Younge, D. F. (1992). Funds of knowledge for teaching: Using a qualitative approach to connect homes and classrooms. *Theory into Practice, 31*(2): 132-141.

Mollenkopf, J. (1983). *The contested city.* Princeton, NJ: Princeton University Press.

Monahan, R. G. (1982). Education of "high risk" infants. In L. W. Abramczyk (Ed.), *Proceedings of the South Carolina Conference on Children and Youth* (pp. 120-123). Columbia: University of South Carolina.

Morris, M., & Williamson, J. B. (1982). Stereotypes and social class: A focus on poverty. In A. G. Miller (Ed.), *In the eye of the beholder: Contemporary issues in stereotyping* (pp. 411-465). New York: Praeger.

Morris, M., & Williamson, J. B. (1986). *Poverty and public policy: An analysis of federal intervention efforts.* Westport, CT: Greenwood Press.

Morris, M., & Williamson, J. B. (1987). Workfare: The poverty/dependence trade-off. *Social Policy, 18*(1), 13-16, 49-50.

Morse, C. W., Sahler, O. J. & Friedman, S. B. (1970). A three-year follow-up study of abused and neglected children. *American Journal of Diseases of Children, 120,* 439 - 446.

Mott, F. L., & Marsiglio, W. (1985). Early childbearing and completing of high school. *Family Planning Perspectives, 17,* 234-237.

Mucciaroni, G. (1991). Unclogging the arteries: The defeat of client politics and the logic of collective action. *Policy Studies Journal,* 19(3-4), 474-494.

Murphy, J. M., Bishop, S. J., Jellinek, M. S., Quinn, D., & Poitrast, F. G. (1992). What happens after the care and protection petition? Reabuse in a court sample. *Child Abuse and Neglect, 16,* 485-493.

Murray, C. (1984). *Losing ground: American social policy, 1950-1980.* New York: Basic Books.

Murray, C. (1993). Welfare and the family: The U.S. experience. *Journal of Labor Economics, 11*(1, Pt. 2), S224-S262.

Musick, J. S. (1993). *Young, poor, and pregnant: The psychology of teenage motherhood.* New Haven, CT: Yale University Press.

Nakamura, R. T., & Smallwood, F. (1980). *The politics of policy implementation.* New York: St. Martin's Press.

National Alliance for the Mentally Ill (NAMI). (1995). National health care should include mental health benefits. In W. Barbour (Ed.), *Mental illness: Opposing viewpoints* (pp. 252-258). San Diego, CA: Greenhaven Press.

National Center for Health Statistics. (1991). *Vital statistics of the United States, 1991: Vol. 1, Natality.* Washington, DC: U.S. Department of Health and Human Services.

National Center on Child Abuse and Neglect. (1989). *State statutes related to child abuse and neglect.* Washington, DC: Author.

National Commission on Children. (1991). *Beyond rhetoric—A new American agenda for children and families: Summary.* Washington, DC: Government Printing Office.

National Commission on Excellence in Education. (1983). *A nation at risk.* Washington, DC: Author.

National Institute of Mental Health (NIMH). (1992). Mental health, United States, 1992. In R. N. Manderscheid & M. A. Sonnenschein (Eds.), *DHHS publication no. (ADM)*

90-1708. Washington, DC: Superintendent of Documents, Government Printing Office.

Neisser, U. (1979). The control of information pickup in selective looking. In A. D. Pick (Ed.) *Perception and its development: A tribute to Eleanor Gibson.* Hillsdale, NJ: Erlbaum.

Norris, D. F., & Bembry, J. X. (1995). Primordial policy soup: Bureaucratic politics and welfare policy making in Maryland. In D. F. Norris & L. Thompson (Eds.), *The politics of welfare reform* (pp. 147-82). Thousand Oaks, CA: Sage Publications.

Novoco, R. (1975). *Anger control: The development and evaluation of an experimental treatment.* Lexington, MA: Lexington Books.

O'Connell, J. C., & Sontag, E. (1992). Parental choice and early intervention: A proactive policy of reform. *The Special Education Leadership Review, 1*(1), 97-113.

Offe, C., & Heinze, R. G. (1992). *Beyond employment: Time, work, and the informal economy.* Philadelphia: Temple University Press.

Ogbu, J. U. (1990). Cultural model, identity, and literacy. In J. W. Stigler R. A. Shweder & G. Herdt (Eds.), *Cultural psychology: Essays on comparative human development* (pp. 520-541). New York: Cambridge University Press.

Oliver, T. R. (1990). *The politics and performance of community health care reforms.* Unpublished doctoral dissertation, University of North Carolina, Chapel Hill, NC.

Oliver, T. R. (1991a). Ideas, entrepreneurship, and the politics of health care reform. *Stanford Law & Policy Review, 3*(Fall), 160-180.

Oliver, T. R. (1991b). Health care market reform in Congress: The uncertain path from proposal to policy. *Political Science Quarterly, 106*(3), 453-477.

Oliver, T. R. (1993). Analysis, advice, and congressional leadership: The Physician Payment Review Commission and the politics of medicare. *Journal of Health Politics, Policy and Law, 18*(1), 113-174.

Olson, M. (1965). *The logic of collective action: Public goods and the Theory of groups.* Cambridge, MA: Harvard University Press.

Olson, M. (1989). Is Britain the wave of the future? How ideas affect societies. *LSE Quarterly, 3*(Winter), 279-304.

Osborne, D. E., & Gaebler, T. (1992). *Reinventing government: How the entrepreneurial spirit is transforming the public sector*, Reading, MA: Addison-Wesley.

O'Toole, R., Turbett, P., & Nalepka, C. (1983). Theories, professional knowledge and diagnosis of child abuse. In D. Finkelhor, R. J. Gelles, G.T. Hotaling & M.A. Straus (Eds.), *The Dark Side of Families.* Beverly Hills, CA: Sage.

Paul, G. L. & Lentz, R. J. (1977). *Psychosocial treatment of chronic mental patients.* Cambridge: Harvard University Press.

Pavetti, L. (1993). *Learning from the voices of mothers: Single mothers' perceptions of the trade-offs between welfare and work.* New York: Manpower Demonstration Research Corporation.

Payne, C. M. (1984). *Getting what we ask for: The ambiguity of success and failure in urban education.* Westport, CT: Greenwood.

Pearson, P. D. & Johnson, D. D. (1978). *Teaching reading comprehension.* New York: Holt, Rinehart, & Winston.

Peck, C., Odom, S., & Bricker, D. (Eds.) (1993). *Integrating young children with disabilities into community programs: Ecological perspectives on research and implementation.* Baltimore: Paul H. Brookes Publishing Co.

Phelan, P. & Davidson, A. L. (eds.), *Renegotiating cultural diversity in American schools*. New York: Teachers College Press.

Phelan, P., Davidson, A. L., & Yu, H. C. (1993). Students' multiple worlds: Navigating the borders of family, peer, and school cultures. In P. Phelan & A. L. Davidson (Eds.). *Renegotiating cultural diversity in American schools* (pp. 52-88). New York: Teachers College Press.

Phillips, E., & Garfinkel, I. (1993). Income growth among non resident fathers: Evidence from Wisconsin. *Demography, 30*, 227-241.

Pirog-Good, M. A., & Good, D. H. (1994). *Child support enforcement for teenage fathers: Problems and prospects* (Discussion Paper No. 1029-1094). Madison, WI: Institute for Research on Poverty.

Piven, F. F., & Cloward, R. A. (1971). *Regulating the poor: The functions of public welfare.* New York: Pantheon.

Piven, F. F., & Cloward, R. A. (in press). Welfare reform and the new class war. In M. B. Lykes, R. Liem, A. Banuazizi & M. Morris (Eds.), *Unmasking social inequalities: Victims, voice, and change.* Philadelphia: Temple University Press.

Pollio, H. R. (1981). *Behavior and existence.* Monterey, CA: Brooks/Cole. Polit, D., & Kahn, J. (1986). Early subsequent pregnancy among economically disadvantaged teenage mothers. *Journal of Public Health, 76*, 167-171.

Polit, D., & O'Hara, J. J. (1989). Support services. In P. H. Cottingham & D. T. Ellwood (Eds.), *Welfare policy for the 1990s* (pp. 165-198). Cambridge, MA: Harvard University Press.

Polsby, N. W. (1984). *Political innovation in America: The politics of policy initiation.* New Haven, CT: Yale University Press.

Polsgrove, L., Skiba, R., Wilhite, K. L., Marra, R., Jackson, C., Quick, L., & Dare, M. J. (1993). Designing a comprehensive system of services for Indiana: Project CONNECT, Phase I. *Severe Behavior Disorders of Children and Youth, 16*, 90-101.

Popkin, S. J., Rosenbaum, J. E., & Meaden, P. M. (1993). Labor market experiences of low-income black women in middle-class suburbs: Evidence from a survey of Gautreaux program participants. *Journal of Policy Analysis and Management, 12*, 556-573.

Portes, A., Castells, M., & Benton. L. A. (Eds.). (1989). *The informal economy: Studies in advanced and less developed countries.* Baltimore: Johns Hopkins University Press.

Poulton, R., & Harris, M. (Eds.) (1988). *Putting people first: Voluntary organizations and Third World organizations.* London: Macmillan Publishers.

Praeger, D. J. & Scallet, L. J. (1995). Mental health should be part of general health policy. In W. Barbour (Ed.), *Mental illness: Opposing viewpoints* (pp. 239-244). San Diego, CA: Greenhaven Press.

Price, D. E. (1971). "Professionals" and "Entrepreneurs": Staff orientations and policy making on three Senate committees. *Journal of Politics, 33*(2), 316-336.

Prilleltensky, I. (1989). Psychology and the status quo. *American Psychologist, 44*, 795-802.

Quint, J., Fink, B., & Rowser, S. (1991). *New chance: Implementing a comprehensive program for disadvantaged young mothers and their children.* New York: Manpower Demonstration Research Corporation.

Quint, J. C., & Musick, J. S. (1994). *Lives of promise, lives of pain: Young mothers after new chance*. New York: Manpower Demonstration Research Corporation.

Ramamurti, R. (1986). Effective leadership of public sector organizations: The case of "Public Entrepreneurs." In S. Nagel (Ed.), *Research in public policy analysis and management* (pp. 69-88). Greenwich, CT: JAI Press.

Ransby, B., & Matthews, T. (1993). Black popular culture and the transcendence of patriarchal illusions. *Race & Class, 35*(1), 57-68.

Raspberry, W. (1992, December 18). Successful social programs have spiritual element. *Daily Press* p. A22.

Raspberry, W. (1994, August 19). Make communities safe from and for children. *Daily Press* p. A12.

Raths, L., Harmin, M., & Simon, S. (1966). *Values and teaching*. Columbus, OH: Charles Merrill.

Raver, S. (1987). Practical procedures for increasing spontaneous language in language-delayed preschoolers. *Journal of the Division for Early Childhood, 11*, 226-232.

Redman, E. (1973). *The dance of legislation.* New York: Simon & Schuster.

Regan, D. O., Erlich, S. M., & Finnegan, L. P. (1987). Infants of drug addicts: At risk for child abuse, neglect, and placement in foster care. *Journal of Neurotoxocologyand Teratology, 9*, 315-319.

Regeher, E., & Watkins, M. (1983). The economics of the arms race. In E. Regeher, E. & S. Rosenblum (Eds.), *Canada and the nuclear arms race*. Toronto: Lorimer.

Reich, W., Earls, S. M., & Powell, D. (1988). A comparison of the home and social environments of children of alcoholic and non-alcoholic parents. *British Journal of Addictions, 83*, 831-839.

Reinert, H. (1976). *Children in conflict*. St. Louis: C. V. Mosby.

Reischauer, R. D. (1989). The welfare reform legislation: Directions for the future. In P. H. Cottingham & D. T. Ellwood (Eds.), *Welfare policy for the 1990s* (pp. 10-40). Cambridge, MA: Harvard University Press.

Reppucci, N. D. & Haugaard, J. J. (1989). Prevention of child sexual abuse: Myth or reality. *American Psychologist, 44*, 1266-1275.

Reynolds, C. J., & Salend, S. J. (1990). Teacher-directed and student-mediated care reform, in conference proceedings implementation issues and national healthcare reform in conjunction with the Charles Brecher and Josiah Macy Jr., Textbook Comprehension Strategies. *Academic Therapy, 25*(4), 417-427.

Riccio, J., Friedlander, D., & Freedman, S. (1994). *GAIN: Benefits, costs and three-year impacts of a welfare-to-work program—executive summary*. New York: Manpower Demonstration Research Corporation.

Riesman, D. (1991). In J. Sedgwick (Ed.), *The wrenching of America.* Boston: University Press.

Riker, W. H. (1986). *The art of political manipulation.* New Haven, CT: Yale University Press.

Rinehart, S. D. & Welker, W. A. (1992). Effects of advance organizers on level and time of text recall. *Reading Research and Instruction, 32*(1), 77-86.

Rivara, F. P. (1985). Physical abuse in children under two: A study of therapeutic outcomes. *Child Abuse and Neglect, 9*, 81-87.

Roberts, N. C. (1992). Public entrepreneurship and innovation. *Policy Studies Review, 11*(1), 55-74.

Roberts, N. C., & King, P. J. (1989a). The process of policy innovation. A. H. Van de

Ven, H. L. Angle & M. S. Poole (Eds.), *Research on the management of innovation*, (pp. 303-335). New York: Harper & Row.

Roberts, N. C., & King, P. J. (1989b). *Public entrepreneurship: A typology*. Presented at the Annual Meeting of the Academy of Management.

Roberts, N. C., & King, P. J. (1991). Policy entrepreneurs: Their activity, structure and function in the policy process. *Journal of Public Administration Research and Theory*, *1*(2), 147-175.

Robins, P. K., & Frostin, P. (1993). *Welfare benefits and family-size decisions of never-married women* (Discussion Paper No. 1022-93). Madison, WI: Institute for Research on Poverty.

Robinson, F. P. (1946). *Effective study*. New York: Harper & Brothers.

Rock, B., Goldstein, M., Hopkins, M., Quitkin, E. (1990). Psychosocial factors as predictors of length of stay of Medicare patients under the prospective payment system. *Journal of Health & Social Policy*, *2*, 1-17.

Rogers, C. R., & Skinner, B. F. (1956). Some issues concerning the control of human behavior: A symposium. *Science*, *124*, 1057-1066.

Rogers, E. M. (1983). *Diffusion of innovations* (3rd edition). New York: Free Press.

Rogers, E. M., & Kim, J. (1985). Diffusion of innovations in public organizations. In R. L. Merritt, & A. J. Merritt (Eds.), *Innovation in the public sector* (pp. 85-108). Beverly Hills, CA: Sage Publications.

Rooney, E. (1992). Business coalitions in healthcare: An evolution from cost containment to quality improvement. *AAOHN Journal*, *40*, 342-351.

Rooney, K. (1988). *Independent strategies for efficient study*. Richmond, VA: J. R. Enterprises.

Rosen, I. (1991). Self-esteem as a factor in social and domestic violence. *British Journal of Psychiatry*, *158*, 18-23.

Rosenblatt, A. (1994). Doomed and double doomed? Health care reform and the mental health policy challenge. *American Psychologist*, *49*(1), 71, 72.

Rossi, P. H. (1989). *Down and out in America: The origins of homelessness*. Chicago: University of Chicago Press.

Rother, John. (1992, June). *Consumer concerns and the implementation of health foundation*. Washington, DC: Robert F. Wagner Graduate School of Public Service, New York University.

Rothman, D. (1971). *The discovery of the asylum: Social order and disorder in the new republic*. Boston: Little, Brown.

Rothman, D. J. & Rothman, S. M. (1980). *Conscience and convenience: The asylum and its alternatives in progressive America*. Boston: Little, Brown.

Roberts, N. C. (1992). Public Entrepreneurship and Innovation. Policy Studies in a state-wide program for adolescent mothers with outcomes in a national sample. *Family Planning Perspectives*, *24*, 66-71, 96.

Ruch-Ross, H. S., Jones, E. D., & Musick, J. S. (1992). *Comparing outcome strategies*. New York: Doubleday.

Rumberger, R. W. (1994). High school dropouts: A review of issues and evidence. In J. Kretovics & E. J. Nussel (Eds.), *Transforming urban education* (pp. 187-210). Boston: Allyn & Bacon.

Rumberger, R. W., & Larson, K. A. (1994). Keeping high-risk Chicano students in school. In R. J. Rossi (Ed.), *Schools and students at risk: Context and framework for positive change* (pp. 141-162). New York: Teachers College Press.

Ryan, V. L., & Gizynski, M. (1971). Behavior therapy in retrospect: Patients' feelings about their behavior therapies. *Journal of Consulting and Clinical Psychology, 37,* 1-9.

Salisbury, C., & Smith, B. (1991). The least restrictive environment: Understanding the options. *Principal, 71*(1), 24-27.

Salisbury, R. H. (1969). An exchange theory of interest groups. *Midwest Journal of Political Science, 13* (February), 1-32.

Salisbury, R., & Shepsle, K. (1981). U.S. congressman as enterprise. *LegislativeStudies Quarterly, 6*(4), 559-576.

Sarason, I. G. (1976). Using modeling to strengthen the behavioral repertory of the juvenile delinquent. In J. D. Krumboltz, & C. E. Thorsen (Eds.), *Counseling Methods.* New York: Holt, Rinehart, Winston.

Sarason, S. (1990). *The predictable failure of school reform; Can we change course before it's too late?* San Francisco: Jossey-Bass.

Sarason, S., Simon, S., Howe, L. W., & Kirschenbaum, H. (1972). *Values clarification.* New York: Hart Publishing.

Sassen-Koob, S. (1989). New York City's informal economy. In A. Portes M. Castells & L. A. Benton (Eds.), *The informal economy* (pp. 60-77). Baltimore: Johns Hopkins University Press.

Schacter, S., & Singer, J. (1962). Cognitive, social, and physiological determinants of emotional state. *Psychological Review, 69,* 379-399.

Schattschneider, E. E. (1960). *The semisovereignpeople.* New York: Holt, Rinehart, & Winston.

Scheerenberger, R. C. (1983). *A history of mental retardation.* Baltimore: Books.

Scherl, D., English, J., & Sharfstein, S. (Eds.) (1988). *Prospective payment and psychiatric care.* Washington, DC: American Psychiatric Press.

Schmidt, J. D. & Sherman, L. W. (1993). Does arrest deter domestic violence? *American Behavioral Scientist, 36,* 601-609.

Schneider, M., & Teske, P. (1992). Toward a theory of the political entrepreneur: Evidence from local government. *American Political Science Review, 86*(September), 737-747.

Scholz, J. K. (1994). The earned income tax credit: Participation, compliance, and anti-poverty effectiveness. *National Tax Journal, 47,* 63-85.

Schon, D. A. (1971). *Beyond the stable state.* New York: Random House.

Schorr, L. B. (1988). *Within our reach: Breaking the cycle of disadvantage.* New York: Doubleday.

Schorr, L. B. (1993). What works: Using what we already know about successful social policy. *The American Prospect,* pp. 43 - 54.

Schumaker, J. B., Deshler, D. D., Alley, G. R., Warner, M. M., & Denton, P. H. (1982). Multipass: A learning strategy for improving reading comprehension. *Learning Disabilities Quarterly, 5*(3), 295-304.

Schumpeter, J. A. (1934). *The theory of economic development.* Cambridge, MA: Harvard University Press.

Schumpeter, J. A. (1939). *Business cycles: A theoretical, historical, and statistical analysis of the capitalist process.* New York: McGraw-Hill.

Schumpeter, J. A. (1942). *Capitalism, socialism, and democracy,* New York: Harper &

Row.

Schumpeter, J. A. (1947). The creative response in economic history. *Journal of Economic History*, *7* (November), 149-159.

Schumpeter, J. A. (1949). Economic theory and entrepreneurial history. In A. H. Cole (Ed.), *Change and the entrepreneur: Postulates and patterns for entrepreneurial history* (pp. 63-84). Cambridge, MA: Harvard University Press.

Scialabba, G. (1992). Civic liberalism's debut. *Chicago Tribune*, sec. 14, p. 3.

Senge, P. M. (1990, Fall). The leader's new work: Building learning organizations. *Sloan Management Review*, *6*, 7-23.

Sethuraman, S. V. (1985). The informal sector in Indonesia: Policies and Prospects. *International Labour Review*, *124*(6), 719-735.

Shadish, W. R., Lurigio, A. J., & Lewis, D. A. (1989). After deinstitutionalization: The present and future of mental health long-term care policy. *Journal of Social Issues*, *45*(3), 1-15.

Shafer, B. E. (1989). "Exceptionalism" in American Politics? *PS: Political Science and Politics*, *22*(3), 588-594.

Sherman, L. W., Schmidt, J. D. & Rogan, D. P. (1992). *Policing domestic violence: Experiments and dilemmas.* New York: Free Press.

Shoben, E. J., Jr. (1965). Psychology: Natural science or humanistic discipline? *Journal of Humanistic Psychology*, *5*, 210-218.

Shumer, R. (1994). Community-based learning; Humanizing education. *Journal of Adolescence*, *17*(3).

Sivard, R. L. (1991). *World military and social expenditures, 1991.* Washington, DC: World Priorities.

Skrtic, T. M. (1991). *Behind special education: A critical analysis of professional culture and school organization.* Denver: Love Publishing.

Slavin, R. E. (Eds.) (1983). *Cooperative learning.* New York: Longman.

Slavin, R. E. (1989). Cooperative learning models for the 3 R's. *Educational Leadership*, *47*, 22-28.

Sleeter, C. (1992). *Keepers of the American dream: A study of staff development and multicultural education.* Bristol, PA: Palmer.

Sloan, T. (1992). Psychologists challenged to grapple with global issues. *Psychology International*, *3*(4), 1, 7.

Stapleton, C., & Richman, P. (1978). *Barter: How to get almost anything without money.* New York: Scribner's.

Starfield, B. H. (1989). Child health status. Paper presented at the 1989-1990 seminar series of the Vanderbilt Institute for Public Policy Studies, Vanderbilt University, Nashville, TN.

Starfield, B. H. (1992). Effects of poverty on health status. *Bulletin of the New York Academy of Medicine*, *68*, 17-24.

Starfield, Barbara. (1992). Primary care, concept, evaluation, and policy. New York: Oxford University Press.

Starfield, B., Gross, E., Wood, M., Pantell, R., Allen, C., Gordon, B., Moffatt, P., Drachman, R., & Katz, H. (1980). Psychosocial and psychosomatic diagnoses in primary care of children. *Pediatrics*, *66*, 159-166.

Starfield, B., Shapiro, S., Weiss, J., Liang, K., Ra, K., Paige, D., & Wang, X. (1991). Race, family income, and low birth weight. *American Journal of Epidemiology*, *134*,

1167-1174.

Starr, Paul. (1982). *The social transformation of American medicine*. New York: Basic Books.

Starr, P. (1994). *The logic of health care reform*. New York: Penguin Books.

Staub, E. (1992). Turning against others: The origins of antagonism and group violence. *Peace Psychology Bulletin, 1*(2), 11-14.

Stigler, J. W., Shweder, R. A., & Herdt, G. (Eds.). (1990). *Cultural psychology: Essays on comparative human development*. New York: Cambridge University Press.

Stoodt, B. D. (1988). *Teaching language arts*. New York: Harper & Row.

Stoskopf, C., & Horn, S. (1992). Predicting length of stay for patients with psychoses. *Health Services Research, 26*, 743-766.

Straus, M. (1973). A general systems theory approach to a theory of violence between family members. *Social Science Information, 12*, 105-125.

Stroul, B. A., & Friedman, R. M. (1986). *A system of care for severely emotionally disturbed children and youth*. Washington, DC: NIMH Child and Adolescent Service System Program Technical Assistance Center, Georgetown University Child Development Center.

Suarez-Orozco, M. M., & Suarez-Orozco, C. E. (1993). Hispanic cultural psychology: Implications for educational theory and research. In P. Phelan & A. L. Davidson (Eds.), *Renegotiating Cultural Diversity in American Schools* (pp. 108-138). New York: Teachers College Press.

Subcommittee on Health and Scientific Research. (1979). *Testimony*. Washington, DC: House Committee on Aging, U.S. Congress.

Sullivan, J. M. (1992). Health care reform: Toward a healthier society. *Journal of Health Services Administration, 37*(4), 519-532.

Sum, A. (1986). Analyses of data on basic skills levels of teens: The national longitudinal survey of young adults. Unpublished papers, conference for Laser Market Studies, Northeastern University, Boston, MA.

Surber, R. W., Shumway, M., Shadoan, R., & Hargreaves, W. A. (1986). Effects of fiscal retrenchment and public mental health services for the chronic mentally ill. *Community Mental Health Journal, 22*(3), 215-229.

Szanton, P. (1981). *Not well advised*. New York: Russell Sage Foundation and Ford Foundation.

Taube, C., Lee E., & Forthofer, R. (1984). Diagnosis-related groups for mental disorders, alcoholism, and drug abuse: Evaluation and alternatives. *Hospital & Community Psychiatry, 35*, 452-455.

Tenenbaum, S. (1991). The Progressive legacy and the public corporation: Entrepreneurship and public virtue. *Journal of Policy History, 3*(3), 309-330.

Terr, L. C. (1986). The child psychiatrist and the child witness: Traveling companions by necessity, if not by design. *Journal of the American Academy of Child Psychiatry, 25*, 462-472.

Thomas, C. (1994, April 6). Goals 2000 will dumb down next generation, *L.A. Times Syndicate*, 47.

Tiano, S. (1987). Gender, work and world capitalism: Third world women's role in development. In B. Hess (Ed.), *Analyzing gender* (pp. 216-243). Newbury Park, CA: Sage.

Tischler, G. (1966). Decision-making process in the ER. *Archives of General Psychiatry*,

14, 69-78.

Todaro, M. P. (1989). *Economic development in the Third World.* New York: Longman.

Torrey, E. F. (1988). *Nowhere to go: The tragic odyssey of the homeless mentally ill.* New York: Harper & Row.

Torrey, E. F. (1994, July 11). Shrinking mental health. *National Review, 46*(13), 38-39.

Trattner, W. I. (1984). *From poor law to welfare state: A history of social welfare in America* (3rd ed.). New York: Free Press.

Tropman, J. E., & Morningstar, G. (1989). *Entrepreneurial systems for the 1990s: Their creation, structure, and management.* New York: Quorum Books.

U.S. Department of Health and Human Services. (1992). *Serious mental illness and disability in the adult household population: United States, 1989. Advance Data No. 218.* Washington, DC: Centers for Disease Control.

U.S. General Accounting Office (1993). *Self-Sufficiency: Opportunities and disincentives on the road to economic independence.* Washington, DC: Author.

U.S. General Accounting Office. (1994a). *Families on welfare: Focus on teenage mothers could enhance welfare reform efforts.* Washington, DC: Author.

U.S. General Accounting Office. (1994b). *Families on welfare: Sharp rise in never-married women reflects societal trend.* Washington, DC: Author.

U.S. General Accounting Office (1994c). *Families on welfare: Teenage mothers least likely to become self-sufficient.* Washington, DC: Author.

VanDenBerg, J. E. (1992). Individualized services for children. In E. Peschel, R. Peschel, C. W. Howe, & J. W. Howe (Eds.), *Neurobiological disorders in children and adolescents* (pp. 97-100). San Francisco: Jossey-Bass.

Vasquez, J. A. (1994) Contexts of learning for minority students. In J. Kretovics, & E. J. Nussel (Eds.), *Transforming urban education* (pp. 291-300). New York: Teachers College Press.

Vigil, J. D. (1993). Gangs, social control, and ethnicity: Ways to redirect. In S. B. Heath & M.W. McLaughlin (Eds.), *Identity and inner-city youth* (pp. 94-119). New York: Teachers College Press.

Vitz, P. C. (1994). *Psychology as religion: The cult of self-worship* (2nd ed.) Grand Rapids, MI: Erdmans.

Walby, S. (1986). *Patriarchy at work.* Cambridge: Policy Press.

Walker, L. E. (1979). *The battered woman.* New York: Harper & Row.

Walker, L. E. (1984). Violence against women: Implications for mental health policy. In L. E. Walker (Ed.), *Women and mental health policy* vol 9. Sage Yearbooks in Women's Policy Studies. Beverly Hills: Sage.

Walker, L. E. (1987). *The cycle theory of violence.* New York: Harper & Row.

Walker, J. L. (1974). Performance gaps, policy research, and political entrepreneurs. *Policy Studies Journal, 3*(Autumn), 112-116.

Walker, J. L. (1977). Setting the agenda in the U.S. Senate: A theory of problem selection. *British Journal of Political Science, 7*(October), 423-445.

Walker, J. L. (1981). The diffusion of knowledge, policy communities, and agenda setting: The relationship of knowledge and power. J. E. Tropman, M. J. Dluhy & R. M. Lind (Eds.), *New strategic perspectives on social policy*, (pp. 75-96). New York: Pergamon Press.

Wall Street Journal (1995). National health care should not include mental health benefits. In W. Barbour (Ed.), *Mental illness: Opposing viewpoints* (pp. 252-258). San Diego,

CA: Greenhaven Press.

Wang, M. C., Haertel, G. D., & Walberg, H. J. (1993). Toward a knowledge-base for school learning. *Review of Educational Research, 63*(3), 249-294.

Ward, M. J. (1946). *The snake pit.* New York: Random House.

Warner, S. (1961). Criteria for involuntary hospitalization of psychiatric patients in a public hospital. *Mental Hygiene, 45,* 122-128.

Warren, D. I. (1981). *Helping networks: How people cope with problems in the urban community.* Notre Dame, IN: University of Notre Dame Press.

Warshaw, C. (1993). Domestic violence: Challenges to medical practice. *Journal of Women's Health, 2,* 73-80.

Wattenberg, E. (1987). Establishing paternity for nonmarital children: Do policy and practice discourage adjudication? *Public Welfare,* Summer, 8-13.

Watts, H. (1993). Human capital: The biggest deficit. In J. A. Chafel (Ed.), *Child poverty and public policy* (pp. 245-271). Washington, DC: Urban Institute Press.

Wehlage, G. G., Rutter, R., Smit, G. A., Lesko, N., & Fernandez, R. (1989). *Reducing the risk: Schools as communities of support.* Philadelphia: Falmer Press.

Weiner, L. (1993). *Preparing teachers for urban schools: Lessons from thirty years of school reform.* New York: Teachers College Press.

Weiss, C. H. (1989). Congressional committees as users of analysis. *Journal of Policy Analysis and Management, 8*(3), 411-431.

Weissert, C. S. (1991). Policy entrepreneurs, policy opportunists, and legislative effectiveness. *American Politics Quarterly, 19*(2), 262-274.

Weissman, H. N. (1991). Forensic psychological examination of the child witness in cases of alleged sexual abuse. *American Journal of Orthopsychiatry, 61,* 150-154.

Werner, E. E., & Smith, R. S. (1992). *Overcoming the odds: High risk children from birth to adulthood.* Ithaca, NY: Cornell University Press.

Wescott, H. (1991). Children's ability as witnesses. *American Journal of Orthopsychiatry, 61,* 154-157.

Whittington, H. (1966). *Psychiatry in the American community.* New York: International Universities Press.

Wiegand, B. (1993). *Off the books: A theory and critique of the underground economy.* Dix Hills, NY: General Hall.

Wilenski, R., & Kline, D. M. (1988). *School reform and community renewal. Boulder, Co: Bolder Ideas Group* (revised version published as *Renewing Urban Schools: The Community Connection.* Boulder: Education Commission of the States).

Willesman, L., Broman, S. H., & Fiedler, M. (1970). Infant development, preschool IQ, and social class. *Child Development, 41,* 69-77.

Williams, B., & Newcombe, E. (1994, May). Building on the strengths of urban learners. *Educational Leadership, 51*(8), 75-78.

Williams, D. H., Bellis, E. D., & Wellington, S. W. (1980). Deinstitutionalization and social policy. *American Journal Orthopsychiatry, 50*(1), 54-64.

Williams, K. R., & Hawkins, R. (1989). Controlling male aggression in intimate relationships. *Law and Society Review, 23,* 591-612.

Williams, M. R. (1989). *Neighborhood organizing for urban school reform.* New York: Teachers College Press.

Willis, P. E. (1977). *Learning to labour: How working class kids get working class jobs.* Hampshire, UK: Gower Press.

Wilson, E. O. (1978). *On human nature.* Cambridge, MA: Harvard University Press.

Wilson, J. Q. (1973). *Political organizations.* New York: Basic Books.

Wilson, J. Q. (1980). The politics of regulation. In J. Q. Wilson (Ed.), *The politics of regulation,* (pp. 357-394). New York: Basic Books.

Wilson, J. Q. (1989). *Bureaucracy.* New York: Basic Books.

Wilson, J. Q. (1990). Interests and deliberation in the American republic, or, Why James Madison would never have received the James Madison Award. *PS: Political Science and Politics, 23*(4), 558-562.

Wilson, R. S. (1985). Risk and resilience in early mental development. *Developmental Psychology, 21*(5), 795-805.

Wilson, W. J. (1987). *The truly disadvantaged.* Chicago: University of Chicago Press.

Wiseman, M. (1993). *The new welfare state initiatives.* (Discussion Paper No. 1002-93). Madison, WI: Institute for Research on Poverty.

Wright, F. L. (1947). *Out of sight out of mind.* Philadelphia: National Mental Health Foundation.

Wright, J. D.(1988). The mentally ill homeless: What is myth and what is fact? *Social Problems, 35*(2), 182-191.

Wong, B. Y. L., & Jones, W. (1982). Increasing meta comprehension in learning disabled and normally achieving students through self-questioning training. *Learning Disabilities Quarterly, 5,* 228-240.

Wong, Y. I., Garfinkel, I., & McLanahan, S., (1993). Single-mother families in eight countries: Economic status and social policy. *Social Service Review, 67,* 177-197.

Wood, J. W., & Wooley, J. A. (1986). Adapting textbooks. *The Clearing House, 59,* 332-335.

Wynne, E. & Ryan, K. (1993). *Reclaiming our schools: A handbook on teaching character, academics, and discipline.* Columbus, OH: Merrill Publishing.

Young, G. H., & Gerson, S. (1991). New psychoanalytic perspectives on masochism and spousal abuse. *Psychotherapy, 28,* 30-37.

Zaleski, J., Gale, M., & Winset, C. (1979). Extended hospital care as treatment of choice. *Hospital & Community Psychiatry, 30,* 399-401.

Zilboorg, A. & Henry, G. W. (1941). *A history of medical psychology.* New York: W. W. Norton.

Zuckman, J. (1993, May 8). Funding fights to dominate in Chapter 1 rewrite. *Classroom Quarterly,* pp. 1146-1151.

Index

Contributing Authors

Alfred Baumeister is a professor of psychology at Vanderbilt University with a focus on child health, developmental disabilities, and health policy. Dr. Baumeister has served as advisor to three administrations on child health policy, has been awarded $40 million in research grants from the National Institute of Health (NiH), and has been an expert witness in twenty class-action lawsuits. He has published over 400 articles, chapters, and books including, *Final Report of an Evaluation of the Six Institutes for Juvenile Offenders in the Tennessee Department of Corrections for the Attorney General of the State of Tennessee, Preventing the "New Morbidity": A Guide for State Planning Efforts to Prevent Mental Retardation and Related Disabilities Associated with Socioeconomic Factors* (President's Committee on Mental Retardation), and *Guide to State Planning for the Prevention of Mental Retardation and Related Disabilities Associated with Socioeconomic Conditions.*

Nina J. Christopher is a graduate student at Northwestern University Medical School, where she is pursuing a doctorate in clinical psychology. Ms. Christopher is also a research assistant at Northwestern University Medical School's Mental Health Services and Policy Program.

Laura Ptak Cook is a research assistant at Forest Health Systems, Inc. in Des Plaines, Illinois. She attended Eastern Illinois University for bachelor and master's work in psychology with a focus on behavior modification theory and education. Ms. Ptak is an associate professor in the Department of Education at Northeastern Illinois University, Chicago and student teacher orientation facilitator. She also does consultative work in statistics and computer applications as well as for facility start-up concerning managed healthcare.

E. Rae Harcum is an associate professor in the Department of Psychology at the College of William and Mary. Dr. Harcum has published *Serial Learning and Paralearning* (Wiley-Interscience), *Psychology for Daily Living* (Nelson-Hall), *The Gatekeepers of*

Psychology (Praeger), and most recently on the relation between social behaviors and the perception of human dignity in *A Psychology of Freedom and Dignity* (Praeger). Dr. Harcum is an elected Fellow of the American Psychological Association, American Psychological Society, and the American Association for the Advancement of Science.

Wanda Jones, President of the New Century Healthcare Institute, received her masters in public health (MPH) from University of California - Berkeley. She works with hospitals and healthcare systems in twenty states on strategic planning and healthcare system development, population-based planning, program planning, bionics, genetics, primary care networks, program management, computer simulation, and advanced facility design. As the principal investigator on area-wide studies of healthcare demand and health status of populations and work, she is responsible for direct planning process design and management with boards, management teams, program groups, medical groups, professional associations, foundations, and not-for-profit community health services. Ms. Jones has published *The Practice of Planning* (American Hospital Association) and *New Century Hospital Patient-Focused Planning and Design* (NCHI).

Nelson W. Keith is the director of the Institution of International Development and a professor of psychology at West Chester University, Pennsylvania. He has a doctorate in political economy and obtained a barrister-at-law degree from Inner Temple, London. Dr. Nelson co-authored *Social Origins of Democratic Socialism in Jamaica* (Temple University Press) and *Globalism and the New World Orders: The Unshackling of Dependence* (Sage Publications).

Novella Zett Keith is the director of Urban Education at Temple University, Philadelphia, with a focus on urban education and community development. She has a doctorate in sociology and has presented widely in local and national conferences. Dr. Keith has co-authored *Social Origins of Democratic Socialism in Jamaica* (Temple University Press) and *Globalism and the New World Orders: The Unshackling of Dependence* (Sage Publications).

Donna R. Kemp is a professor and graduate coordinator of the Health Administration Program at California State University at Chico. Dr. Kemp has worked as a health planner and program manager, practiced as a family counselor, and engaged in research dealing with mental health public policy. Her previous works include *Supplemental Compensation and Collective Bargaining, International Handbook on Mental Health Policy*, and *Employee Assistance Programs: An Annotated Bibliography*, as well as numerous articles dealing with mental health in professional journals.

Cassandra Kisiel is the project coordinator of the Mental Health Services and Policy Program at Northwestern University Medical School. Ms. Kisiel is completing her doctoral studies in clinical psychology and has clinical and research training with an emphasis on children with particular focus on child abuse as well as policy and decision-making issues. She has co-authored the article "Borderline Personality Disorder: A Review of Data on *DSM III* Descriptions" in *The Journal of Personality Disorders*.

Franklin D. Kupstas completed bachelor and master level work at the Virginia Commonwealth University in the Departments of Special Education and Educational Administration. He received his doctorate in Clinical Psychology from Vanderbilt University, Nashville, Tennessee. Dr. Kupstas currently is a staff psychologist at the Vanderbilt University Psychological and Counseling Center. Past positions include Project Coordinator/Research Analyst at the John F. Kennedy Center for Research in Education and Human Development, Vanderbilt, as well as Assistant Program Manager in the Department of Mental Health and Retardation at Southside Virginia Training Center in Richmond, Virginia. Dr. Kupstas has co-authored numerous publications and presented on topics such as state planning and disabilities, perspectives on psychological, legal, and ethical issues, and AIDS.

John S. Lyons is the Director of the Mental Health Services and Policy Program at Northwestern University Medical School. He is also an associate professor of psychiatry and medicine at Northwestern. Dr. Lyons has written over 100 peer-reviewed publications and two books.

Sheila B. Marino received her bachelor and master of science degree in elementary and early childhood education from the University of Tennessee. She also earned her doctorate in education with a focus on curriculum and instruction from University of Tennessee, with post-graduate study of human development at West Virginia University. Dr. Marino has been in teaching and administration for twenty-six years and is a professor and the Assistant Dean of the School of Education at Lander University in Greenwood, South Carolina.

Rosemary Miller is an adjunct assistant professor for special education and reading at the University of South Carolina and also serves as special education coordinator for Beaufort County Schools, Hilton Head Island, South Carolina. Dr. Miller attended Syracuse University for her bachelor of science work in Sociology, obtained a master's in education from Georgia State University, and received her doctorate in special education from the University of Arizona. Dr. Miller has made numerous presentations and has written many papers on topics related to teaching and learning, including effective learning strategies, reading instruction, inclusive education, the teaching-learning process, language development, and reading success.

Robert G. Monahan works in the field of special education as an associate professor within the School of Education at Lander University in Greenwood, South Carolina and has been in the teaching and administration arena for twenty-nine years. He received his bachelor's in education from Morehead State University, did master's work in special education at Marshall University, and obtained a doctorate in education with a focus on special education from the University of Southern Mississippi. Dr. Monahan has published the chapter, "Inclusion and Young Children At-Risk" in *Youth at Risk: Reaching for Success* and "From Research to Real Life: Adapting Text to Meet the Literacy Needs of At-Risk Learners" in *Addressing the Problems of Youth at Risk: Approaches that Work.*

Michael Morris is a professor of psychology at the University of New Haven. Dr. Morris has co-edited the to-be-released book *Unmasking Social Inequalities* (Temple University Press), co-authored "Poverty and Public Policy," and has authored a variety of other publications addressing the topics of poverty, welfare policy, and social class (including the underclass).

Thomas Richard Oliver is an assistant professor in the Policy Sciences Graduate Program at the University of Maryland in Baltimore County. Dr. Oliver attended Stanford University and received his bachelor's degree there in Human Biology. He earned a master's degree in health administration from Duke University and received his doctorate in political science from the University of North Carolina at Chapel Hill. He was a postdoctoral fellow in the Pew Health Policy Program at the University of California, San Francisco. Dr. Oliver currently holds an Investigator Award in Health Policy Research from the Robert Wood Johnson Foundation for a study of "Public Entrepreneurship and Health Policy Innovation." His published research includes articles in the *New England Journal of Medicine, Political Science Quarterly, Stanford Law & Policy Review, Journal of Health Politics, Policy, and Law*, and *Health Affairs.*

Daniel J. Rybicki is a clinical psychologist in the Occupational Health and Safety Division of the Department of Personnel in Los Angeles, California, with a focus on marital and family therapy, addictions, forensic psychology, and occupational and personnel psychology. Dr. Rybicki has authored a chapter, "Critical Issues in Differential Diagnosis of Psychiatric Inpatients: Selected Topics and Tests," in *Current Advances in Inpatient Psychiatric Care: A Handbook.* He is a certified addictions counselor and registered custody evaluator, a clinical member of the American Association of Marriage and Family Therapists, and a charter member of the American Association of Christian Counselors.

Michelle Shasha is a graduate student in the doctoral program at Northwestern University, where she is also a research assistant in the Mental Health Services and Policy Program. Ms. Shasha's focus is on clinical psychology.

Chris E. Stout received his education at Purdue University and Forest Institute. He was awarded "Distinguished Alumni if the Year from Purdue University" in 1991. He obtained post-doctoral experience at Harvard Medical School as a Fellow in neuro-developmental behavioral pediatrics and he is working on his MBA at the University of Chicago's Graduate School of Business. Dr. Stout, a licensed clinical psychologist, is the senior vice-president of Clinical Applications, Policy, and Development of Forest Health Systems, Inc. He is also a contributing editor and national columnist on managed care in *The Psychotherapy Letter* and he maintains an active practice in research and consultation. Dr. Stout has published or presented over 300 papers and fifteen books/manuals on various topics in psychology. He has lectured across the nation and internationally in eight countries. He is an associate professor of clinical psychology. He was appointed by the Secretary of the US Department of Commerce to the Board of Examiners for the Baldrige National Quality Award and he served as a consultant to The White House on national education matters under the Bush Administration. Dr. Stout has a diplomate from the American Board of Medical Psychotherapists, is a member of the American College of Healthcare Executives, and is a member of the National Register of Health Service Providers.

Jerry A. Theis, a former managed care executive and board member of a nationally recognized research center, is President of Mid-America Managed Care Consultants, Inc. of Wisconsin. Mr. Theis is co-author of *Trade Association's Draft Report Card* and author of *Quality, Outcomes, and Case Management in Mental Health*.

John T. Vessey completed his master's work in statistics and earned his doctoral degree in methodology and evaluation research from Northwestern University Medical School. Dr. Vessey is currently an assistant professor in the Mental Health Services and Policy Program also at Northwestern University Medical School.

Kathi L. Wilhite, formerly with the Indiana Department of Education, Division of Special Education, is currently an adjunct faculty member at Indiana University, Purdue University at Indianapolis, and Ball State University, and the president of K. L. Wilhite and Associates, a consultation and training resource. Ms. Wilhite has a masters degree in special education and licensure in the areas of mentally handicapped, learning disabled, and emotionally disturbed, and special education administration. She is an active contributor to numerous professional organizations, including elected General Member-at-Large for the International Council for Children with Behavior Disorders and Past-President of the Indiana Subdivision of the Council for Children with Behavioral Disorders. Ms. Wilhite has co-authored several journal publications and has presented widely on topics of special education and special education administration with a special interest in systems change.

Pamela Woodley-Zanthos is a research associate at Vanderbilt University with a focus on behavioral aspects of developmental disabilities. Her doctoral training included study of psychology-mental retardation special education. Dr. Woodley-Zanthos has served a consultant in public school and residential facility class action lawsuits involving deinstitutionalization, behavior and medical treatment, and medicaid provisions to children. She has published *The New Morbidity: Recommendations for Action and an Updated Guide to State Planning for the Prevention of Mental Retardation and Related Disabilities Associated with Socioeconomic Conditions* (U.S. Department of Health and Human Services).

ISBN 0-275-95011-5

90000>

EAN

9 780275 950118

HARDCOVER BAR CODE